John Dee's Actions With Spirits

22 December 1581 to
23 May 1583

Volume II

Christopher Whitby

GARLAND PUBLISHING, INC.
NEW YORK & LONDON 1988

Library of Congress Cataloging-in-Publication Data

Whitby, Christopher.
John Dee's actions with spirits : 22 December 1581 to 23 May 1583 : volume I, volume II / Christopher Whitby.
p. cm. — (Garland publications in American and English literature)
Thesis (Ph.D.)—University of Birmingham, 1981.
Bibliography : p.
ISBN 0-8240-6399-6
1. Dee, John, 1527-1608. 2. Spirit writings. I. Title. II. Series.
BF 1598.D5W47 1988
133.9'3—dc 19 88-16428

Printed on acid-free, 250-year-life paper
Manufactured in the United States of America

GARLAND PUBLICATIONS IN AMERICAN AND ENGLISH LITERATURE

Editor
Stephen Orgel
Stanford University

GARLAND PUBLISHING, INC.

CONTENTS

Conventions and Usages in the Transcription

1. Foliation and blank pages. The transcription follows the folio numeration made in pencil in the top right corner of each recto side of the manuscript by the Manuscript Department of the British Library. For ease of reference the recto and verso sides of each folio have been designated 'a' and 'b' in the transcription and the folio number with its side designation has been noted in square brackets in the top right corner of each page of the transcription. Where a page of the transcription contains text which proceeds from one folio side to another, both folio sides are noted (e.g. [62a-62b]). Except in the case where a folio side has no marginal notes and the text of that side ends with a happy coincidence at the bottom of a page of the transcription, the end of each folio side is designated by a continuous line across the page, after which follow the marginal notes, separated from the next folio side by another continuous line. Blank pages are indicated by the word 'blank' within slanting brackets between the continuous lines that mark the beginning and end of a folio side.

2. Lineation. The transcription provides a line by line reproduction of the original text and every fifth line of each folio side has been numbered down the right hand side of each page of the transcription. I have attempted as far as possible to maintain the relative indentations of the lines. Where a complete line cannot be contained in one line of transcription, the text of that line is continued below the beginning of that line, but separated by single spacing in contrast to the double spacing between each line.

3. <u>Marginal entries</u>. These are reproduced between the continuous lines which mark the end of one folio side and the beginning of another and are prefixed by the letters 'MN' together with the number of the line by which they are to be found. Where an Action ends in the middle of a folio, the marginal notes to that Action are reproduced at the end of the Action rather than at the end of the folio and are separated from the main text by dotted lines across the page. Unless otherwise noted, marginal entries occur in the left hand margin. Where they occur elsewhere their location is either noted in full, or else by the abbreviation 'RH' for right hand margin (e.g. MN30RH signals a right hand marginal note to line 30). On occasions a multiplicity of marginal notes to one line has led to the use of 'LH' to designate a location in the left hand margin.

4. <u>Interlineations</u>. Some interlineations which constitute later corrections are reproduced in the marginal notes at the end of each folio side, but most are reproduced in the relevant line of the text. Superscriptions are noted by the signs /¯ 7 and interlineations that occur below the line by the signs /̲ ./. The use of a caret is shown by a superscribed 'c' (e.g. a superscription of the word 'and' using a caret is marked /^{c}and7).

5. <u>Rules, underlinings and flourishes</u>. Rules and underlinings have been reproduced in pen. Dee frequently ends an Action with a large flourish and this has been noted by the word 'flourish' within slanting brackets.

6. Lines joining words and phrases. Dee quite frequently joins words and phrases on different lines of a folio side by freehand lines when he considers that there is some significance in comparing the parts of the text. This has been noted at the end of the marginal notes to each folio side.

7. Deletions and erasures. These are marked within square brackets. An illegible deletion or an erasure is marked by dots between the brackets.

8. Brackets. Dee's use of ordinary brackets and square brackets has been reproduced in the text, but in order to differentiate Dee's square brackets from those I have used to signify deletions and erasures, I have lengthened Dee's (e.g. [   ] in contrast to [   ]).

9. Minuscules and majuscules. It is often difficult to distinguish Dee's minuscules and majuscules, particularly with the letters S, L, V, W and Y. In the case of the first two letters I have made a decision according to relative size only, but in the case of the other three letters I have taken only the forms V, W, and Y as opposed to v, w, and y, to be majuscules irrespective of their size.

10. Use of I and J and long s. In the transcription I have changed Dee's form J for both 'I' and 'J', when it occurs, to either 'I' or 'J' according to whether the sound is a vowel or a consonant. I have consistently changed long 's' to short 's'.

11. Contractions and abbreviations. I have reproduced the contractions and abbreviations used by Dee, noting the full form in the Commentary when difficulty might arise. An exception is ꝧ which I have always transcribed in full as 'the'. The most common contractions and abbreviations are listed below:

a) a line over a vowel, usually 'e', for a missing 'n' or 'm' (e.g. saeculorū for saeculorum).

b) a line over a word indicating a contraction (e.g. oīm for omnium).

c) ꝑ for 'per' (ꝑceyue for perceyue), ꝓ for 'pro' (ꝓpose for propose) and ꝓ̄ for 'pre' (ꝓ̄sent for present).

d) ꝫ for 'ner' (e.g. mannꝫ for manner).

f) ꝗ for 'que' (e.g. expertiꝗ for expertique).

12. Ampersands and ligatures. Dee uses three forms of ampersand, &, c and ɔ, and I have transcribed them all as '&'. I have used the transcription '&c' for the form &c and 'etc' for the form &c . Dee consistently uses ligatures on 'oe' and 'ae' and I have ignored these when they are miniscules. I have also ignored the ligatured long 's' and 't' which Dee sometimes uses. Consequently the only ligature which is noted is capital 'AE'.

13. Marginal and textual crosses and asterisks. These have been reproduced as in the original.

14. Diagrams. I have reproduced all diagrams as close to their original size as possible, but dimensions are also noted in the Commentary. When a marginal note is accompanied by a

small diagram of a hand with the finger pointing to the relevant line, I have noted 'with hand' in slanting brackets at the end of the marginal note.

15. Inks. The manuscript is written in black ink and I have noted the occasional use of red ink in the Commentary.

16. Readings from elsewhere. Where a word is illegible or the manuscript has suffered damage, I have turned to Ashmole's transcript (Sloane MS 3677). Where this has proved fruitful, readings of words or parts of words taken from Ashmole's transcript have been placed within pointed brackets (e.g. < the>). Where Ashmole's transcript has failed to provide the answer because the original had suffered damage even by the time that it came into his hands, I have reproduced within pointed brackets the line of dots that he has used for illegible or missing text, thus indicating that his transcript does not provide any further information (e.g. <....>). Where it has been possible to turn to another source, as when a quotation from a printed work has suffered damage, the missing words or letters are contained within slanting brackets. I have also used slanting brackets when I have made a conjecture over a word, either because it is illegible and Ashmole's transcript does not help, or because the word is missing but may reasonably be guessed.

17. Hands in the manuscript. The manuscript is in Dee's hand with the exception of certain words and inserted leaves in

Ashmole's hand and fol. 99, which apart from a marginal note by Dee, is in Kelly's hand. Ashmole's hand is indicated by a wavy underlining (e.g. the), except in the case of fols 2-3 (his preface to the MS) where it is noted in the Commentary only. Kelly's hand is noted in the Commentary and in the transcription of fol. 99b, where there is a marginal note by Kelly and a marginal note by Dee, the authors being noted in slanting brackets after each marginal entry.

The Transcription

Be it remembred, That the 20th of August 1672. I received by the hands of my Servant Samuell Story, a parcell of Dr Dee's Manuscripts, all written with his owne hand; vizt: his Conference with Angells, wch first began the 22th of Dec: an^{o} 1581. & continued to the end of May an^{o} 1583. where the printed Booke of the remaining Conferences (published by Dr Cawsabon) begins, & ⌈[..]⌉ are bound vp in this Volume.

Beside these, the Booke intituled, the 48 Claves Angelicae, also Liber Scientia Terrestris Auxilij & Victoria (These two being those very individuall Bookes, wch the Angells comanded to be + burnt, & [af] were after + restored by them, as appeares by the printed Relation of Dr Dee's Actions with Spirits pag: 418. & 419.) The Booke intituled De Heptarchia Mystica Collectaneorum Lib: primus, and a Booke of Invocations or Calls, begining with the Squares [Letters] filled with Letters, about the Black Cross. These 4 Bookes I haue bound vp in another volume.

All wch were a few daies before delivered to my said Servant, for my pervsall (I being then at Mr William Lillies house at Horsham in Surrey) by my good freind Mr Thomas Wale, one of his Maties Warders in the Tower of London.

Marginal note:

line 14: + 10. Apr. } 1586
++ 30. Apr: }

[2b]

The 5t of Sept: following Mr Wale (having heard of my retourne to Towne) came to /my Office in/ the Excise Office in Broadstreete, & told me he was content to exchang all the foresaid Bookes, for one of myne, vizt: The Institution, Lawes & Ceremonies of the most Noble Order of the Garter, to this I agreed, and provided one, wch I sent him fairly bound, & gilt on the Back.

On the 10th of the sd Sept; Mr Wale came thither to me againe, & brought his wife with him, from her I received the following account of the preservation of these Bookes, even till they came to my hands, vizt: That her former Husband was one Mr Jones a Confectioner, who formerly dwelt at the Plow in Lumbardstreet London, & who, shortly after they were married, tooke her with him into Adle Streete among the Joyners, to buy some Houshold stuff, where (at the Corner house) they saw a Chest of Cedar wood, about a yard & halfe long, whose Lock & Hinges, being of extraordinary neate worke, invited them to buy it. The Master of the shop told them it had ben parcell of the Goods of Mr John Woodall Chirurgeon (father to Mr Tho: Woodall late Serjant Chirurgeon to his now Matie King Charles the 2^{d} [&] (my intimate freind) and tis very probabble he bought it after Dr Dee's death, when his goods wer exposed to Sale.

Marginal note:

line 7: As a further Testimo= / ny of the Sence of M^{r} / Wales kindnes; shortly / after his death, I sent / for his Son, & bestowed / on him, one of my depu= / ties places in the Excise, / with an allowance / of 80^{l} p Añum.

[3a]

Twenty yeares after this (& about 4 yeares before the fatall Fire of London) she & her s^{d} husband occasionally removing this Chest out of its vsuall place, thought they heard some loose thing ratle in it, toward the right hand and, vnder the Box or Till thereof, & by shaking it, were fully satisfied it was so: Herevpon her Husband thrust a peece of Iron into a small Crevice at the bottome of the Chest, & therevpon appeared a private drawer, wch being drawne out, therein were found divers Bookes in Manuscript, & Papers, together with a little Box & therein a Chaplet of Olive Beades, &

a Cross of the same wood, hanging at the end of them.

They made no great matter of these Bookes &c: because they vnderstood them not, wch occasioned their Servant Maide to wast about one halfe of them under Pyes & other like vses, wch when [they] discovered, they kept the rest more safe.

About two yeares after the[se] discovery of these Bookes, Mr Jones died, & when the fire of London hapned, /^{c}though7 the Chest perished in the Flames, because not easily to be removed, [but] /^{c}yet7 the Bookes were taken out & carried with the rest of Mrs Jones her goods into Moorefields, & being brought safely back, she tooke care to preserve them; and after marrying with the fores^{d} Mr Wale, he came to the knowledge of them, & therevpon, with her consent, sent them to me, as I haue before set downe.

E Ashmole.

/blank7 [3b]

[4a]

ANNO 1581 : 1582

Mysteriorum

Liber Primus.

Mortlaci

+ 1 +

[blank] [4b]

[5a]

Praeter alias meas extemporaneas preces, et eiaculationes
ad Deum vehementiores: Haec vna, maximè
Vsitata fuit.

Ōro mea Matutina, Vespertinaq; : pro Sapientia.
In nomine Dei Patris, Dei Filij, Dei Spiritus Sancti.
Amen

Omnipotens, Sempiterne, Vere, et Viue Deus, in adiutorium meum
intende: Domine Dominantium, Rex Regum, Jeouah
Zebaoth, ad adiuuandum me festina:
Gloria Deo, Patri, Filio, [spir] et spiritui Sancto: Sicut erat in
principio, et nunc, et semp : et in saecula saeculorū: Amen.
Recte sapere, et intellegere doceto me (ô rerum ōim Creator,) Nam
Sapientia tua, totum est, quod volo: Da Verbum tuum in ore meo,
ô rerum ōim Creator,) et Sapientiā tuā in corde meo fige.
O Domine Jesu Christe (qui sapientia Vera es, aeterni et Omnipotentis
tui Patris) humilimè tuam oro Diuinam Maiestatem, expeditum
mihi vt mittere digneris, alicuius pij Sapientis expertiq; Philosophi
auxilium, ad illa plenissimè intelligenda perficiendaq; , quae maximi
Valoris erunt ad tuam laudem et gloriam amplificandam: Et si
Mortalis nullus iam in terris viuat, qui ad hoc munus aptus sit: Vel
qui ex aeterna tua prouidentia, ad istud mihi praestandum beneficium

assignatus fuerit: Tunc equidem humilimè, ardentissimè et constan=tissimè a tua Diuina Maiestate requiro, vt ad me de caelis mittere digneris bonos tuos Spirituales Ministros, Angelosq, Videlicet Mi=chaëlem, Gabrielem, Raphaëlem ac Vrielem: et (ex Diuino tuo fauore) quoscunq alios, veros, fidelesq tuos Angelos, qui me plene et perfecte informent et instruant, in cognitione, intelligentiaq vera et exacta, Arcanorum et Magnalium tuorū (Creaturas omnes tuas, illarumq naturas proprietates, et optimos vsus, concernentium) et nobis Mortalibus Scitu necessariorum; ad tui nōis laudem, honorem, et gloriam; et ad solidam meam, aliorumq, (per me) plurimorum tuorum fidelium consolationem: et ad Inimicorum tuorum confusionem, et subversionem. Amen. Fiat Jeouah Zebaoth: Fiat Adonay, fiat Elohim. O beata, et superbenedicta Omnipotens Trinitas, Cōcedas mihi (Joanni Dee) [petititione] petitionem hanc, modo tali, qui tibi maximè placebit.

Amen

[flourish]

Ab anno 1579. hoc fere modo: Latinè, vel Anglicè; (ast circa annū 1569 alio et peculiari, particulari modo: interdum pro Raphaële, interdum pro Michaële) ad Deum preces fundere: mihi gratissimum fuit: [et] [est.] Mirrabilem in me faciat Deus Misericordiā suam

Amen.

[flourish]

[blank] [5b]

John Dee his Note

Angelus siue In=
telligentia nunc
toti Mundo prae=
dominans ——— ANNAEL ——— Etymologia: Gratiosa, Afflicta, Misericors } Dei

4. Angeli praesidẽtes
4. Cardinibus Caeli:
vt Agrippa notat
in scala Quater=
narij ——— Michael — Gabriel — Raphael — Vriel
Etymologiae ——— Fortitudo Dei — Prevalescentia, siue praepotentia, siue Fortitudo praevalescens } Dei — Medicina Dei — Lux Dei.

——— אָנָּא et אָנָּה Anna, et Annah, obsecr̄atis et confitentis particula est.
hac tōe, non absurdè innuĕre videtur,
orantem et confitentem Deum.

⌜blank⌝ [6b]

[7a]

<.....i> censia

<.....rig >

Ad Deum Omnipotentem Protestatio fidelis:

ad perpetuam rei memoriam A^o. 1582:

O God Almighty, thow knowest, ⌜&⌝[c] art my director, and witnes herein, That I haue from my youth vp, desyred & prayed vnto the for pure and sownd wisdome and vnderstanding of ⌜some of⌝[c] thy truthes naturall and artificiall: such, as by which, thy wisdome, goodnes & powre bestowed in the frame of the [whorld] world might be browght, in some bowntifull measure vnder the Talent of my Capacitie, to thy honor & glory, & the benefit of thy Servants, my brethern and Sistern, in, & by thy Christ ō Saviour: And for as much as, many yeres, in many places, far & nere, in many bokes, & sundry languagis, I haue sowght, & studyed; and with sundry men conferred, and with my owne reasonable discourse labored, whereby to fynde or get some ynckling, glyms or beame of such the forsaid radicall truthes: But, (to be brief) after all my forsaid endevor I could fynde no other way, to such true wisdome atteyning, but by thy extraordinary gift: and by no vulgar Schole doctrine, or humane Invention. And, Seing, I haue red in thy bokes, & records, how Enoch enioyed thy favor and conversation, with Moyses thow wast familier: And allso that to Abraham, Isaac, and Jacob,

Josua, Gedeon, Esdras, Daniel, Tobias, and sundry other, thy good Angels were sent, by thy disposition, to instruct them, informe them, help them, yea in worldly and domesticall affaires, yea and sometimes to satisfy theyr desyres, dowtes & questions of thy Secrets: And furdermore Considering, the Shew stone, which the high preists did vse, by thy owne ordering: wherein they had lights and Judgements in theyr great dowtes: and considering allso that thow (O God) didst not refuse to instruct thy prophets, (then, called Seers) to give true answers to common people of things aeronomicall, as Samuel, for Saul, seeking for his fathers asses being gon astray: and of other things vulgar true predictions, whereby to wyn credyt in ⌜some[c] thy⌝ waightier affayres: And thinking wth my self, the lack of ⌜thy[c]⌝ wisdome, to me, to be of more importance, then the Value of an Asse or two, could be to Cis, (Saul his father): And remembring what god cownsayle thy Apostle James giveth, saying, Si quis autem vestrûm indiget sapientia, postulet a Deo &c And that Salomon the Wise, did so, euen immediately by thy self, atteyne to his wonderfull wisdome: Therfore, Seeing I was sufficiently towght and confirmed, that this wisdome could not be come by at mans hand or by humane powre, but onely from the (Ô God) mediately or immediately) And having allwayes a great regarde & care to beware of the filthy abvse of such as willingly and wetingly, did invocate and consult (in diuerse sorts) Spirituall creatures of the damned sort: angels of darknes, forgers & patrons of lies & vntruthes: I did fly vnto the by harty prayer, full oft, & in sundry mann)s: sometymes Crying vnto the, Mittas lucem tuam et veritatem tuam, quę me ducant &c sometymes Recte sapere et intelligere doceto me, Nam sapientia tua totum est quod volo: &c sometymes, Da verbum tuum in ore meo et sapientiam, tuam in

---

[7b]

tuam in corde meo fige, &c. And having perceyued by sōme sligh<t> experience with two diuerse persons, that thow hadst a speciall care <to> give me thy light, and truth, by thy holy and true Ministers Ang<elic> and Spirituall: and at length hearing of one, (A Master of Art<s,> a preacher of thy word admitted) accownted ^as^ a good Seer, and skryer of Spirituall apparitions, in Christalline receptacles, or in open ayre, by his practise, procured: and trusting to frame him, by my ernest & faithfull prayers vnto the (my God) to some my help in my forsayd Studies: tyll, thow (o hevenly father) woldest by thy unserchable provydence, send me sōme [better] apter man or means thereto. Therevppon trying him and vsing him, I fownd great diuersity betwene his /private7 ^c^ usuall mann), and intents of practise, and my pure, sincere, devowte, & faithfull prayer vnto the onely. And therefore often & fervently I exhorted him [& rebuked him] to the good; and reproved both him, and his ministers, with my no small daunger, but that thow (in manner vnhard of) didst pitch thy holy tents to my defence, and cumfort, in conflict most terrible: as thow best knowest O God, and I willed him ⌜^{c}therevppon⌝ to preach thy Mercyes, & the verity of the kingly prophet his testimony Castra metatur Angelus Domini, in Circuitu timentiū eum. And out of Roger Bachon his boke written De mirabili potestate Artis et Naturae, [I warned] (where he writeth against the wycked Diuel Callers) I noted vnto him that sentence, Facilius (sine comparatione a * Deo impetrandum foret, vel a bonis spiritibus, quicquid hom⌜o⌝ vtile reputare &c which my cownsayle he promised me to follow, as thow art witnes, ô our true & almighty God. And [albeit] ⌜as⌝ thy good Spirituall Creatures neyther had delight in the man, neyther wold so playnely & preistly give me theyr answers or informations by him, that he might be hable to ꝑceyve the pith therof: So was he at length very vnwilling to here him self rebuked for his nawghtynes, and to be barred from the Mysteries of ⌜thy⌝ [Gods] truthes vnderstanding; which were the onely things that I desyred, throwgh thy grace, o our most mercifull God. Therfore, as well for a Memoriall, answerable to the premisses, as for the better warrant of my Such exercises to be made accownt ⌜^{c}of,⌝ hereafter: (leaving all vnto thy infinite mercies, and vnserchable providence,) I haue thowght it not imꝑtinent, to note downe, even in this place one of the last Actions, which I had wth ⌜^{c}the⌝ forsayd preacher: when I made ernest & faythfull petition vnto the (o the true & Almighty God) for sending, vnto my comfort & eridition, (yf it wer thy blessed will,) thy holy, & mighty Angel Annael: of whome as ⌜^{c}of⌝ all the Hierarchies hevenly all prayer /[c]honor &7 thanks, be rendred vnto thy divine maiestie: now & euer: & worlde without ende. Amen. Amen. Amen.

/flourish7

Marginal note:

line 24: * Numquid non est / Deus in Israël, / vt eatis ad con= / sulendum Beelze= / bub, deum Accaron: / Reg. 4. cap. 1.

[8a]

Anno 1581. Decembris 22. Mane. Mortlak

Δ After my fervent prayers made to God, for his mercifull cumfort and instruction, throwgh the Min[i]^stery of his holy and myghty Angel, named Anael, (yf it wer his diuine pleasure) I willed, the Skryer, (named Saul) to loke into my great Chrystaline Globe, yf God [has] had sent his holy Angel Anael, or no: And Saul loking into my forsayd Stone, (or Chrystall Globe) for to espie Anael, he saw there one, which answered to that name. But being ernestly requested of me to tell the Truthe yf he were Anaël, An other did appere very bewtifull, with apparell yellow, glittering, like gold, and his hed had beames like star beams, blasing, and spredding from it; his eyes fyrie. He wrote /in the [c] stone very7 much [hebrue] in hebrue letters, and the letters seamed all transparent gold. which, Saul was not able eyther presently to reade, that I might write after his voyce, neyther to imitate the letters in short tyme.

A bright star, did go up [ad] and down by him.

There appeared allso a white dog, with a long hed.

And many other visions appeared, with this second; the first being voyded quite away. Therevppon I sayd, as followeth

Δ——In nomine Jesu Christi, Quis tu es? he answered to Saul his hearing

AN.——Potestas omnis, in me sita est

Δ——Quae ?

An——Bona, et mala.

Δ——Then appeared in the stone, these two letters M. G.

I then axing him some questions, de Thesauro abscondito: he answered,

AN.——Ne perturbes: Nam hae sunt Nugae.

And withall appeared many dedd mens skulls, on his left hand.

He sayd to me,

AN.-[V]——Vbi est potestas tua?

Δ——Cur quaeris de potestate aliqua mea?

AN.——Cur? Signifi, non mihi placet.

Δ——I, therevppon, set by him, the stone in the frame: and sayd.

Δ——An bonus aliquis Angelus, assignatus est hinc speculo?

AN.——Etiam.

Δ——Quis?

AN.——מִיכָאֵל——he answered, by the shew of these letters in ye stone

Δ——Bonus ne ille Angelus, de q̊ in scripturis fit mentio?

AN——Maximè.

Δ——Fieri non potest, quòd ego eundem videam, et cū illo agam?

AN.——Ita. and therewith appeared this character—— 

Δ——Quid per hoc, significare velis?

AN——Alterius Angeli character est.

Δ——Cur hîc, et nunc ostendis?

AN——Causam ob magnam Make an ende: It shalbe declared, but not by me.

Δ——By whome then?

AN.——By h<m>

Marginal notes:

line 4: ANAEL

line 9: Δ. Note / An illuding / intrucer euen / at the first, / putting him / self, as an / Angel of light. / Take hede / allwayes of / vndue secu= / ritie ∴

line 19: Δ There / <Ther>e appeared a great / <gre>at number of dead / <de>ad mens skulls, like= / <li>kewise

---

[8b]

AN——By him that is assigned to the stone: but not, tyll after the feast. And then thow

must prepare thy self, to prayer and fasting

In the Name of God, be Secret: and in all thy doings praying, tyll thow hast thy

desyre: which shall not be far of.

After Newyeres tyde, Deale, But not on the Sabaoth day

Pray continually.

When it shall pleas god, to stir the vp, Then procede. In the brightest day,

When the Sonne shyneth: In the morning, fasting, begynne to pray.

In the Sonne Set the stone.

Deale both Kneeling, and sitting. I haue done for this tyme.

My name is ANNAEL.

I will speak ones more to [the] the: and than fare well: for thow shalt not

haue me any more.

Be not to hasty in wrath.

Δ——Is this, that, you ment to speak?

AN.——I. Do good to all men. God hath sufficient for the, and for all men

Fare well.

Δ——Gloria patri et filio et spiritui Sancto. Sicut erat in principio,

et nunc et semper: et in saecula saeculorū

Amen.

Δ—Remember, that diuerse other particulars, mowght haue byn Noted of this dayes

Action: but these may suffice: And yet it is not to [be][c] forgotten, that

as he sayd his name was Annael (with a dubble n) so he allso confessed

him self to be the same Annaël which is prepositus orbis veneris:

and allso Chief governor Generall of this great period, as I haue

Noted in my boke of Famous and rich Discoueries.

[flourish]

Consider and Remember.	That this Note, of the Action, (had with holy ANNAEL), is, of Prince Befafes, (otherwise called Obelison) accownted

as the Prolog of my first boke of mysticall exercises

A^{o} 1582. Nouembris 20——— vide post.

[flourish]

Marginal notes:

line 2: Prayer

line 3: Fasting

[9a]

At Mortlak

In nomine Jesv CHRISTI. Amen.

Anno 1582. Martij die .10. hora 11½ Ante meridiem. Saterday

Δ One Mr Edward Talbot cam to my howse, and [^{c}he] being willing and desyrous to see or shew sōme thing in spirituall practise, wold haue had me to haue done sōme thing therein. And I truely excused my self therein: as not in the vulgarly accownted Magik, neyther studied, or exercised: But confessed my self long tyme to haue byn desyrous to haue help in my philosophicall studies throwgh the Cumpany and information of the blessed Angels of God. And there= vppon, I browght furth to him, my stone in the frame, (which was given me of a frende) and I sayd vnto him, that I was credibly informed, that to it (after a sort) were answerable Aliqui Angeli boni. And allso that I was ones willed by a Skryer, to call for the good Angel Anchor, to appere in that stone to my owne sight. And therfore I desyred him, to call him: and (yf he wold) Anachor and Anilos likewise, accownted good Angels. for I was not prepared therevnto. etc He then settled him self to the Action: and on his Knees att my desk (setting the stone before him) fell to prayer and entreaty &c In the mean space, I, in my Oratory did pray, and make motion to god, and his good Creatures for the furdering of this Action. And within one quarter of an howre (or less) he had sight of one in the stone. but he still expected for two more: deeming this to be one of the three (namely Anchor Anachor Anilos). But I then cam to him, to the stone: And after some thanks to God, and Wellcome to the good Creature, vsed; I required to know his name. And he spake plainly, (to the hearing of E.T.) that his name is VRIEL.

Δ——Are you one of them (sayd I, John Dee) that are answerable, (vppon due observations performed) to this stone?

VRIEL——I am.

Δ——Are there any more besyde you?

VR——Michaël and Raphaël. But, Michaël est princeps in operibus nostris.

Δ——ys my boke, of Soyga, of any excellency?

VR——Liber ille, erat Adae in Paradiso reuelatus, per Angelos Dei bonos.

Δ——Will you give me any instructions, how I may read those Tables of Soyga?

VR——I can——But solus Michaël illius libri est interpretator.

Δ——I was told, that after I could read that boke, I shold liue but two yeres and a half.

VR ——Thow shallt liue an Hundred and od yeres.

Δ——What may I, or must I do, to haue the sight, and presence, of Michael, that blessed Angel?

VR——Praesentias nr̄as postulate et invocate, sinceritate et humilitate. Et Anchor, Anachor, et Anilos, non sunt in hunc lapidem invocandi.

Δ——Oh, my great and long desyre hath byn to be hable to read those Tables of Soyga.

VR——Haec maximè respiciunt Michaëlem. Michaël est Angelus, qui illuminat gressus tuos. Et haec revelantur in virtute et veritate non vi.

Δ——Is there any speciall tyme, or howre to be observed, to deale for the enioying of Michael?

VR——Omnis hora, est hora nobis.

Δ——After this, there appered in the stone a strange seale, or Characterismus of this fashion ensuing:

Marginal notes:

line 4: Note: he / had two dayes / before made the / like demaunde / and request vnto / me: but he went / away vnsatisfied. / for,his comming / was to entrap / me, yf I had had / any dealing with / Wicked spirits / as he confessed / often tymes after: / and that he was / set on. &c.

line 10: [a sketch of the stono in its frame]

line 49: Δ / An illuding / spirit straight / way intruded / him self, and / this charac= / ter: as may / appere libri / Quinti appendice / Where the / character is / described exactly.

[9b]

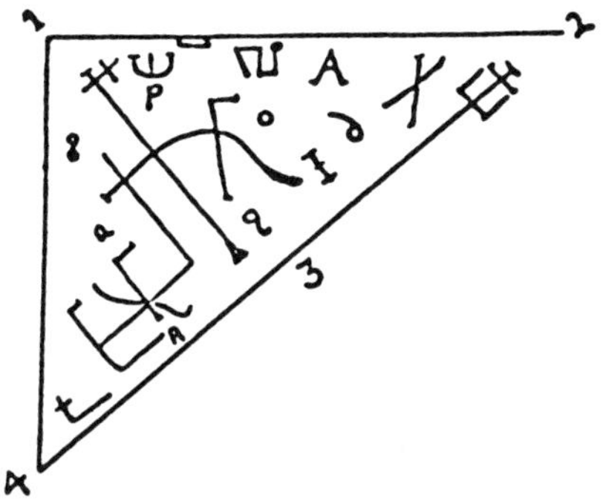

Δ——what is the intent, or vse of this?

*VR~~~~ Sigillum hoc in auro sculpendum, ad defensionē corporis, omni loco, tempore et occasione. et in pectus gestandum.

Δ—— So we ceased, with thanks to god: and I mused much vppon this Action: and layd all vp in mynde, and writing.

Δ——Soli Deo Honor omnis, et gloria.

Amen.

[flourish]

Marginal note:

line 3: *This was not / True Vriel: / as may appere / A° 1583: Maij 5.

The same Saterday afternoon. Hora .5.

Δ——After that Mr E.T. had called Vriel, and I was cōme to the stone

and had vsed a short speche of thanks giving to God: [an] I then required

some instruction for the purpose of Soyga

VR———Peace. you must Vse Michaël.

Δ——I know no meanes or order to vse in the invocating of Michaël

VR——— He is to be invocated by certayn of the psalmes of Dauid, and

prayers. The which psalmes, are nothing els, but a means vnto the

seat and Maiestie of God: whereby you gather with your selues due

powre, to apply your natures to the holy Angels. I mean the psalmes,

commonly called the Seven psalmes. You must vse pleasant sauours

with hand and hart: whereby you shall allure him and wynn him

(thorowgh Gods fauour) to atteyn vnto the thing, you haue long sowght for.

There must be Coniunction of myndes in prayer, betwyxt you two, to

God contynually.

Yt is the wyll of God, that you shold, ioinctly, haue the knowledge

of his Angells togither

You had atteyned vnto the Sight of Michaël, but for the imperfection

of Saul.

Be of good Cumfort.

Δ——The chayre cam into the stone againe: and I axed what

it ment.

VR——— This is a seat of perfection: from the which, things shall be shewed vnto the, which thow hast long desyred.

Δ Then was there a square Table browght into the stone: and I demaunded, what that Table betokened.

VR——— A Mysterie, not yet to be known. These two, shall remayn in the stone, to the sight of all vndefyled Creatures.

you must

Marginal note:

line 15: Note. / Δ— in this time / there appered / in the stone, / a rich chayre: / and after a little / while, it was / out of sight.

[10a]

you must vse a fowre square Table, two cubits square: wherevppon must be set Sigillum [Diuinitatis] /Dei/, which is allready perfected in a boke of thine: Blessed be God, in all his Mysteries, and Holy in all his works. This seal must not be loked on, without great reuerence and deuotion. This seale is to be made of perfect wax. I mean, wax, which is clean purified: we haue no respect of cullours. This seal must be 9 ynches in diameter: The rowndnes must be 27 ynches, and somwhat more. The Thicknes of it, must be of an ynche and half a quarter. and a figure of a crosse, must be on the back side of it, made thus:

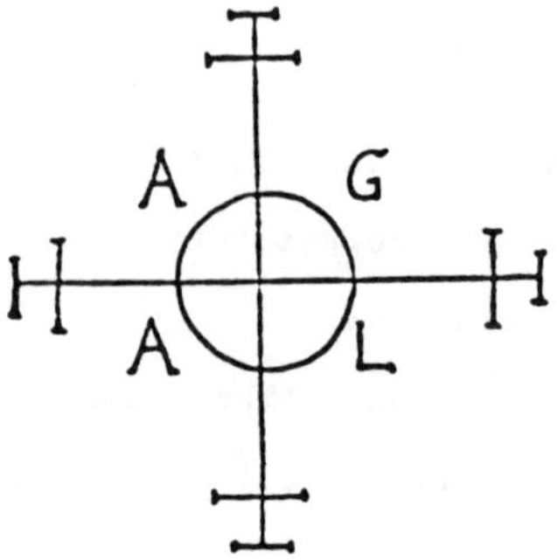

The Table is to be made of swete wood: and to be of two Cubits high.

with 4 feete: with 4 of the former seales vnder the 4 feet.

Δ——The fashion of the 4 feet, standing vppon the foresayd rownd seales,

was shewed: so as the vttermost circle conteyning the letters, did seme to be

clean without the cumpas of the fete, equally rownd abowt the same fete.

And these seales were shewed much lesser than the principall seal.

Vnder the Table did seme to be layd red sylk, two yardes square.

And ouer the seal, did seme likewise red sylk to lye fowr square: somwhat

broader then the Table, hanging down with 4 knops or tassells at the

4 corners thereof.

Vppon this vppermost red silk, did seme to be set the stone with the frame: right

ouer, and vppon the principall seal: sauing that the sayd sylk was betwene

the one and the other.

The Table was shewed to haue on the fowre sides of it, <u>Characters and names</u>,

these, that are here in a schedule annexed, in 4 diuerse rowes.

VR——The Characters and words on the sides of the square Table, are to

be written with yellow, made of perfect oyle, vsed in the church.

Δ——What oyle is that

VR——[of] That oyle shalbe opened vnto you. The oyle, is perfect prayers:

of other oyle I haue no respect.

We sanctifie, bycause we are holy: and you sanctify bycause of your holines.

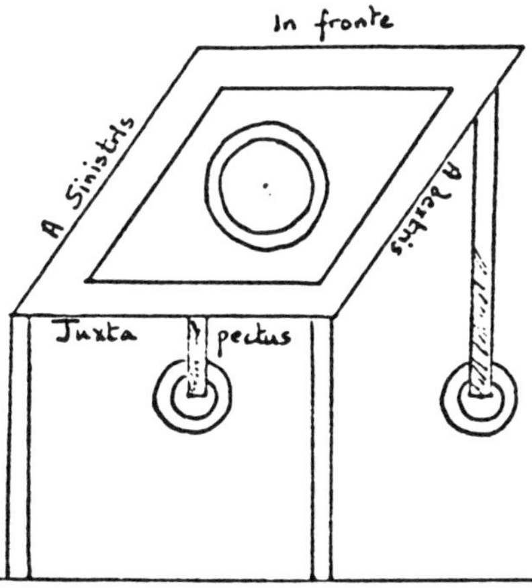

Marginal notes:

line 2: * erronicè, / contra igno= / ratiā meā. / vide post.

line 16: *Note this point.

line 25: <*> Caue: quia / angelus tenebra= / rum se intrusit / hic vt libri / Quinti appendice / apparavit.

VR——— There is a spirit, named Lundrumguffa vsing you.

who seketh your destruction, in the hatred of men, in the hurt of thy goods. Discharge him to morrow with Brymstone.

He haunteth thy howse, and seketh the destruction of thy dowghter.

His pretence was to haue maymed the in thy Sholder the last night,

and long ago. Yf thow do not dischardg him to morrow he will hurt, both thy wife and thy dowghter.

He is here* now

Giue him a generall discharge from your familie and howse

He will seke Sauls death, who is accursed.

Δ——I know no means, or art to do this by. For I did burn in flame of Brymstone, Maherion his name and Character, whan I found Saul priuilie dealing with him (which manner of wicked dealing I had oft forbydden him) and yet he came after, and wold haue carryed Saul away quick: as Robert Hilton, George, and other of my howse can testify.

VR——— The Cursed will co̅me to the cursed.

Δ——I besecne you to discharge him: and to bynde him somwhere where far of, as Raphael did (for Thobias sake) with the wycked spirit Asmodeus.

VR——— But Thobias did his part. Art is Vayne, in respect of of God his powre. Brymstone is a mean

Δ——Whan shall I do this?

VR——— To morrow at the tyme of prayers.

Δ———Gl<or>ia P̅ri et filio et Spiritui Sancto <sicu>t &c. Amen.

[flourish]

Marginal notes:

line 7: Δ Note:

line 8: * so is it evidēt / who went abowt / to hinder the / truth before in / the character / and in the bor= / der of the Table, / falsly cownter= / feating &c as it / allso in the next / action may appere. / [rule]

line 15: Saul in dan= / ger of being / carried away / quick

1582 Martij 11

Sonday. a Meridie hora .3.[a] circiter

Δ——Vriel being called by .E.T. there appeared one, clothed with a

long robe, of purple: all spanged with gold. and on his hed, a

garland, or wreath of gold: his eyes sparkling. Of whome [asked] I axed

Whether the characters noted for the Table, wer perfect:

He answered,

——They are Δ* perfect: There is no question

Δ—— Are you Vriel.

Than presently cam in One, and threw the brave spirit down by the

sholders: and bet him mightyly with a whip: and toke all his robes,

and apparell of him: and then he remayned all heary and owggly.

and styll the spirit was beaten of him, who cam in after him. And

that spirit, which so bet him, sayed to the hearing of my Skryer,

Lo, thus are the wycked skourged

Δ—— Are you Vriel, who speaketh that?

VRI———I am he. Write down and mark this: for it is

worthy

Marginal note:

line 35: Δ • / Hereby may appere / that this wycked / spirit foysted in / the shew of the / fals character / and names before

---

[11a]

worthy of the Noting.

This was thy persecutor Lundrumguffa. I browght him hither: to let the see, how God hath ponished thy enemy

Lo, thus, hath God delt for the: Lo thus haue I delt for the: Thank God.

Δ——blessed be his holy name, and extolled, world with out ende.

E.T.—he drew the wycked spirit away, by the leggs, and threw him into a great pitt. and washed his hands, as it were, with the sweat of his [hed] own hed. for he seamed to be all in [/c....7] [sweat.] a sweat.

Δ—— Here vppon, my skryer saw Vriel go away: and he remayned out of sight a little while. Then he cam in agayn: and an other with him: and iointly these two said to gither. Glorifie God for euer.

And than Vriel did stande behinde: and the other did set down in the chayre, with a sworde in his right hand: all his hed glystring like the sonne. The heare of his hed was long: He had wings: and all his lower parts seamed to be with fethers. He had a roab ouer his body: and a great light in his left hand. he sayd

Michaël—We are blessed from the begynning: and blessed be the name of

God for euer.

Δ—My skryer saw an innumerable Cumpany of Angels abowt him:

And Vriel did lean on the square Table by.

He that sat in the chayre (whom we take to be Michaël) sayd

Than

———Go forward: God hath blessed the

I will be thy Guyde

Thow shallt atteyne vnto thy seching

The World begynns with thy doings

Prayse God.

The Angels vnder my powre, shall be at thy commaundement.

Lo, I will do thus much for the

Lo, God will do thus much for the

Thow shalt see me: and I will be seen of the

And I will direct thy liuing and conversation.

Those that sowght thy life, are vanished away.

Put vp thy pen.

Δ—so he departed.

Δ—— Gloria, laus, honor, virtus et Imperium

Deo immortali, invisibili, et

Omnipotenti, in saecula saeculorū

Amen

[flourish]

Marginal notes:

line 1: Note / Lundrumm / guffa skourged / spiritually.

line 34: Lundrum= / guffa.

[11b]

Martij 14. Wensday. mane circa horā 9[a]

Δ— Being desirous to procede in this matter, by consent, we bent our selues to the Action. And after that [E T] had called Vriel and saw him, I cam to the desk from my oratorie.
There did contynually appeare, the chayre and the Table.
I than being affrayde that any other shold cōe into the stone, in stead of Vriel, did ernestly require the spirituall creature appearing, to shew who he was, and what was his name.
At length he answered, and sayde to the hearing of E. T.

Vriel is my name, with diuerse called Nariel.

Stay.

Δ— Then he went away, for a while: and cam agayn, and sayd thus,

Vr.— The strength of God, is allwayes with the.
Dost thow know, what thow writest?

Δ— In two senses, I may vnderstand it: eyther that [God] the good Angel ^ Gabriel is allwayes with me, thowgh invisibly: or els, that the strength, and mighty hand of God, allwayes is my defense

Vr— Fortitudo Dei, tecum semper est.

Δ— He went away agayn, and cam agayn, following or wayting vpp<on> an other. and before that other, was a man hauing his hed all couered with blak. Then he that cam so in the middle, did sit down in the chayre, and spake this worde following:

Mi— Note

Δ— This was Michael, with his sword in his right hand

Then cam Vriel to the man (hauing his hed all hyd, as it were in a blak hode) and toke of that blak hode: and then lifted vp the Table cloth. He looked vnder it, and put it down againe: and lifted it vp again. The man stode still before Michael. Then Michael rose; and toke of all the mans clothes, and left him, as it were, onely in his shirt Then Vriel toke a little rownd Tablet, as it were, of the bignes of a sixpence, hauing two letters in it thus: and gaue it to Michaël.

Vriel lifted Vp the Table cloth: and, from thence, seamed to take apparaile, and put on the man. it semed to be sylk: and very full of wrynkles, or plights. And the man kneeled, and held vp

up his hands. Vriel toke like a lawrel bush, and set vppon the mans hed. And than the man kneeled before Michaël. Michaël toke the rownd thing, with the letters: and gaue it the man to eat: and he did eat it

Vr——Lo, things are covered.

Δ——Then he couered the Table and pluckt the cloth over it, down to the grownd, on euery side. The man rose vp: And Michaël dubbed him on the hed with his sworde. Then the man stode vp

Then

Marginal notes:

line 10: *Agrippa hath so,/ Cap. 24. Lib. 3. / Occultae phiae.

line 16: Δ—potius erat di= / cendum Michaël: / Na̅, Gabriel est / Praevalescentia / Dei: et ita forti= / tudo quidem, sed / altioris gradus.

[12a]

Then the man turned his face toward E. T. the skryer. and the man did resemble me (John Dee) in cowntenance. And then he turned to Michaël agayn.

Michael wrote vppon the mans back, thus,

ANGELVS TVAE PROFESSIONIS.

Δ—Then .E. T. asked me, yf there were such Angels of a mans Profession: and I answered yea; as in ·Δ· Agrippa and other, is declared.

Mi——Leaue your folly: Hold thy peace.

Haue you not red, that they that cleaue vnto God, are made like vnto him.

Δ—yes, forsoth.

Mic——Thow camst hither to lern, and not to dispute.

Laudate Dominum in operibus suis.

Δ—The man kneled down, and so went out of sight.

Mi——He hath eaten strength against trubble. He hath eaten nothing: and in eating, he hath eaten all things. The name* NA, be praysed in trubbles.

Δ—Now Michael thrust out his right arme, with the sword: and bad the skryer to loke. Then his sword did seame to cleaue in two: and a great fyre, flamed out of it, vehemently. Then he toke a ring out of the flame of his sworde: and gaue it, to Vriel: and sayd, thus

Mic——The strength of God is vnspeakable. Praysed be god for euer and euer.

Δ——Then Vriel did make cursy vnto him.

Mi——After this sort, must thy ring be: Note it.

Δ——Then he rose, or disapeared, out of the chayre, and by and by, cam again, and sayde, as followeth.

Mi——I will reveale the this ring: which was never revealed since the death of Salomon: with whom I was present. I was present with him in strength, and mercy.

Lo, this it is. This is it, wherewith all Miracles, and diuine works and wonders were wrought by Salomon: This is it, which I have revealed vnto the. This is it, which Philosophie dreameth of. This is it, which the Angels skarse know. This is it, and blessed be his Name: yea, his Name be blessed for euer.

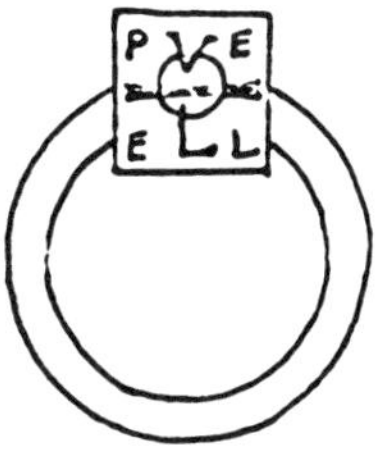

Δ——Then he layd the Ring down vppon the Table: and sayd, Note

Δ——It shewed to be a Ring of Gold: with a seale graued in it. and had a rownd thing in the myddle of the Seale and a thing like an V, throwgh the top of the circle: and an L, in the bottome: and a barr  cleane throwgh it: And had these fowre letters in it, P E L E

After that, he threw the ring on the borde, or Table: and it semed

to fall

Marginal notes:

line 7: <*vi>de Agrippam / <de> Triplici hoīs / <Cu> stode. lib. 3°. / cap 22.

line 16: # Vide Reuclinū / de verbo mirif / fico, de nōie / NA.

line 46: Vide Reuclini Librum / librū de Verbo Miri= / mirifico, de nōie / Nōie PELE

[12b]

to fall throwgh the Table: and then he sayde, thus,

Mi——— So shall it do, at thy commaundement.

Without this, thow shalt do nothing

Blessed be his name, that compasseth all things:

Wonders are in him, and his Name is WONDERFVLL:

His Name worketh wonders, from generation, to generation.

Δ—— Then he went away: and cam in agayn by and by.

Mi——— Note

Δ—— Then he browght in the Seale, which he shewed the other day: and opened his sworde, and bad the skryer reade; and he red E M E T H

[illegible] the sword closed vp agayn: and he sayde

[illegible]——This [do] I do open vnto the, bycause thow mervayledst at SIGILLVM DEI. This is the Name of the Seale: Which he blessed for euer. This is the seale self. This is Holy: This is pure: This is for euer. Amen.

Δ—— Then the seale Vanished away. And I sayde to my frende (the Skryer) In dede, this other day, I considered diuerse fashions of this seal: and I fownd them much differing, one from an other: and therfore I had nede to know, which of them I shall imitate: or how to make one perfect of them all.

Mi——Dowt not for the making of it: God hath perfyted all things. Ask not the cause of my absence, nor of my apparell: for that Mysterie, is known to God. I haue no cloathing, as thow thyself shalt see. I am a Spirit of Truth, and Vertue. Yea you shall see me in Powre, and I will viset you in HOPE

Bless you the Lorde, and followe his wayes, for euer

Δ Then he went away: and Vriel followed him.

And then I sayde to my skryer: It were good, we had euer some watch word, when we shold not loke for any more matter at theyr hands, euery tyme of theyr Visitting of vs. Wherevppon, (vnlooked for, of vs,) he spake agayn

Mi——We lead tyme, Tyme leadeth not vs:

Put vp thy pen

The Name of God, be blessed for euer.

Δ—Then they lifted vp theyr hands to heuen ward (which heven, appeared allso in the stone) and turned toward vs, and sayd

Valete:

Δ—So they departed: and at theyr going, the chayr, and the Table, in the stone, did seme to shake

Δ——Soli Deo oīs honor

Laus et Gloria.∴

Amen.

[flourish]

Marginal notes:

line 3: The vse of the Ring

line 11: De Sigillo Emeth / vide Reuclini Artē / Cabalisticā. lib. 3. / et Agrippā lib. 3. / Cap. 11.

[13a]

Martij 15. Thursday. Hora 1¼ a meridie

Δ——After [E T] his calling into the stone, appeared a tall man, with a sceptre (very great) of gold, glittring. His body all red: and out of his hed, did shote out beames of light, like the sonne beames.

Δ——[I] being desirous, to know who he was, and his name, I requested him ernestly thereto. but he answered, as followeth.

——Invocate nomen Domini, et agnoscetis eum

Δ——Then I prayed the psalme, Deus misereatur $\overline{\text{nri}}$, et benedicat nobis etc after that he sayd

——I am mighty:

Δ——Bycause he delayed to declare his name, [E T] the Skryer did require him, in the name of God the father, Jesus Christ his Sonne, and of the holy ghost, to expresse his name: and he answered in speche

——So I will by and by

Δ——Then he seamed to take from his hed little bright sparcks, like little candells endes: and to stick them abowt the chayre: and he went rownd abowt the chayre: and than he spake, as followeth.

——I am mighty, and working wonders: I am SALAMIAN.

I rule in the hevens, and beare sway vppon erth in his name, who be

blessed for euer. Thow doost dowt at me. I am the servant of God,

in his light: I serve him. I say, I serve him, with [reverence and] feare.

and reverence. My name is SALAMIAN: Mighty in the Sonne,

worker of wordly actions, as well internall, as externall: known vnto

God: whose name I know, and bless for euer.

Δ——Then appeared a big flame of fyre by him in the ayre

Sal.——Thow knowest not, or thow wilt not know, that Mamon, with

his servants, are present abowt the: whose presence doth hinder the presence

of the vertues Adonay our comming. Blessed be God, in the highest

Amen.

Δ——He toke the forsaide flame of fyre, and flung it vp vnto the heven

ward

Sal——Mamon is a king whome God hateth: whose sect, contynually

tempt, provoke and stir vp wickednes, against the lord, and against

his annoynted. But he dyeth: blessed be God for euer. Driue him away

Δ——It is incomparably more easy for you to do. And as for my parte,

I fele neyther in body, nor sowle, any token of his presence or working.

Therevppon he caused the whole chamber (which /we/[c] were in) to appere very

playnely in the stone: and so there shewed a great cumpany of wycked spirits to be in the chamber: and among them, One, most horrible and

grisely thretting, and approaching to our beds: and skorning and gnashing

at vs.

Sala——God determines his mysteries, by Arte and vertue

Δ——Then he willed me very egerly, to drive them away. And I prayed

fervently. And there seamed One to cōme into the stone, which

had very long armes: and he draue them away courragiously: And

so they were driuen away.

After that presently, cam one into the stone, all white.

Salamian reached this white one a Cup.

The white man held vp the cup: and sayd, as followeth,

————Lo, this is my name.

God shall bless you. Fear not, your faithfullness provoketh me to tell

my name, and this it is: (putting furth the Cup again) for, I am called

Medicina Dei. I will shew the, and I will shew you, the Angel of

your

Marginal notes:

line 18: SALAMIAN.

line 20: Δ— of Salamian you / may rede, in the / Call. Diei Dominicae / in Elemētis Magicis / Petri de Abano. / There called Sa= / lamia.

line 32: Mamon.

line 52: Raphaël

your Direction, which is called OCH

Δ—— This name he spake: he shewed it allso on the Table (before him) written.

Raph —— He is mighty in the sonne beams. He shall profit the hereafter.

Δ—— Then cam in an other, and sat down in the chayre: and he sayde, as

followeth

———— The strength of God liueth: and God raigneth for euer

I am Fortitudo Dei.

Δ—— Why then, you are Gabriel: and I toke you hitherto to be Michaël

Michael How shall I then amend my boke, in respect of your name, allwayes

waies before, written Michaël?

For. Dei — What thow hast written, that thow hast written, and it is true

/is true.c/ Write down this name POLIPOS.

Dost thow vnderstand it?

Δ—— No, God knoweth

For. Dei — When that day commeth, I will speak with the: Yf thow observe that which I haue* commaunded the.

As truely, as I was with SALOMON, so truely I will be with the

Δ—— /thee c/ Then cam in an other: whom we toke to be Vriel. for he went

went allso, as he was wont and leaned at the Table.

For. Dei — Search for wisdome and lerning, and the lord will deliuer it vnto you.

Δ—— I wold to god, I knew your name truely, or what peculier letter I might set for you, to Note your words and Actions by.

[For.Dei]—Name I haue none, but by my Office.
SALAMIAN cam not hither, but by me
He is a mighty Prince, governing the hevens, vnder my powre.
This is sufficient for thy Instruction.
I was with Salomon, in all his works and wonders:
and so was this, whome God had appointed vnto him.
The Diuines know his name: and he is not hidden from the face
face of the erth: His name is written in the boke which lyeth in
in the Wyndow

Δ—Do you mean Agrippa his boke? And is it there expressed
by the name SALAMIAN?

[For.Dei]—I haue sayde.

Δ—What order will you appoint vnto vs two, in respect of
our two beings to gither? My frende here, may haue other
intents and purposes of his affayres, then will serve [for]
me for
for his ayde hauing in these Actions?

[For Dei]—Joyne in prayers. For God hath blessed you. Dowt not.
Consider these Mysteries.

Δ—Then they in the stone vsed to talk to gither: but not well
to be
be discerned of the eare of [E.T]
At length [F.D] talked very much, and spedily to [E.T] and
disclosed vnto him (which he expressed not to me, at the stone
but afterward) all the manner of the practise, and Circumstance
abowt the Action intended, with the Gold lamin, the ring, the
seales etc. And after I had spoken somwhat, in requesting him,
to shew me the manner, How I shold artificially prepare euery
thing

spoken of, he sayd

F. D

Marginal notes:

line 1: De OCH, vide in / libello Arbatel / in ⊙

line 16: Δ* / Perchaunce he / meaneth the / cownsayle of / Annael: before / specifyed.

line 33: Δ——It is in Elementis / Magicis Petri de Abano / printed with Clauis / Agrippae, which / <1>ay in my Oratorie / amost vnder my / wyndow.

[14a]

Blessed be God who revealeth all Mysteries etc [caret]

I am strength in nede

And Lo, here is Medicine for the sore

We bless the lord: We gouern the erth, by the societie of Gabriel:

Whose powre, is with vs: but he not here. etc

Vse Patience

Vr——I liued with Esdras: I liued in him, in the lord, who liueth for euer.

Raph.——I liued with Tobie: Tobie the yonger.

Δ——This was the white creature, that spake this.

F. D——We liue in the lorde: who be praysed for euer.

Δ——I stode silent a good while.

F. D——What wilt thow?

Δ——I did attend, what you wold say.

F. D——I haue sayd.

Δ—I haue byn long at this tyme, in my dealing with you. I trust, I do not offend you therewith. But, for my parte, I coulde finde in my hart to contynue whole dayes and nights in this manner of doing: euen tyll my body shold be ready to synk down for wearines, before I wold giue ouer. But I feare, I haue caused wearines to my frende here.

F. D—In vertue is no wearines.

Δ—Now [they] /$\overset{c}{\text{he}}$/ stode vp, out of his chayr: and he, and they all, ioinctly blessed vs, stretching theyr hands toward vs, Crossingly. And so they went away. The Table and the Chayre remayned. and the glyttring sparckles, or drops of streaming little lightes were of the chayre immediately.

Δ—Glorie, thanks, and honor
be vnto the Almighty Trinitie
Amen

/flourish/

Marginal note, written vertically in left-hand margin:

<God will be re>vendged vppon Saul: for he hath abvsed his names in his Creatures / <He hath sinn>ed agaynst kinde. His ponishment is great: and so I ende.

/blank/ [14b]

Mysteriorum Liber Primus, booke
ending here (as I conceive) after w^{ch}
followes Mysteriorum+Liber: [Pr]
secundus, but the begining thereof
is vtterly perished.

\+ So it appears to be by diu s
Quotations in the foll^{g} Books

Marginal note:

line 3 [+so by the / Citation 28 / Ap. 1582.]

[blank] [15b]

[16a]

Mysteriorum Liber
secundus.
[rule]

[blank] [16b]

[17a]

<in> <My>steryes,
<....>ow toward a thing <........>
<... h>owse is hollow, it is empty and voyde <............ ...>
<..>ants: The God of heuen and erth, will send in<to ....>
NOTE. We bring tydings*of light. The Lord is o<ur..........>
you and we prayse to gither. His name be praysed for eu<O ....>

in his Mysteries O holy and eternall God.

Δ. he bowed down to the Chayre and then to the table, and sayd, Bene dictus qui venit in (and there stayed a little) and sayd agayn Bene dictus qui venit in nōie Domini

Δ Than came in Michael, with a sword in his hand, as he was wont and I sayd vnto him, are you Michael.

Mich. Dowt not: I am he which reioyce in him that reioyceth in the For= titude and Strength of God.

Δ Is this Forme, for the Great Seale, perfect?

Mi The forme is true and perfect

Thow shalt sweare by the liuing God, the strength of his Mercy, and his Medicinall vertue, powred into mans sowle neuer to disclose these Mysteries

Δ yf No man, by no means, shall perceyue any thing herof, by me, I wold think that I shold not do well.

Mi. Nothing is cut from the Churche of God. We in his Saincts are blessed for euer.

We Separate the, from fyled and wycked persons: we move the to God.

Δ I Vow, as you require: God be my help, and Gwyde, now and euer amen.

MIC. This is a Mystery, skarse worthy for vs our selues, to know, muche lesse to Reueale. Art thow, then, so Contented?

Δ I am: God be my strength.

Mic. Blessed art thow among the Saincts: And blessed are you both.

I will pluck the, from among the wycked [he spake Δ to my Skryer]

Thow Commyttest Idolatry

But take hede of Temptation:

The Lord hath blessed the. This is a Mystery,

Dee, what woldest thow haue?

Δ Recte Sapere et Intelligere. etc.

Mic. Thy Desyre is graunted the.

Vse

Marginal notes:

line 5: < * / ..... / .....>

line 13: <M>ichael / Fortitudo / <D>ei

line 17: <My Oa>the / <or> vow / <r>equired / for secresie

line 32: ▲To, E.T. / he spake

line 36: Dee

[17b]

wit<h>

<. . . . . . . t>hey are corrupted <. . . . . >

<. . . They > haue byn vsed to the wycked <Ther. . . . >

<. . . . . >

<But> I will shew the in the mighty hand and strength of God, <.....>

his Mysteries are. The true Circle of his aetern<ity>

Comprehending all vertue: The whole and Sacred Trinitie.

Oh, holy be he: Oh, holy be he: Oh, holy be he.

Vriel answered. Amen.

MIC. Now what wilt thow? Δ I wold full fayne procede according to the matter in hand.

Mi. Diuide this outward circle into 40 aequall partes: whose greatest numbers are fowre. See thow do it presently.

Δ I did so. Diuiding it first into fowre: and then euery of them into ten. He called, Semiel. and one cam in and kneled down: and great fyre cam out of his mowth: Michael sayde, To him, are the Mysteries of these Tables know<ne.> Michael sayde, Semiel (agayn) and by and by, /he said,7 O God [c] thow hast sa<id> and thow liuest for euer. Do not think here I speake to him. Δ he spake that to vs, least we might dowte of his last speches; as being spoken to Semiel: which he directed to the aeternall god and not to Semiel. Semiel stode vp, and flaming fire cam out of his mowth: and than he sayd, as followeth.

Sem. Mighty lord, what woldest thow with the Tables?

Mi. It is the will of God, Thow fatche them hither.

Sem. I, am his Tables

Behold these are his Tables. Lo where they are.

Δ There cam in 40 white Creatures, all in white sylk long robes and they like chyldern: and all they fallyng on theyr knees sayd Thow onely art [Holy Ho] Holy among the highest. O God, Thy Name be blessed for euer.

Δ Michael stode vp out of his chayre, and by and by, all his leggs semed to be like two great pillers of brass: and he was as high as half way to heven. And by [b] and by, his sword was all on fyre and he stroke, or drew his sworde ouer all theyr 40 heds.

The Erth quaked: and the 40 fell down: and Michael called Semiael, with a thundring voyce, and sayd,

Declare the Mysteries of the Liuing God, our God, of one that liueth for euer.

Sem. I am redy. Δ Michael stroke ouer them, with his sword

Marginal notes:

line 6: <The> Circle / of AEterni / tie

line 12: 40

line 15: Δ / Semiel / this etymo= / logie, is as= / though he / wer the secre= / tarie, for / the Name / of God

line 17: The Tables

line 26: Semiael

line 28: 40 White / Creatures

line 41: Δ / Semiel — forte significat Nomen meū Deus: Ita quod Tabulae istae sint Nomen Dei / Vel Noia Diuina
[with line from 'meū' to 'Name' (line 31)]

[18a]

his sword agayne: and they all fell down, and Vriel allso <on his> knees And commonly at the striking with his Sword, flamyng <fier> like lightening did flash with all.

Mi. Note: here is a Mysterie.

Δ Then stept furth, one of the 40, from the rest, and opened his brest, which was couered with sylk, and there appeared a great T all of Gold.

Mi. Note the Number. Δ ouer the T, stode the figure of 4, after <this> manner $\overset{4}{\mathrm{T}}$

<T>he 40, all, cryed, Yt Liueth and Multiplyeth for euer: blessed be his name.

Δ That Creature did shut vp his bosome, and vanished away, like vnto a fyre.

MI. Place that, in the first place. It is the name of the Lorde.

Δ Than there seamed a great clap of thunder to be.

Then stepped (before the rest) one other of the 40, and kneled as the other did before: and a voyce was herd [saying], Prayse God, for his name is reuerent.

Michael sayd to me, say after me thus

Deus Deus Deus noster, benedictus es nunc et semper: amen

Deus Deus Deus noster, benedictus es nunc et semper: amen

Deus Deus Deus noster, benedictus es nunc et semper: amen

Δ Then this Creature opened his breast, and fyre cam oute of the stone as before and a great romayne G appeared

Mi. Write with reuerence, These Mysteries are wunderfull, the Number of his name, and knowledge

Lo, this it is. 9. Behold, it is but one, and it is Marveylous

Δ Then this Creature vanished away . . . .

Mi. The Seale of Gods Mercy: blessed be thy name.

Δ It semed to rayne, as thowgh it had rayned fyre from heuen.

Then one other of the 40 was browght furth: The rest all fell down and sayd. Lo, thus is god known.

Then he opened his brest, and there appered an n, (not of so big pro=portion as the other), with the number of 7 over it.

MI. Multiplicatum est Nomen tuum in terra

Δ Then that man vanished away as it were in a golden smoke

MI. Thou must not write these things, but with great devotion.

He Liueth. Δ Then cam another furth: Then all falling downe sayde Vidimus Gloriam tuam Domine. They were prostrate on theyr faces. Then this Creature opened his breast and he had there a Tablet all of Gold (as it were) and there appered a small t vppon it: and the figure of 9 vnder this letter t.

Mi. Mark it, for this is a Mysterye. Δ Then that Shewer (of the 40)

seamed to fly vp into the ayre, like as it were a white garment.

Mi. Illius Gloria sit nobiscum. Δ All sayd; amen: and fell down.

Δ Then stode vp another, and opened his bosom, and shewed on his brest

bare (being like syluer) a small h; and he pointed to it, and ouer it

was the number of 22.

Mi. Et est numerus virtutis benedictus. Δ This Shewer went away like a

Videte Angelos Lucis white Cok flying vp.

Δ There cam an other in, and sayd

Et sum Finis et non est mihi Numerus. Sum Numerus in numero.

Et omnis Numerus est mihi Numerus. Videte

Δ There appeared a small n on his skyn, being all spotted with Gold

Then he

Marginal notes:

line 6: <the> very fas<hion> / of ye / <of> the T, w<as> /

thus / <t>hus T

line 12: △ T. / △ T, in the holy Lan / Language is na / named Gisg. vide / vide lib. 5. / post. et est Vl= / Vltima Al= / phabeti litera

line 21: △ △ / G,: alr Ged. / lib. 5.

line 30: N, alr, Drux:

line 39: △ / Gisg.

line 45: △ / Na

line 48: Angeli / Lucis

line 52: △ / Drux

[18b]

Then he went away like three fyres, red flaming, and comming to gather <againe>

in the myddst of the firmament. △ you must Note that in th<e stone>

the whole world in [a] manner did seme to appeare, heuen, and erth. etc

Mi. (△ he cryed with a lowde voyce) Et est Vita in caelis

△ Then stepped furth one and sayd, Et ego viuo cu bene viuentibus, and withall he

kneeled down: and Michael stepped furth and toke of his veale on his brest

and he made Cursy and stode vp.

Mi. Viuamus Halleluyah O Sanctum Nomen

△ All fell down on theyr faces, and Michael stroke ouer them <with his> sword

and a great flash of fyre: And this man his brest semed ope<n, so that> his

hart appeared bleading, and therein the letter m, and 6, over it thus <$\frac{6}{m}$>

Mic. Benedictus est Numerus Agni

Δ Herevppon they all fell down

Mi. Orate invicem Δ Herevppon we prayed a psalme; [one] /my skryer7 saying one verse, and I the other etc

Mi: Omnia data sunt a Deo. Δ Then cam one in, hauing a rownd Tablet in his forhed and a letter o in his forhed: and 22 ouer it.

Mi. Et non est finis in illo.

Benedictus es tu Deus Δ and then that shewer vanished away: He flew vp, like a rownd raynbow knyt togither at the ends.

Mi. Angeli a nomine tuo procident Domine

Tu es primus O Halleluyah.

Δ. One stode vp and the rest fell down, and out of his mouth that stode, cam a sworde: and the point, a [Δ] Triangle, and in the myddest of it a small a thus Δ(a), of pure gold, grauen very depe:

Et Numerus tuus viuit in caeteris, sayd the shewer. The nūber
20
was 22 over the a

This shewer went away with great lightening covering all the world.

Mi. Nomen illius est nobiscum Δ He stroke agayne with his sword ouer them Then stode one vp: who, vppon his garment had an n: and he turned abowt: and on his back were very many (ens) n

Mi Creasti tu Domine Angelos tuos ad Gloriam tuā Δ ouer the, n, was the number of 14 ouer that n (I meane) which was onely on his brest

Mi Et te primus Creauit Deus Δ. Then the shewer flew vp like a star

And an other cam in, all his cloth being plucked vp: and so seamed naked: He

hath a little, a,. This, a, did go rownd abowt him: begynning at
his feete: and so spirally vpward: and he seemed to be all Clay
ouer the, a, was the number 6.

Mi. Et Creata sunt et pereunt in Nomine tuo. △ and therewith
this shewer fell down all into dust on the Earth: and his white
garment flew vp, like a white smoke: and allso a white thing did
fly out of his body

Surgit Innocentia ad faciem Dei.

△ Michael did ouer them agayn with his sworde, and it seemed to lighten
He began to speak, and he stopped suddenly, and fyre flew from his mowth

Mi. Innocentium Nomina, et sanguinem vidisti Domine a Terra, et Iustus
es in operibus tuis △ Then cam one in, [all] with a garment
all bluddy: he was like a chylde, he had a ball in his hand of perfume
which smoked: and he hath vppon his forhed a little, h,. He bowed
to Michaël and Michael sayd, Numerus tuus est infinitus; et erit
finis rerum. △ This shewer seemed to powre him self awaye
like

Marginal notes:

line 3: stone

line 11: △ / Tal

line 17: △ / Med

line 25: △ / Vn.

line 27: Corrected thus, / after, by / Vriel / to be 20

line 30: △ / Drux

line 36: Δ / Vn

line 40: Note these 3 / parts

line 49: Δ / Na

[19a]

like a flud of blud: and his garment flew vpward

Mi: Non est illi numerus

Omnia pereunt a facie Dei, et a facie Terrae:

Δ Then stepped one furth, and like a water running rownd abowt him,

and he cryeth miserably, O benedictum Nomen tuū Domine.

Numerus perijt cum illis. Δ A little, o, with 18 ouer it, appered

Δ This shewer seemed to vanish away, and to cause a great water remayn

ouer all.

Mi. Lux manet in tenebris. Gloriosum est Nomen tuum

Δ Then stept one furth from the rest, who fell down, as theyr manner was.

Δ Note: All the Cumpanies of these 40, stode, five to gither, and five to gither, and so in eight Cumpanyes; each, of fiue

Δ This was a very white one: The vpper partes of his throate, seemed open

and there seemed to cum out of it fyre, in very many and diuerse cullours.

he sayd Trinus sum.

Mi. Benedictum sit nomen El

Δ Than in the myddle of the fyres or smoke seemed an, 1, thrise placed,

on a bluddy Cross. and ouer the, 1, the number 26.

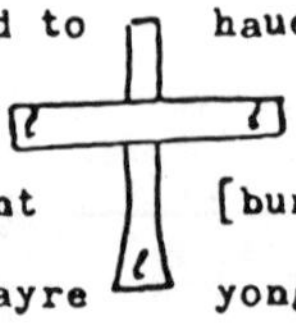

△ This shewer seemed to haue three mens heds and to vanish away in a myst with a thunder.

Mi. Labia mea laudant [bunt] Dominum

△ Then cam a very fayre yong one in with long heare hanging on her (or his) sholders: and on her belly appeared a great scotcheon: to hir, or him, Michael gaue a flame of fyre and she, or he, did eat it

Mi Et hic est El: and so appeared a little, 1, on the scotcheon and it waxed bigger and bigger: and a fyre did seeme to go rownd abowt it

Mi. Benedicta sit aetas tua: △ and there appeared, 30, vnder the 1.

△ There cam a great many of little fyers and did seeme to eleuate this yong woman (or child) out of sight.

Michael stroke his sword ouer them agayn, and sayd

Natus est illa Lux

Ille est Lux noster.

△ Then stept out an other and opened his white silk garmēt vppermost: and vnder it, he seemed to be sowed vp in a white silk cloth He had in his forhed an, n, in his brest an, n, and in his right hand an, n

Mi. Numerus tuus est benedictus △ They all fell down, saying

Numerus tuus est Nobiscum: Nec adhuc nouimus finem [eius] illius

Venies cum numero tuo O vnus in aeternum

△ and they all fell down agayn. This shewer departed clyming vp into the ayre, as if he had clymed on a ladder.

Mi. Linguis suis cognouerunt eum

Δ All sayd, Benedictus est qui sic et sic est, throwing vp in the ayre thre cornerd trenchers of this fashion  all of Gold. The one side of the trenchers was thus marked, and the other side had nothing on.

Δ Then stept one oute: and fyre cam out and in of his mowth: he kneeled, the rest fell down. This seemed a transparent body and he had in his eyes a small 1: and in his forhed the figure of 8.

Mi. Note this, vnder. I meane the figure 8. thus, $\overset{1}{8}$.

Δ All sayd

Marginal notes:

lines 3 to 6: [A cross]

line 6: Med

line 17: Δ/ Vr.

line 36: Δ/ Drux

line 49: Vr

[19b]

Δ All sayd, Et es verus in operibus tuis. and so he vanished away in a flame of fyre

Mi Gaudete omnes populi eius, gaudete omnes populi eius, ab hinc Gaudete. Δ All sayd, Amen.

Δ: one stept furth saying, Incipit virtus nostra. he being covered vnder his robe, all with armor: and he hath a great G on his armor.

and the figure of, 7, ouer it. He went behynde Michael and so vanished away

Mi. Recte viuite omnes Sancti eius

Δ One stept furth: and opening his brest, there appered a boke, and turning ouer the leaves there appeared nothing but a little, r, and 13 over it. He went behinde the Chayre and so vanished awaye.

Mi. Hic est Angelus Eccliae meae, qui doceat Ille viam meam.

Δ There stept oute a playn man, and vnder his garment, a gyrdel, and vnder his gyrdle a Rod: and in his hand he had a Sworde, and in his mowth a flame of fyre: he had a great H vppon his Sworde and vnder it 22. he went behynde the Chayre etc

Michael standing vp still vppon his leggs, like pillers of brass.

Δ I axed yf I shold not cease now, by reason of the folk tarrying for Vs to co̅me to supper

Mic Lay away the world, Contynue your work:

Coniunxit spiritum mentibus illorum

Δ Then stept out one, hauing vnder his garment a little Chest, and therein a mans hart raw: and the hart was thus with two letters, one on the one side, [and the] o, and on the other a, g,: ⊔ Δ as in scotcheons of armes, where the man and [th] his wifes armes ar ioyned ꝑ pale, as the heraulds term it This shewer shut vp the chest

and went his way.

Mi. Numerus illius est sine numero

△ Than cam in an other, saying

Tempus est Deum vestrum agnoscate.

△ This shewer his armes reached down to his feete: he shewed furth his right hand and in it a little, t, and 11 vnder it

Mi Stay, place this, in the second place. This went away.

Mi /17/ Ymago tua, (mors,) est amara.

△ Then cam one in, with a big belly, and fat cheekes: an half sword perced his hart, and a little, y, written on it.

Iustus es malis deus nr △ The number of 15 vnder it.

Mi Place it in the former place

Mi Opera fidelium, Delectatio mea [△ Then cam one in]

Hic est Deus nr He shewed the letter of o on his naked brest and the figure of 8 vnder it. He went away.

Mi Ecce, Iniquitas regnat in domo mea

△ Then stept one oute very lean, all his body full of little e, and vnder euery one of them, 21. He went away behynde the chayre.

Mi. Bestia deuoravit populum meum, peribit autem in aeternum.

△ Then stept out one in bluddy apparell. all his body full of serpents heds and a b on his forhed, and the number of 10 ouer it. He went away.

Mi Iniquitas Abundat in templo meo, et sancti viuunt cu Iniquis.

△ One very lean, hunger sterued cam out, an A on his brest, and, 11, over it and so

---

Marginal notes:

line 3: Δ / Ged — G.

line 7: Δ. Note / this to be / the first / that vanished / away, going / behynde / Michael

line 11: Δ / Don:

line 16: Δ / Na:

lines 24 to 26: Δ / ⟨ Med / ged

line 33: Δ / Gisg.

line 35: Δ / Gon — cū puncto, Y / Δ Imago. I / writ first but, / aunciently, and / vulgarly both in / writing and / print, you shall / fynde ymago / thowgh not / according to the / Latine Imag

line 41: Δ / Med.

line 44: Δ / Graph

line 48: Δ / Pa — b

[20a]

and so went away

Δ <u>There cam in an other</u>

MI. Iniqua est Terra malitijs suis

Δ Then cam in one who drew out a bluddy sworde: on his brest a great romayn

<u>I</u>, and 15 over it. he went his way.

Mi. Angeli eius ministrauerunt sanctis. Δ Then stept one oute with a

Target and a little <u>a</u> on it, and ouer it the number of 8: he went away.

Mi Regnabit Iniquitas pro tempore. △ They all cryed Halleluyah

△ Then stept one furth with a golden crown, and a great arming sworde his clothing all of gold with a letter A· on his sword and, 16, ouer it and so he went away.

Mi. Nulla regnat virtus sup terrā. △ Then stept one oute, hauing all his body vnder his white sylken habit (as they all, had) very braue after the fashion of these dayes, with great ruffs, cut hose, a great bellyed dubblet a veluet hat on his hed, with a feather: and he advanced him self braggingly. He had burnt into his forhed a little n, and Michael sayd. Non est numerus illius in Caelis. △ He went awaye.

Mi. Antiquus serpens extulit caput suum deuorans Innocentes. Halleluyah

△ Then cam one who put of his white habit: and he toke a sword, and smote vp into the ayre, and it thundred: and he had a seal (suddenly there) very gorgeous of gold and precious stone. he sayd

Regnum meum: Quis Contradicet?

△ He hath proceding out of his mowth, many little (enns) n. and on his forhed, a great A

Mi non quòd est A, sed quòd contradicit A.

Nec portio, nec numerus eius inventur in caelo

Habet autem Numerum terrestrem

Mysterium

△ He shewed three figures of, 6, in triangle thus

6
6 6

Mi. Vobis est Mysterium hoc, posterius reuelandum.

Δ And there cam a fyre and consumed him, and his chayre away, suddenly.

Mi Perturbatur terra iniquitate sua

This shewer, his garments, white, vnder: his face as brass: his body gre=

vous with leprosy: hauing vppon his brest, an o, with the number of

.10. vnder it: and so he departed.

Mi. Surgite O Ministri Dei. Surgite (inquam) Pugnate: No=

men Dei est aeternum

Δ Then cam two oute togither: they had two edged swords in theyr hands

and fyre cam oute of theyr mowthes. One had a G, and 5

ouer it, the other had

[Δ We fell to prayer. Wherevppon Michael blessed vs.]

The other had an h on his sword, and 14 vnder it: and so they

went away.

Mi. Omnis terra tremet ad vocem tubae illius

Δ One stept out, and vnder his habit had a trumpet. he put it to his

mowth, and blew it not. On his forhed a little, o, and 17 vnder

it. He went awaye.

Mi Serua Deus populum tuum, serua Deus populum tuum Israel, ser=

ua (inquam) Deus populum tuum Israel. Δ He cryed this, alowde.

Δ One appeared with a fyry sword, all bluddy, [his vesture all bluddy]

his vesture all bluddy. and he had ι

Est numerus in numero. Δ he went away

Δ I vnderstand it to be a letter, and the number 5 allso. Mi: So it is

---

Marginal notes:

line 2: Δ I think / it be / supfuous

line 10: Δ / Vriel / corrected / it after, / to be ynder

line 30: Mysterium / nobis reue= / landum.

line 32: Δ My Skry= / < er> had omit= / ted to tell / me this, or / els, it was / not told / and shewed / but Vri=/ el did after / supply it / by the / Skryer: / The first / letter of / Perturba= / tur, doth not make / shew, of / the letter / following / as other / before / did

line 51: Δ / Fam

[20b]

Δ There cam one in with diuerse owgly faces, and all his body skabbed

Mi Nunc sunt Dies tribulationis Δ he had an a on his [face] forhed and the Number 5 vnder it.

Mi hic est Numerus predictus

Mi Audite, Consummatum est This had a great pot of water in his hand and vppon the pot, grauen, a with 5 vnder it <: he> departed in fyre

Mi Angele preparato Tubam tuam

Δ Then cam one out with a Trumpet. Venit Tempus.

Δ He offered to blow, but blew it not. on the ende of his Trumpet was a little a and 24 vnder it: he went away.

Δ They all now seemed to be gon: Michael and all. He cam in agayn and two with him. And he sayd, Hij duo Caelati sunt adhuc. They two went away.

Mi. Vale. Natura habet terminum suum

Δ He blessed vs and florished his sword towards, and ouer vs. and so went away: and Vriel after him. who all this while appeared not.

[flourish]

Marginal note:

line 6: Δ / Vriel also / did correct / this place / with deliue= / ring this / [for] in the / place of / the other des= / cription / before

---

Δ After supper Mr Talbot went vp to his chamber to prayers: and Vriel shewed himself vnto him: and told him that somwhat was amyss, in the Table or seale which I had [Noted] byn occupyed abowt this day. And therevppon Mr Talbot cam came to me into my study: and requyred the Seale (or Tables) of of me: for he wished to correct somthing therin, (sayd he) I deliuered him the Seal and he browght it agayn within a little tyme after, corrected: both in the numbers, for quantyt< y > and some for place ouer or vnder: and also in one letter or place omitted. Which I denyed, of any place omitted by me, that was expressed vnto me. And the rather I dowted, vppon Michael his words last spoken, vppon two places then remay= ning yet empty: saying Hij duo Caelati sunt adhuc. But

If I had omitted any, there shold more than two haue wanted.
Wherevppon we thowght good to ax Judgmēt and dissoluing
of this dowte, by Michael. And comming to the Stone
He was redy: I propownded this former Dowte. he answered
Mi Veitas est sola in DEO. Et haec o̅i̅a vera sunt
you omitted no letter or history that was told you. But the
skryer omitted to declare vnto you. _ May I thus recorde it?
Yt is iustly reformed by Vriel: the one being omitted of the descrier
and the other not yet /to/ [by] vs declared, might make that phrase
meete to be spoken, Hij duo Caelati sunt adhuc.
Mi Thow hast sayd. △ I pray you to make vp that one
place yet wanting. Then he stode vp on his great brasen leggs
agayn: He called agayn: Semiael Semieil Than he cam,
and kneled down.
Consummatum est. △ The shewer (a white man) pluckt
oute

Marginal note:

line 39: The descryer or, / The Skryer / omitted to / tell
/A line joins 'Hij' (line 13) to 'two' (line 31),
which is itself joined by a line to 'Hij' (line 32)/

[21a]

oute a trumpet, and put it to his mowth, as thowgh he wold blow: but blew
not: and there appeared at the ende of the Trumpet the greke ω
There arose a myst, and an horrible Thunder.
MI. It is done. △ Then of the three 6 6 6 before Noted, with his
finger he put oute the two lowermost: and sayd Iste est numerus suus.

and Michael did put his finger into the Trumpets ende: and pulled furth a rownd plate of Gold, wheron was the figure of .1. With many circles abowt it, and sayd Omnia vnum est.

Δ The forme of the World which appered before, vanished away: and Semyeil went away. And Michael cam and sat in his chayr agayn: and his brasen leggs wer gone.

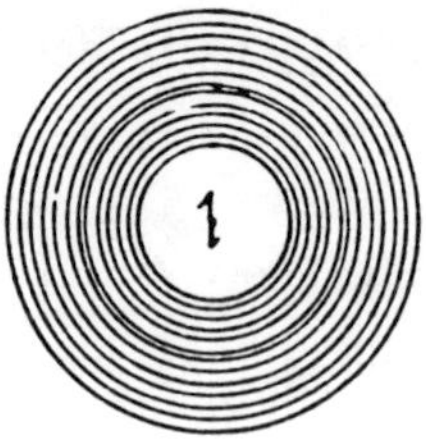

and vppon our pawsing he sayd

Mic. Go forward. Do you know what you haue allready written? Laudate Dominum in sanctis eius.

Note: The Circumference (which is done) conteyneth 7 names:

7 names, conteyn 7 Angels:

Euery letter, conteyneth 7 Angels:

The numbers are applyed to the letters.

When thow dost know the 7 names, thow shalt vnderstand the 7 Angells.

The Number of 4, pertayning to the first T, is a Number significatiue: signifying, to what place thow shalt next apply thy eye: and being placed aboue, it sheweth removing toward the right hand. Taking the figure for the number of the place applyable to the next letter to be taken. The vnder number, is significatiue: declaring to what place thow shalt apply the next letter in the Circumference, toward the left hand.

Which thow must reade, vntyll it light vppon a letter, without nūber, not signifying. This is the Whole. so shalt thow fynde the 7 principall Names: known with vs, and apply= able to thy practise.

Make experience.

△ Then telling from T (^{4}), 4 more places (toward the right hand) exclu= siuely, I finde in that fowrth place, from T, (but /being/ [c] the fifth frō the beginning, and with the begynning) this letter h: with 22, ouer it. Therfore, I procede to the right hand, 22 places: and there I finde A, and 11 over it. Going then toward the right /hand/ [c] 11 places furder: I finde a little a with 5 vnder it: by reason of which vnder place of 5 I go toward the left hand, 5 places, exclusively; where I finde o with 10, vnder it: whervppon I procede to the left hand, farder by 10 places and there I see the letter t, and 11, vnder it: and therfore going to the left hand 11 places, I see there the letter h alone without any number. Wherfore, that letter, endeth my word, and it is in all ThAaoth: ys this, as it shold be?

Mi. That is not the name. Thow shalt vnderstand all in the next Call. The Rule is perfect. Call agayn within an h<ou>re and it

△ Note these doings to be accownted Calls

Marginal notes:

line 12: SemiEl1

line 24: The decla / ration of / the num= / bers.

line 48: Call

[21b]

and it shalbe shewed

[flourish]

△ The howre being come we attended Michael his retorn to mak<e>
make the Practise euydent of his first Rule.
Mi Saluete.
Thow diddest erre: and herein hast thow erred: and yet notwithstanding
=ding no error in the, bycause thow knowest not the error.
Vnderstand that the 7 Names must Comprehend, as many letters
letters in the whole, as there are places in the Circle: Some letters are
are significatiue of them selues: in dede no letters, but dubble numbers,
=bers being the Name of God. Thow hast erred in the first
name, missetting downe A a, that is, twise a togither, w[ch]hich
differ the word. Which thow shalt Note to the ende of
thy work: Where soeuer thow shalt finde two a a togither
ther the first is not to be placed within the Name, but rather with
with his inward powre. Thow shalt fynde 7 Names proceding <from>
[from] three generall partes of the Circumference: My meaning is fr<om>
[from] three generall letters: and onely but one letter, that is, this
[this] letter A. Accownt thow, and thow shalt finde the names
iust. I speak not of any that come in the begynning of the word
[word] but such as light in the myddest: Proue: proue: and thow shalt s<ee>

/shalt see.7 Whereas thow hast [go,] it is to be red [og]. This is the whole

Δ I haue red in Cabala of the Name of God of 42 letters: but not y<et> yet of any, of 40 letters: That of 42 letters is this

אב אלהים בן אלהים רוח [אלהים]הקדש אלהים
שלשה באחד אחד בשלשה

[id est]

id est: Pater Deus, Filius Deus, Spiritus Sanctus Deus: Tres in vno, [vel vnitas] et vnus in tribus. vel Trinitas in vnitate et vnitas in Trinitate

or this אב אל בן אל [ו]רוח הקדש לא אכל לא שלשה
אלהים כי אם אלוה אחד

which in Latin, is, Pater Deus, Filius Deus, et Spiritus Sanctus, Deus, attamen non tres Dij sed vnus Deus.

And /as7 this is of God, Vnitie in Trinitie, so of Christ onely (the second persone of the Diuine Trinitie) the Cabalists haue a name explained of 42 letters, on this maner.

כאשר הכפש המשכלת והבשר אדם אחד
כן האל והאדם משיה אחד

That is in Latine Sicut anima rationalis, et caro, homo vnus, ita Deus Deus et homo, Messias vnus.

I am not good in the hebrue tung, but, you know my meaning.

Mi. The letters being so taken oute, being a name, and a nūber, doth certifye the old rule of 42 letters, whan you restore them in agayn:

Mi. Note, Oute of this Circle shall no Creature pass, that entreth,

/treth/ yf it be made vppon the earth. My meaning is, if he be defyled:

This shalt thow proue to be a mysterie vnknown to man.

Beastes

Marginal notes:

line 10: Dubble / Nubers /with hand/

line 13: Note

line 16: Δ / Note / 7 Names, pro / ceding from / 3 generall / places of the / Circumferece. / or 3 generall / letters, being / but one letter, / and that, A.

line 29: Δ / Vide Gala= / tinu, lib° / 3°. cap. 11.

line 44: Δ / 42, are here / in Potetia / but, non Acta

line 47: the / Vertu / of this / Circle. /with hand/

[22a]

Beasts, birds, fowle and fish do all reuerence to it. In this they were all Cre=

ated. In this, is all things conteyned. In tyme thow shalt find it, in ADAMS

Treatise from Paradise. Looke to the Mysteries: for they are true.

A and ω :Primus et Nouissimus; Vnus solus Deus viuit nunc et

semper: Hic est, et hic erit: Et hîc, sunt Nomina sua Diuina

Dixi.

Thow art watcht all this night: who is euen now at the Dore:

Clerkson.

Blessed are those, whose portion is not with the wicked

Benedictamus Dominum. Halleluyah.

/flourish/

Marginal note:

line 21 <ADAM>s / <TREA>t= / <ISE, Δ He me>a / <neth my> / <Booke that> / <I cal>l / Soyga

---

†

Tuesday the 20 of Marche circa $10^{\bar{a}}$ mane //ers to thee / and corrected certayn pray= —Δ. I had made, and written, [caret]

Δ Are you Vriel?

Vr. I am. We thank the for thy great goodwill

We cannot viset the now. At the twelfth howre thow shalt vse vs.

Δ Fiat voluntas Dei. [flourish]

A meridie: circa $2^{\bar{a}}$

Δ At the twelfth howre, my partner was busyed in other affayres, and so contynued tyll abowt 2 of the Clok: when, we comming to the stone, fownd there Michael and Vriel. but Michael straight way rose vp and went out, and cam in agayn, and one after him, carrying on his right shulder, 7 little baskets, of gold they seamed to be

Mi. — shut vp your doores. Δ I had left the vttermore dore of my study, open: and did but shitt the portall dore of it.

Δ He toke the 7 Baskets, and hanged them rownd abowt the border of a Canapie, of beaten gold, as it were.

Mi. Ecce, Mysterium est. Benedictus Dominus Deus Israel.

Δ Therewith he did spred oute, or stretch the Canapy: whereby it seamed to couer all the world [which seamed to be in the stone allso, heven, an erth ⌐ so that the Skryer could not now see the heven

And the baskets, by equall distances, did seeme to hang in the border of

the horizon.

Mi. What wold you haue Δ Sapientiam

Mi. Rede the names thow hast written _ I had written these

according to the Rule before giuen, as I vnderstode it.

Th[a]aoth

Gal[a]as

Gethog

Horlωn

Innon

c
A[a]oth

Galetsog

Mi. Loke to the last name. Δ I had written, (as y^t appeareth) Galetsog

---

Marginal notes:

line 23: <B>askets.

line 24: <Shut> }
<dor>es }

---

by misreckeing the numbers. Where I fownd it shold be Galethog [wh] [22b]

with an h and not s.

Mi. Lo, els thow hadst erred. They are all right, but not in order The second is the first (his name be honored for euer: The first here, must be our third. and the third here must be our second: thus set downe.

1. Galas.
2. Gethog.
3. Thaoth.
4. Horlωn.
5. Innon.
6. Aaoth.
7. Galethog.

Mi work from the right, toward the left, in the first angle next vnto the circumference

△ He shewed than, thus, this letter

M. Make the number of 5 on the right hand, (that is, before it) at a reasonable distance, thus  5

△ After that [he] shewed the second letter, a great roman A, thus  24

Then he shewed  30

Then  21

Then  9

Then he shewed  14

Then he shewed this compownd letter, with the circle and cross. 

He willed me, at each corner of these Segmēts, to make little Crosses and so I did.

△ After euery of the 7 letters shewed he did put them vp in his bosom assone as he had shewed them fully. The plates wheron those letters were shewed [were as the figure principall seale] hath the forme of the segment of a circle, thus  and seemed to be of pure gold. When the 7 letters were placed, he sayd

Omnia vnum est.

Then he pulled all the 7 plates out of his bosom: and Vriel kneeled down before him. Then the plates did seeme to haue two wings (eche of them) and to fly vp to heven vnder the Canapye.

[Marginal flourish and rule to end of 'heven' (line 35)]

△ After this, one of the 7 baskets, (that which is in the east) cam to Michael. and he sayd.

Mi. Seal this: For This was and is for euer

△ Then he stode agayn on his leggs like brasen pillers, and sayd

Mi Oh how mighty is the name of God, which rayneth in the heavens. O God of the faithfull, for thow raynest for euer.

△ he opened the basket, and there cam a great fyre out of it

Mi

[23a]

Mi. Diuide the 7 partes of the circle next vnto that which thow hast done, euery one, into 7.

Note. (for the tyme wilbe Long.) Seuen, rest in 7: and the 7, liue by 7: The 7, gouern the 7: And by 7, all Gouern=ment is. Blessed be he: yea blessed be the Lord: praysed be our god: His Name be magnified: All honor and Glory be Vnto him now and for euer. Amen

1. △ Then he toke oute of the fire in the basket, a white fowle like a pigeon

That fowle had a  vppon the first of 7 feathers which were on his brest.

that first feather was on the left side

Mi Mote. there is a mysterie in the seuen. which are the 7 gouerning the 7 which 7 gouern the earth. Halleluyah

Mi. Write the letters: Δ Now, a small l in the second fether. Then he couered those first two letters, with the other feathers

The third an l, like the other: then he couered that allso.

The fowrth an R. he covereth that

the fifth a great roman H. he couereth it.

the sixth feather hath a little i. then he hid that feather.

the last feather had a small a.

Mi. Prayse god. [Δ we prayed.]

Δ Then he put the fowle into the basket: and set it down by him. Then he hong it vp in the ayre by him.

Δ Then he lift vp his sworde over vs, and bad vs pray. Δ we prayed.

2. Δ Then he stretched out his hand and there cam an other basket to him. and he pluckt out a white byrd, much bigger than the other: as big as a swan: with .7. feathers on the brest

Mi Dixit, et factum est

Mi. Note. Δ The first feather hath a little a, on it: and it went away: the next a  great as the first

Then a C great

Then a little a

Then an other little a

Then a feather with a little c

Then one with a little b Δ Then he couered them all.

Mi. Thow hast truth.

Δ Then he put vp the fowle into the basket, and hung it vp by the other in the ayre.

Δ Than the third Basket cam to him: and he toke out a byrd all green as grass. like to a peacok in form and bignes

Mi. Et viuis tu cum illo et:

regnum tuum cum illis est

Δ There started out of this birds brest, 7 fethers, like gold, and fyrie.

Mi. Pray

3. Mi. Note. Δ On the first feather a small p

Then a small a

a little u

Then a small p

Then a small n

then a small h

Then a small r. Then he put the fowle vp into the Basket etc

Marginal note:

line 5: Δ / Note of / <the> 7 Baskets

[23b]

Δ Then there cam an other basket to his hand

Mi. Dedit illi potestates in caelis

Potestas illius magna est.

Orate. Δ we prayed

4 △ Then he pluckt out a fowle, greater then any of the other, like like a griphen (as commonly they are [p..] figured) all red fyry. with skales like brass. Then on seuen scales, appered letters.

Mi. Note. △ first a little h.

a little d

a little m

Then a little h

Then a little i

Then a little a

Then a little i

△ Then he put vp the fowle, & hung the basket in the Ayre.

△ Then there cam an other Basket to him.

[△ Note: all this while the firmament was not to be seen.]

Mi. Magnus est DEVS in Angelis suis.

et magna est illorum potestas in Caelis

Orate. △ We prayed

△ Then he pluckt out a bird like an Egle: all his body like Gold and he had a little Circle of feathers on his brest: and in it betwene /betwene7 fowre parrallell lines, twelue equall squares: and on the top, on the myddle, one [equall] like the other twelue, thus.

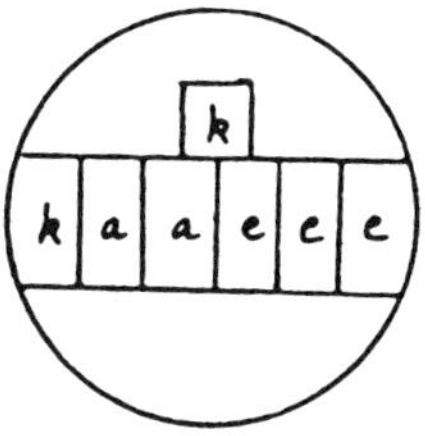

: Then he put vp the Egle etc

Δ Then cam an other Basket.

Mi. Nuncius tuus est magnus in caelis

Orate.

Δ He, and the Basket that wer opened, shut, and set aside, seamed all to be gon: and the Baskets remayning, still hanging on the border of the Canapie. Then he cam agayn. and went awaye agayne. Then cam VRIEL and held the Basket: and his leggs seemed to be such great tall pillers of Brass: as Michael did stand on before.

VR <u>This is a Mysterie</u> He <u>is here,</u> and not here which was here before.

Δ He opened the Basket and pluckt out like a phenix [or Δ pelican]
6. of the bignes of a swan: all fyrie, sparkling: His byll is bent into his brest: and it bled. In his brest was a quadrangle made with his own feathers, thus. He put it vp, and hung it by the other Baskets

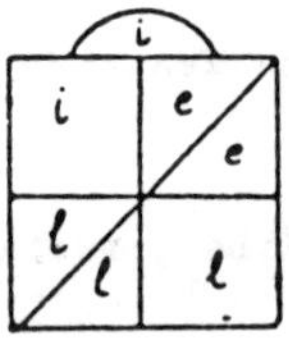

Then

Marginal note:

line 36: Δ. Michael / Was the / sixth name / vide post

Then cam the last basket. Vriel stode still: and sayde

VR. Dedit angelis potestatem in lumine Caeli.

Orate Δ we prayed

7. Δ Then cam Michael and toke the Basket of Vriel: and becam standing on the great brasen Legs, as before.

Δ He toke out of the basket a strange fowle with many wings: This fowle had in his forhed a Tablet of this fashion

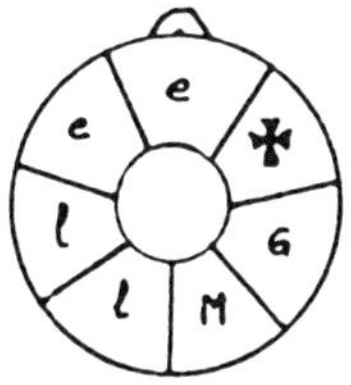

Mi. Et Coniunxit illos DEVS in vnum

Δ All the Basket flew vp: and so the Canapie vanished away: and the Heaven appeared.

Δ. Now he cam and sat down in his chayre

Δ. Michael sayd to Vriel: it is thy part, to expownd these Mysteries:

Go to, in the name of our God.

Δ Vriel cam and stode before him and sayde: What will you: Ô our fellows, and seruants to God? What will you?

Δ Perfect knowledg and Vnderstanding, such as is necessary for vs.

VR. Looke vppon, and see if thow canst not vnderstand it: we will depart for a little space: and come to the agayne

Δ So they went: and left all the stone in fyre, so that neyther the Chayr or the Table could be seen in it

Δ After a quarter of an howre, Michael and Vriel cam both agayne

Mi Loke into the 7 angles next vnto the vppermost Circumference

△ Vriel cam and stode before Michael

VR. Those 7 letters, are the 7 Seats of the One and everlasting GOD. His 7 secret Angels proceding from euery letter and Cross so formed: referred in substance to the FATHER: in forme, to the SONNE: and Inwardly to the HOLI GHOSTE. Loke vppon it: it is one of the Names, which thow hast Before: euery letter conteyning an Angel of brightnes: comprehending the 7 inward powres of God; known to none, but him self: a Sufficient BOND to vrge all Creatures to life or death, or any thing els conteyned in this World. Yt banisheth the wicked, expelleth euyll spirits: qualifieth the Waters, strengthe neth the Just, exalteth the righteous, and destroyeth the Wicked. He is ONE in SEVEN. He is twise THREE He is seuen in the Whole. He is Almighty. His Name is euerlasting: His Truth can not fayle. His Glory is incomprehensible. Blessed be his name. Blessed be thow, (our GOD) for euer.

Marginal notes:

line 13: Vriel

line 17: <M>y contynuall & / and auncient p= / prayer

line 26: △ / Note these / these ma= / manifold & / and great Mi= / Mysteries & / and make th / these 7 diuerse / Crosses wth / the 7 letters.

line 34: Note / this / Bond.

line 38: Δ~He is twice / twice three & / and one

[24b]

VR. Thow must refer thy numbers therin conteyned, to the Vpper Circle. For, From thence, all things in the inward partes, shalbe comprehended

Looke if thow vnderstand it

Δ I finde it to be GALETHOG

Vr. [So] it is so. Δ. I thank God and you, I vnderstand now (also) the numbers annexed.

Vr. As this darknes is lightened, by the spirit of God, herein: So will I lighten, Yea so will the Lord lighten your Imperfections, a glorifie your myndes to the sight of innumerable most holy and vnspeakable Mysteries.

Vr. To the next part. Δ Michael sat still, with his sword in his hand

Vr. The parte wherein thow hast labored, conteyneth 7 Angels.

Dost thow vnderstand it? Δ Not yet: Vr. Oh how far is mans Judgmēt from Celestiall powres? Oh how far are these secrets hidden from the wycked? Glory be vnto him, which seeth for euer. Δ. Amen, Amen, Amen.

VR. Note. we can not tarry long.

Thow must set down these letters onely, by 7, in a spare paper: thus.

VR. Rede ———————— Begyn at the first, and rede downward Z l l R H i a Δ I rede thus, Zaphkiel Zadkiel, Cumael a Z C a a c b Raphael, Haniel, M< i >

chaël, Gabriel	p a u p n h r	Vr. Thow hast red right
	h d m h i a i	
∠ praysed be God.	k k a a e e e	Vr. Thus dost thow see, how
mercifully God dea=	i i e e l l l	leth with his servants.
	e e l l M G ✠	

Euery letter here, conteyneth or comprehendeth the number of 72 Vertues. Whose names thow shalt know: Skarse yet revealed to the world.

Vriel and Michael iointly togither pronownced this blessing on vs.

VR. }
We bless you: your { sowles / Harts / Bodyes / and all yo[r] doings.
Mi. }

Δ Michael with his sword, and flame of fyre florished ouer our heds.

Yet I will thus ^much shew you, for your Cumfort beside. What seest thow? Δ he spake to the skryer. and he saw an innumerable [angels] multitude of Angels, in the Chāber or study abowt vs. very bewtifull with wings of fyre. Then he sayd, Lo, thus you shalbe shaddowed from the wicked Kepe these Tables secret. He is secret that liueth for euer.

Man is frayle Fare Well. ⁋ He must

Marginal notes:

line 7: [hand]

line 14: 7. Angels.

line 21: Δ—I haue hitherto / forgotten to ax / wher Vriel / his name may / appere.

line 26: Δ / 48. letters / are here: / and One is / noted by a / Cross: which / maketh the 49.th / Vide / A° 1584 / Junij 25 / of this Crosse and Angels

line 29: 72: / vertues / multiplyed / by 48: giue / 3456

line 37: [hand]

line 40 : Innumerable / multitudes of / Angells:

Below line 44 under 'He must': ℭ of this sentence / cam no frute mor / furder information / Therfore consider

---

[25a]

go for the bokes, els they will perish. Δ He ment that my partner Ed. Talbot, shold go to fatch the bokes from Lancaster (or theroy) which were the L. Mowntegles bokes. which Mr Mort yet hath: whereof mention is made before

ended hor. 5. a meridie

Tuesday the 20 Martij

1582

[flourish]

Marginal note

line 1: The L / Mownteglés / bokes.

Wensday. 21. Martij, circa 2ā a meridie

After appearance was had, there cam in one before Michael (who sat in his seat) and Vriel leaned on the table (as he, vsually did). This seemed to be a Trumpeter: he was all in white, and his garments bespotted with blud he had nothing on his hed. his heare very long hanging behynde him on his sholders. The Trumpet seamed to be gold. The sownd therof was very playne.

C I axed of my Skryer [caret], [How] [in what manner] Vriel now shewed, (and Michael likewise.)

Then Michael sayd, I warned the for axing of my apparell or manner

Et haec est Gloria illius, quae non cōmouebitur ab impijs

Mi. Quid vultis? Δ Juxta voluntate Dei, Sapiētiam

nobis necessarium etc

Mi Sapientia mundi, nihil est, peribit autem in aeternum

Veniat aeternitas Domini, ab vniuersis mundi partibus.

Venite, venite, sic vult DEVS ADONAI

fac officium Phanaël

Δ This Phanael was the Trumpeter, (above mentioned) who therevpon blew his Trumpet, lustily, turning him self rownd abowt, to all the world.

Then from 7 partes of the world, (being equally diuided abowt the Horizon,) cam 7 Cumpanyes of Pillers all of fyrye cullour glittring: And euery Cumpany of pillers high and great and as thowgh they were Pillers of fyre.

The Heauen, the Sonne, and, Mone [and] sterrs seemed to tremble.

Mi. Multiplex est Deus noster

Mi Mark this Mystery Seuen comprehendeth the Secrets

of Heven and erth: seuen knitteth mans sowle and

body togither (3, in sowle, and 4 in body)

In 7, thow shalt finde the [Trinitie] Vnitie:

In 7, thow shalt finde the Trinitie

In 7, thow shalt finde the Sonne, and the proportion of the

Holy Ghoste. O God, O God, O god, Thy Name (O God) be praysed euer, from thy 7 Thrones, from thy 7 Trumpets, and from thy 7 Angels. △ Amen, Amen, Amen.

Mi. In 7, God wrowght all things.

Mi. Note

Marginal notes:

line 12: Note this / Trumpeter.

line 17: We were / commaunded / Not to ax / of the appa / rayle of / Michael.

line 24: <Ph>anaël

lines 38 and 39: 7 < Thrones / Trumpets / Angels

[25b]

Note. In 7, and by 7 must you work all things

O Seuen tymes Seuen, Veritie, vertue and Maiestie I Minister by thy licence This expownd by thy Vertue (△ Michael spake that, pointing to Vriel.)

△ Michael and Vriel both kneeled down, and the Pillers of fyrie and brasen cullour, cam nere, rownd abowt them vniformely

Mi Sic est DEVS noster

△ One of the pillers leaned [down] toward the skryer, and had like a pommel or mace hed, on the top of it. And Michael with great reuerence toke out of the top of it a thing like an S

△ Then leaned down 6 Pillers more: and Michael, cryed lowd

Vnus est DEVS noster, Deus Deus noster.

Δ Then orderly he opened all the pillers heds: and then the 7 ioyned

all togither, distinctly to be discerned

Mi, Note. Δ. There appeared a great S

A

A

I

Δ Then the sides closed vp, and hid those letters first shewed.

After that appered two letters more E

M

Δ He made Cursy, and semed to go fromward, and vanished away.

Μοτεριογ est E 8

Δ The Pillers all ioyned togither at the tops, making (as it were) One

Mace or Pommell, and so flew vp to heven wards.

Δ There seamed two Pillers more to <u>come down from</u> heven

(<u>like the other</u> in forme) and toke place there, where the

other 7, stode, which went away.

Δ Michael with his sword, Cut them asunder: and cryed out,

<u>Away you workers of Iniquitie</u>

Perijt Malus cum malis

Δ The pillers fell down, and the grownd swallowed them vp.

Tanta est tua <u>audacia Sathan</u>

sed DEVS noster viuit.

Δ The Pillers which before ascended, cam down ioyntly: and oute of them a Voyce saying NÔN SVM

Δ Then the /77 (c) pillers next his right hand, bowed to Michael, And oute of them, a voyce sayd SVM

Δ Then one of the Pillers stode higher than his fellows, and Michael opened all the tops of them, and sayd

Orate Δ we prayed.

Mi Write the Name down in the Tables

Δ Then he toke of, 3 of the heds of the Pillers, and sett them downe and there appeared, B T Z, great letters in hollow places like square cumfet boxes.

Mi, Ista sunt <u>secreta secretorum</u>

Invocate

Marginal notes:

line 1: [hand]

line 26: NOTE

line 30: Note the / intrusion of / Error by the / Wicked powres / of Sathan.

line 36: Δ / Non Sum / I vnderstand / the refusall of / these two intruded / pillers.

[26a]

Invocate Nomen eius, aut nihil agere possumus.

<u>The key of Prayer</u> openeth all things. Δ we prayed.

Δ Then the other 4 pillers, bowingly shewed 4 letters thus, K A S E, and the number 30 with a prik vnder

Then the Pillers ioyned theyr heds togither very close, and flew vp into the firmament with Thunder

Sic Domine, Sic, Sic.

Mi Place these in the Table. Δ I wrote and he sayd, Thow hast done right Laudate nomen Domini qui viuit in aeternum.

△ A voyce cam out of the next cumpany of the 7 pillers (ioyning them selues togither) saying Ipse.

Mi. Et Misericordia tua Dn̄e magna est

△ Michael kneled whan he sayd this

△ Michael shewed out of 4 of theyr heds, of the pillers, (and with all sayd) NO, NOT the Angels of heuen, (but I,) are priuie of these things: △ so there appeared, 4 letters, H E I D

△ Then the other 3 pillers were opened and had E N E on theyr tops

Dominus collocatur in numero suo.

△ The 7 pillers mownted vp into the ayre, and it thundred at their going

△ Then the fowrth Cumpany of pillers bowed to Michael: out of them cam a voyce. Viuo sicut LEO in medio illorum

Mi. Et tua potestas magna est vbiq̧

△ Then Michael pluckt of, fiue of the tops.

There appered D: then they ioyned all togither: then appered E I M O

Mi Hoc non est sine praece

△ The other two opened, and there appeared 30 A.

△ Then they closed vp, and went away, with a great thunder

△ Then cam 7 other pillers to Michael, and a Voyce oute of them saying Serpens sum, et deuoraui serpentem.

Mi. Et bonis et malis serpens es Domine

△ Then they closed all vp: and Michael sayd, Orate. △ we prayed

△ Then Michael toke of the heds of 4: then appeared first an I then M E G

Then he opened the other 3. and C B E appeared.

Mi. Numerus illius, est nulli cognitus.

Δ They ioyned theyr heds all togither, and ascended vp to heuenward: and

great lightening after them.

Δ Then cam an other Septenarie of Pillers: and oute of them a voyce, saying

Ignis sum penetrabilis

Mi. Et sit nobiscum Ô Deus. Pray. Δ we prayed

Δ Then he opened 4 of theyr heds and appered in them I L A O

Δ They closed togither agayne

Δ Then one other was opened, and I apered

Δ Then $\overset{21}{8}$ appered, and did shut vp agayn.

Δ Then he smote fyre out of the last pyller, and it thundred and

there seemed to come out of it innumerable Angels like little Children

Note these Innumerable Angels

Marginal notes:

line 1:  / Note of / Prayer [with hand]

line 14: [hand]

line 46: Δ / <T>here is / <V>, omitted / <by> our / <ne>glect

---

[26b]

with wings: and there appered N, and suddenly did shut vp.

SIC SIC SIC Deus noster

Δ Then they ioyned all togither, and flew vp.

Mi Note down in the table. Δ I Noted them down.

△ Then cam the last 7 pillers, and out of them this Voyce

Finis

Gaudium et Lux nostra Deus

△ Then they closed all in One

Mi. Orate. △ we prayed.

△ Then /.6. [c] of7 the heds opened and appered I H R L A A

△ Then the seuenth opened: Then seamed trees to leap vp, and hills, and the seas and waters to be trubbled, and thrown vp

△ a Voyce cam out of the Pillers Consummatum est.

△ There appeared in that Piller 21/8

△ They ioyned togither and flew vp to heven ward.

Mi. VNVS VNVS VNVS

Omnis caro timet vocem eius

Pray △ we prayed.

△ Note that my skryer was very faynt, and his hed [da] in manner gyddy, and his eyes dasyling, by reason of the sights seen so bright, and fyrie, etc

Michael bad him be of good cumfort, and sayd he shold do well.

Mi Cease for a quarter of an howre.

△ After we had stayed for a quarter of an howre, we comming to the stone agayne, fownd him cōme all ready to the stone: and Vriel with him. Who, allso, had byn by, all the while, during the Mysterie of the .7. pillers.

Mic. Set two stoles in the myddst of the flowre.

on the one, set the stone: and at the other let him knele

I will shut the eares of them in the howse, that none shall heare vs. I will shew great Mysteries.

Michael than, with a lowd voyce sayd

Adeste Filiae Bonitatis:

Ecce DEVS vester adest:

Venite.

Δ There cam in 7 yong women apparelled <u>all in Grene</u>, hauing theyr heds rownd abowt attyred all with greene silk, with a wreath behinde hanging down to the grownd.

Michael stroke [the] /his/ sword ouer them, no fyre appearing. Then they kneeled: And after, rose agayn.

Mi. Scribe quae vides.

Δ One of them stept out, with a blue tablet on the forhed of her: and in it written El

Δ. She stode a side, and an other cam in, after the same sort, with a great M and a little e, thus, Me

The Third, cam as the other, and had Ese

The fowrth ———————— Iana

The fifth ———————— Akele

The sixth ———————— Azdobn

The seuenth stepped furth with ———— Stimcul

They, all togither

Marginal notes:

line 22: /flourish/

line 27: /hand/

line 32: Filiae Bonita= / tis, / or Filiolae / lucis: vide pagina sequēt.

Δ. They alltogither, sayd Nos possumus in Caelis multa.

Δ Then they went theyr way, suddenly disapering

Mi. Note this in your next place but one Δ I did so

Mi. Go to the next place. Stay.

Mi. Adeste Filiolae Lucis

Δ They [answered] all, cam in agayn, and answered, Adsumus Ô tu qui ante faciem DEI stas

Mi. Hijs nr̄is benefacite

Δ They answered, all, Factum erit.

Mi. Valete.

[E]Mi. Et dixit Dominus, venite Filij Lucia

Venite in Tabernaculo meo.

Venite (inquam): Nam Nomen meum exaltatum est.

Δ. Then cam in 7 yong men, all with bright cowntenance, white appareled,

with white silk vppom theyr heds, pendant behinde, as the women had.

One of them had a rownd purifyed pece or ball of Gold in his hand

One other had a ball of siluer in his hand.

The third a ball of Coper

The fowrth a ball of Tynne in his hand

The fifth a ball of yern

The sixth had a rownd thing of Quicksyluer, tossing it betwene his two hands

The last had a ball of Lead

They wer all apparayled of one sort

Mi Quamvis [caret] in vno generantur tempore, tamen vnum sunt.

Δ. [t]he that had the gold ball, had a rownd tablet of gold on his brest.

and on it written a great I ———

Then he with the syluer ball, cam [he] furth, with a golden tablet on his brest

likewise, and on it written Ih ———

He with the Copper ball, had in his tablet Ilr ———

He wth the tyn ball, had in his tablet Dmal ———

He with the yern ball, had in his tablet Heeoa, and so went asyde —

He with the Mercury ball, had written Beigia ———

The yong man with the leaden ball, had Stimcul ———

Mi. Facite pro illis, cum tempus erit

Δ All answered, Volumus.

Mi. Magna est Gloria Dei inter vos. Erit semper. Halleluyah

Valete.

Δ They made cursy, and went theyr way; mownting vp to heven.

Mi Dixit Deus, Memor esto nōis mei:

Vos autem immemores estis.

I speak to you. Δ Herevpon, we prayed

Mi. Venite, Venite, Venite

Filiae Filiarum Lucis Venite

Qui habebitis filias venite nunc et semper

Dixit

Marginal notes:

line 5: Filiolae / lucis

line 7: Michael / one of them / that are / cownted to / stand before / the face of God

line 10: [flourish]

line 11: Filij Lucis

line 16: Metalls

line 24: <Δ pha>ps here / wa< nte> th / non

line 26: Filij Lucis

line 43: Filiae filiarū

line 44: Note these three, / descents [with line to 'Qui' (line 44), above which is written 'forte quae']

[27b]

Dixit Deus, Creaui Angelos meos, qui destruent Filias Terrae

Adsumus, Δ. sayd 7 little wenches which cam in

They were couered with white silk robes, and with white abowt theyr hed, and pendant down behinde very long

Mi. Vbi fuistis vos? Δ They answered: In terris, cum sanctis et in caelis, cum glorificatis.

Δ These, spake not so playn, as the former did; but as thowgh they had an Impediment in theyr tung

Δ They had, euery one, somwhat in theyr hands, but my Skryer could not iudge what things they were. Mi. Non adhuc cognoscetur Mysterion hoc.

Δ Eache had fowre square Tablets on theyr bosoms, as yf they were white Iuory

/Ivory/ Δ The first shewed on her Tablet a great S

The second ———————— Ab

The third ———————— Ath

The fowrth ———————— Ized

The fifth ———————— Ekiei

The sixth ———————— Madimi

The seuenth ———————— Esemeli

Mi. Quid istis facietis?

Erimus cum illis, in omnis operibus, illorū, Δ they answered.

Mi Valete. Δ They answered, Valeas et tu Magnus O in Caelis Δ. and so they went away

Mi. Orate Δ We prayed.

Mi. Et misit filios filiorum, edocentes Israel

Mi. Dixit Dominus, Venite ad vocem meam

Adsumus, Δ. sayd 7 little Childern. which cam in like boyes couered all with purple, with hanging sleues =es like preists or scholers gown sleues: theyr heds attyred all (after the former manner) with purple silk.

Mi Quid factum est inter filios hominum?

Male viuunt (sayd they) nec habemus locum cū illis tanta est illorum Iniustitia. Veh mundo, scandalis. Veh scandalizantibus, Veh illis quibus Nos non sumus.

Δ These had tablets (on theyr brests) three cornerd, and seemed to be very grene greene and in them, letters. The first had two letters in one thus, of E, L

The first ———— E L —— Δ he sayd Nec nōīe meo tixet Mund/ūs/us

The second ———— An —— Nullus videbit faciem meam

The third ———— Aue —— Non est virgo suꝑ terrā cui dicā, [Δ and pointed to his tablet, wherein that word, Aue was written]

The fowrth ———— Liba — Tanta est infirmitas sanctitudin Diei. Benefacientes decesserūt ab illo

The fifth ———————— Rocle—Opera manuū illorū sūt vana

Nemo autem videbit me.

The sixth shewed his

Tablet and said, Ecce —— Hagonȧ—Qui adhuc Sancti sūt, cū illis viuo.

The seventh

Marginal notes:

line 3: <T>hey<r> Attyre.

line 10: [hand]

line 13: Filiae / Filiarū

line 15: Ath —

line 18: Madimi —

lines 24-25: [flourish]

line 27: Filij filiorū

line 28: Theyr Attyre

line 37: E~

line 44: Rocle

line 47: Hagonel. / (vide de / hoc Hagonel, lib° 4°.

[28a]

The seuenth had on his tablet —Ilemese—Hij imitauerūt doctrinā mea<m>

In me Ōis sita est Dóctrina

△ I thowght my Skryer had missherd, this word Imitauerūt, for Imitati sunt. And Michael smyled and seemed to lawgh and sayd, Non curat numerum Lupus and furder he sayd: Ne minimam detrahet à virtute, virtutem

Mi. Estote cum illis: Estote (inquam cum istis) Estote (inquam) mecum. Valete.

Δ. so they went, making reuerence, and went vp to heuen

Mi. Dictum est hoc tempore.

Mi. Note this in thy Tables:

Dost thow vnderstand it. Loke if thow canst

Δ He sayd to Vriel, it is thy part, to interpretate these things

Vr. Omnis Intelligentia est a Domino.

Mi. Et eius Nomen est Halleluyah.

Compose a table diuided into 7 parts, square.

S	A	A	I $^{21}_{8}$	E [M]	M [E]	E 8
B	T	Z	K	A	S	E 30
H	E	I	D	E	N	E
D	E	I	M	O	30	A
I 26	M	E	G	C	B	E
I	L [A]	A [L]	O	I $^{21}_{8}$	[$^{21}_{8}$] V	N
I	H	R	L	A	A	$^{21}_{8}$

Vr. Those names, which procede from the left hand to the right, are the Names of God, not known to the Angels: neyther can be spoken or red of man. Proue if thow canst reade them

Beatus est qui secrete

nomina sua conseruat.

Vr. These Names, bring furth 7 Angels. The 7 Angels, and Governers in the heuens next vnto vs, which stand allwayes before the face of God.

Sanctus Sanctus Sanctus

est ille DEVS noster.

Vr. Euery letter of the Angels names, bringeth furth 7 dowghters Euery dowghter, bringeth furth her dowghter, which is 7 Euery dowghter her dowghter bringeth furth a sonne. Euery sonne in him self, is 7. Euery sonne

hath

Marginal notes:

line 13: Vrielis / officiū

line 17: Δ Note: this / Table is made / perfecter by / the next side / following

line 25: 7. Names / of God.

line 30: Note these / two orders / of Angels: / and Note / V[i]riel doth / name him self / one of the standers / before the face of God

line 34: Δ / NOTE / well this / Rule of / Arte

[28b]

hath his sonne. and his sonne is 7.

Let vs prayse the God of seuen, which was and is

and shall Liue for euer.

Vox Domini in Fortitudine

Vox Domini in Decore

Vox Domini reuelat Secreta

In templo eius, Laudemus Nomen eius El.

Halleluyah.

See if thow canst now vnderstand this table.

The Dowghters procede from the angle on the right hand, cleaving the myddle: where theyr generation ceaseth.

The Sonnes from the left hand to the right to the middle. So proceding where theyr number endeth in one Centre. The Residue thow mayst (by this Note) Vnderstande

Δ Then /M̄ichael/ he stroke ouer vs ward, with his sword, and the flame mes of fire yssued oute.

Loke to the Corner on the right hand, being the vppermost: where thow shalt finde 8. Refer thyne eye to the vpper number, and the letter aboue it. But the Number must be fownd vnder neth, because his prick so noteth.

Than procede to the names of the dowghters in the Table: and thow shalt see that it is the first name of them: This shall teache the.

Δ Loking now into my first and greatest Circle for 8, I finde it wit<h> with 1 ouer it. I take this to be the first Dowghter

Vr. you must in this square Table set E by the 8. and n<ow> write them Composedly in one letter, thus E.

Nomen Domini viuit in aeternum.

Vr. Giue ouer, for half an howre, and thow shalt be fully instructed.

4 I did so, and after half an howre comming to the stone, I was willed to make a new square table of 7: and to write [do] and note, as it followeth.

S	A	A	I 21/8̣	E	M	E 8̣	— Viuit in Caelis
B	T	Z	K	A	S	E 3̣°	— Deus noster
H	E	I	D	E	N	E	— Dux noster
D	E	I	M	O	3̣°	A	— Hic est
I 2̇6	M	E	G	C	B	E	— Lux in aeternum
I	L	A	O	I 21/8̣	V	N	— Finis est
I	H	R	L	A	A	21/8̣	— Vera est haec tabula

Vera est haec Tabula, partim nobis cognita, et partim omnibus, incognita Vide iam.

The 3̣° by E, in the second place, in the vpper right corner, serueth not in the consideration <u>of the first Dowghters</u>, but for an other purpose.

The 2̇6

Marginal notes:

line 10: Filiae

line 12: Filij

line 13: Note this / manner of / Center accowm= / ted.

line 18: Note of Nūbers / with pricks / signifying letters.

line 25: 1 the first / dowghter

line 27: El

line 44: Note these / other pur= /poses.

[29a]

The 2̇6 by I, <u>serueth for another purpose</u>: but not for this Dowghters

Dowghter.

The 21, is e, and 8 with the prick vnder it is l: which togither maketh

El, or thus compownded as it were one letter, El

The Names in the great Seale must follow the Orthographie of this

Table. Virtus vobiscum est.

Orate. Δ we prayed.

Δ · Then there appeared SAAI$\frac{21}{8}$MEl. here is an E, comprehended in L

Vr. Read now the Table.

Angeli Lucis Dei nostri

Et posuit angelos illius in medio illorum

Vr. In the table are the names of 7 Angels. the first Zabathiel,

beginning from the left vppermost corner: taking the corner letter first,

and then that on the right hand aboue: and than that vnder the first

and than the third from the first, in the vpper row: and then cornerwise

down toward the left hand: and then to the fowrth letter frō the first

in the vpper row: where there is I with $\frac{21}{8}$, which maketh El. So

1. have you <u>Zabathiel</u>.

2. Vr. Go forward. Δ So, I finde next <u>Zedekieil</u>.

Vr. this I in the last Syllable <u>augmenteth the true sownd of it</u>.

3. Δ. Then next I finde Madimiel ———————— Vr. it is so.

4. Δ. Then ———— Semeliel ———— Vr. it is true

5. Δ. Then ———— Nogahel ———— Vr. it is so

6. Δ. Then ———— Corabiel ———— Vr. it is so.

<7.> Δ. Then ———— Leuanael ———— Vr. it is so.

Vr. Write these names in the Great Seal, next vnder the 7 names which thow wrotest last. videlicet, vnder EL , An Aue etc distinctly in great letters.

Vr. Make the E and L of Zabathiel, in one letter compownded, thus ZABATHIEL. In this, so fashion your E and L. And this name must be distributed in his letters into 7 sides of that innermost Heptagonum. For the other, I will teache you to dispose them. you must make for IEL (in this name onely) I with the $\frac{21}{8}$ annexed. So haue you iust 7 places.

Vr. The next fiue names thow shalt dispose in the fiue exterior angles of the Pentacle: euery angle conteyning one whole name

Vr. Set the first letters of these 5 names, (in Capitall letters) within the fiue acute internall angles of the Pentacle: and the rest of eche name following Circularly from his Capitall letter, but in the 5 exterior obtuse angles of the Pentacle.

Vr. Set Z, of Zedekieil within the angle which standeth vp toward the begynning of the greatest Circle. And so procede toward the right hand.

Vr. In the middle now of the Pentacle, make a cross † like a Crucifix and write the last of those 7 names Leuanael

thus

Marginal notes:

line 10: Angeli / Lucis

line 20: The true sownd

line 24 RH: △ This name / Corabiel you / may see in Elem / m̄etis Magicis Petri / De Abano in the / Considerations Diei ☽

[29b]

Vriel Vidit DEVS, opus suum esse bonum
et cessauit a Labore suo.
Factum est.

△ Michael stode vp and sayd

The aeternall Blessing of God the FATHER
The mercifull Goodnes of CHRIST, his SONNE
The Vnspeakable Dignitie of GOD the Holy GHOSTE
bless you, preserue you, and multiply your
doings in his Honor and Glory.

Vriel. AMEN

Vr. These Angels are the angells of the 7 Circles of Heven,
gouerning the Lightes of the .7. Circles
Blessed be GOD in vs, and by Vs
Which stand contynually before
the presence of GOD for euer.

DIXI.

:J Whan may we be so bold, as to require your help agayn.

Mic. Whan so euer you will, we are ready.

Farewell.

Δ Sit Nomen Domini benedictum, ex hoc nunc,
et Vsq in saecula saeculorum:

Amen

[flourish]

Anni Dni 1582. Martij. 21. } At Mortlake by Richemond

[flourish]

Marginal note:

line 14 (at meeting of rules from lines 11 and 15): Note these / the order / of Angels

---

SIGILLVM DEI; AEMAETH EMETH

nuncupatum:· אֱמֶת } hebraicè

DEI אֱמֶת

[30b]

[blank]

[31a]

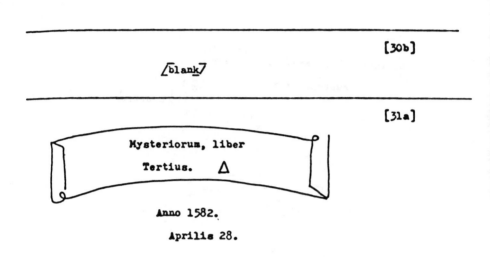

Mysteriorum, liber

Tertius. Δ

Anno 1582.

Aprilis 28.

Liber: 3us

Liber: 4us

[31b]

[blank]

[32a]

A° 1582. Aprilis 28. a meridie hora 4

E T. onely Michael appeared; [Δ^{c}:] and to diuerse my Complayntes, and requests

sayde

Mi. The Lord shall consider the in this world, and in the world to cōme

E T. All the chayre seamed on fyre

Mi. This is one Action, in one person: I speak of you two

Δ You meane vs two to be ioyned so, and in mynde vnited, as yf we wer one man

Mi. Thow vnderstandest

Take heade of punishmet for your last slaknes.

Δ Yf you mean any slaknes on my behalf, Truely it was and is for lak of habilitie to

buy and prepare things, appointed of you. Procure I pray you habilitie, and

so shall I make spede.

E T. A great hill of gold with serpents lying on it appeared: he smyteth it

with his sword, and it falleth into a mighty great water, hedlong.

Mi. Dost thow vnderstand. Δ No verylie.

E T. He razed the hill away, as thowgh there had byn none: and sayd

Mi. Lo, so it is of this worldly habilitie

Δ I pray you how must the lamine be hanged?

Mi As concerning the lamine, it must be hanged vnseen,

in sōme skarf.

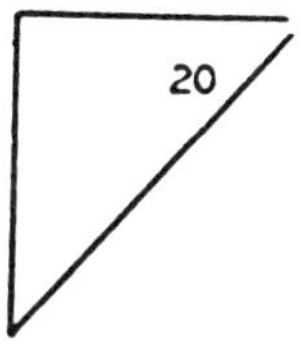

The Ring when it is made, I will lessen it according to

my pleasure

I meane by two Cubites, your vsuall yarde.

Haste, for thow hast many things to do.

Glory be to God, Peace vnto his Creatures, Mercy to the wicked;

Forgivenes to the Faithfull. He liueth, ô he rayngeth, O

thow art mighty, PELE: thy name be blessed. Δ Amen.

Venito Ese, Δ he cryed so with a lowd voyce

E T. he is now couered, in a myghty couering of fyre, of a great beawty.

There standeth a thing before him I cannot tell what it is.

Laudate Dominum in caelis

Orate. △ we prayed.

E T. His face remayneth couered with the fyre, but his body vncovered

Mi Adesdum Ese

Adesdum Iana.

Vobis dedit demonstrationem in Tabulis vr̄is.

E T. There appeare of the figure, (before, imperfect) two little women:

One of them held vp a Table which lightened terribly: so that all the

stone was couered: with a myst.

A voyce cam out of the myst, and sayd,

Ex hijs creata sunt et haec sūt noīa illorū.

E T. The myst cleareth, and one of the women held vp a Table

being thus written vppon.

Numerus Primus.

△ The Table semed square, and full of letters and numbers, and

Crosses, in diuerse places, diuersely fashioned

> △ Remēber, Ese and Iana, ar the thirdth and fowrth of the
> septem Filiae Bonitatis, sūp lib.° 2.° They are thus in
> order these, El, Me, Ese, Iana, Akele, Azdobn, Stimcul.

a finger

Marginal notes:

line 6: <V>nion / of vs < two.>

line 15: Worldly / hability.

line 19: The lamin / not simples / spoken: for / No such

Lamyn / <w>as to be / <m>ad< e >

line 27: PELE

line 28: Ese

line 35: Iana

line 42: Creatio

[32b]

A finger cam out of the mist, and wyped oute, the first Shew, wit<h>
the Cross, letters, and numbers.

The second was in like wise

The third was a b with the tayle vpward thus 

The 52 with the three great B B B, seme to be couered wth Gold

The two Crossed ones he did not wipe oute with his finger.

The next he blotted oute.

He blotted not oute the three b b b with the 8 and ℨ

The two barrs must go clere and not towch the

The  , the square, wherin it standeth, is all gold:

and that he let stand.

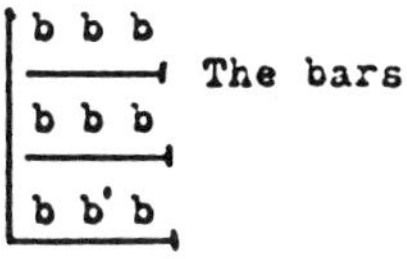

Five cam oute and burnt 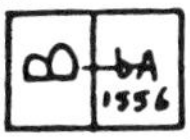

The 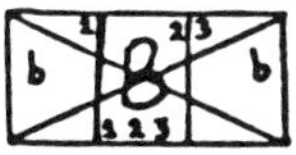 is all of a bright cullour, like the brightnes of the Sonne

and that was not put out.

The places are very black, but where the letters and numbers do stand.

E T. hard a voyce saying Finis Tenebrarū: Halleluyah.

E T There commeth a hand and putteth the little woman into the clowde.

Mi. Prayse God: Be inwardly mery.

The Darknes is comprehended

God bless you: God bless you: God blesse you.

You must leave of for an howre and a half: for you haue .6. other

Tables to write to night.

Prayse God: be ioyfull.

[flourish]

After supper we resorted to our scholemaster.

E T. I here a voyce but see nothing: he sayeth

Initium bonum in nomine eius

et est. Halleluyah.

E T. Three quarters of the stone (on the right side) are dark, the other

quarter, is clere.

Mi. Venite filiae filiarū Ese

The nethermost......

E T There come six yong maydens, all in white apparell, alike.

Now they all be gonne into the dark parte of the stone, except one

There cam a flame of fyre out of the dark, and in the flame written

Vnus on this manner

She that standeth without, putteth her hand into the dark: and pulleth out

a ball of light: and threw it oute: and it waxed bigger and bigger: and

it Thundred.

E T. A voyce sayd———Dies primus

an other voyce———Vbi est Tabula?

an answer ———Est, Est, Est

She wyndeth and turneth her self abowt, begynning at her hed, and s<o>

was Transformed into a Table, rownde

E T. Three faces do shew and shote oute, and ouer returne into one he<ad>

agayne: and with it cam a mervaylous swete sauour

The Table was of three cullours: white, redd, and a mixture of white and red

---

Marginal notes:

line 32: Filiae filiarū / Ese / sup̄ lib'. 2°.

line 33: Δ somewhat / wanting.

line 40: Lux

line 49: The Table / cullored

A line joins 'very black' (line 16) to 'Tenebraru' (line 17).

[33a]

Numerus Primus

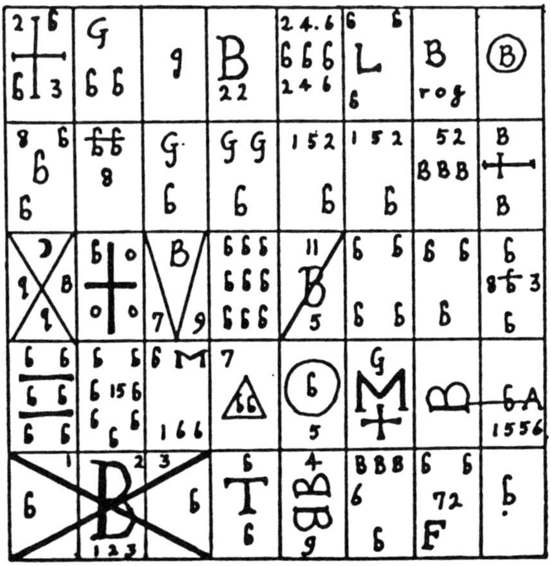

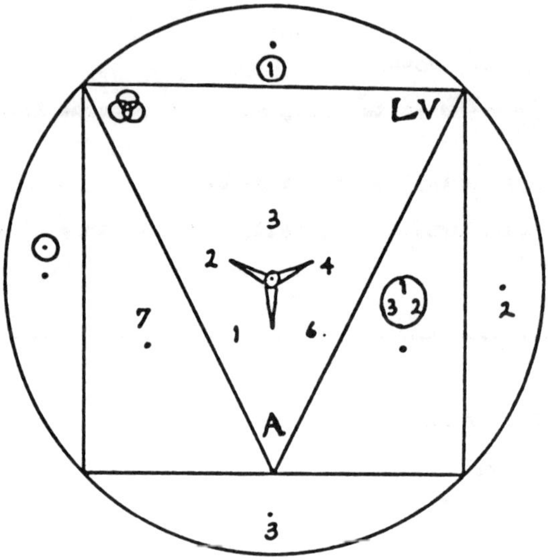

Δ

Of these seven tables, Characters, or scotcheons 5

Consider the words spoken in the fifth boke A.^{o} 1583, Aprill 28

How they are proper to every King and [pin] prince in theyr order.

They are Instruments of Conciliation

Volumine 5°. wher my Character, is fashioned

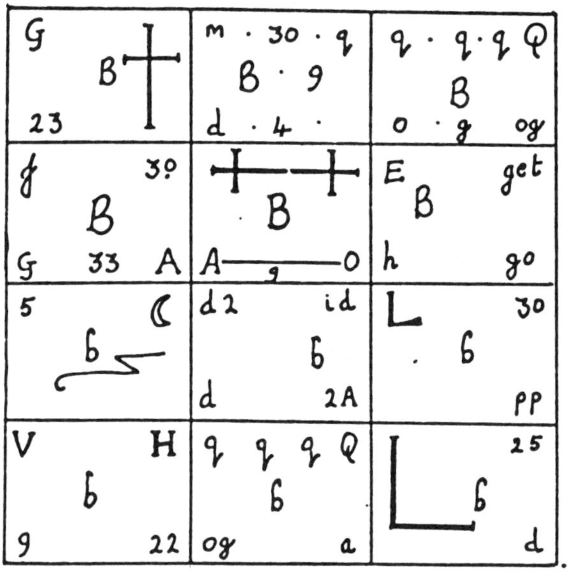

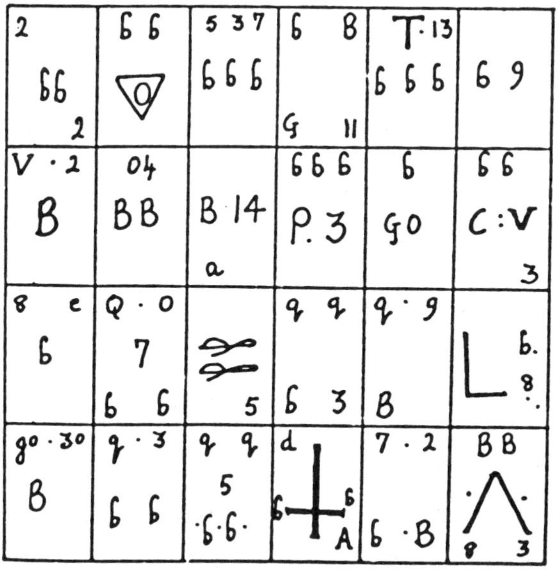

and red, changeably. A strong sownding cam withall, as of clattring of har<ness,>

or fall of waters, or such like.

There cam a sterre shoting oute of the dark, and settled it self in the myd<le>

of the Table: And the fyre which cam oute with the woman, did cumpas

the Table abowt

A voyce sayd. O honor, laus et gloria; Tibi qui es, et eris.

The Table sheweth wunderfull fayre and glorious

Onely seuen priks appeare in the Table.

The three angles of the triangle open, and in the lower point appeared a

great A

And in the right vpper corner LV. (E T. the Table trembled)

And in the other Corner appeared thre circles of aequall bignes, aequally, or

alike intersecting eche other  by theyr centers.

A Voyce——Vnus est, Trinus est; in omni Angulo est

Omnia comprehendit: Fuit, est, et vobis erit.

Finis et Origo (E T. Ô, Ô; with a dullfull sownd he pnown/ced/

E T. The woman sayth, Fui: sum, quod non sum

A voyce————Lux non erat et nunc est

E T The woman being turned, from the shape of the Table, into womans shape

agayn, went into the dark.

Then one part of the darknes diminished, In the dark was a mervaylous

turmoyling, tossing, and stur, a long tyme during.

A voyce————For a tyme Nature can not abyde these sightes.

E T. It is become Quiet, but dark still.

A voyce.——Pray and that vehemently, For these things are not revealed

without great prayer

[flourish]

E T. After a long tyme there cam a woman: and flung vp a ball like glass: and

a voyce was hard saying Fiat

The ball went into the darknes, and browght with it a great white Globe

hollow transparent.

Then she had a Table abowt her neck, square of 12 places

The woman seamed to daunce and swyng the Table:

Then cam a hand oute of the dark: and stroke her and she stode still, and

becam fayrer: She sayd Ecce signū Incomprehensibilitatis

E T. The Woman is transformed into a water, and flyeth vp into the Globe of

Light: [a voyce was hard Est, Est, Est]

[flourish]

E T. A voyce. Est, Est, Est.

E T. One commeth [out], (a Woman) out of the Dark very demurely, and

soberly walking, carrying in her hand a little rownd ball: and threw

it into the dark and it becam a great thing of Earth. She taketh

it in her hand agayne, and casteth it vp into the rownd Globe and sayd

Fiat.

E T. She turned her back toward E T and there appeared a Table diuided

in 24 partes. yt seemeth to be very Square.

A voyce.——Scribe. Veritas est.

E T. A sword cam out of the Dark: and claue the woman asunder and the one half becam a man, and the other a woman: and they went and sat vppon the Ball of clay or erth.

[flourish]

Now seemeth·

Marginal notes:

line 17, over 'sum': Δ forte fui

line 26: Prayer

line 36: Water.

line 42: Erth.

line 49: Man / Woman

[34b]

Now seemeth the Dark part to quake

A voyce ———— Venito Vasedg

E T. There cōmeth a woman oute of the Dark: she sayd

Vita hijs ex mea manū.

E T. She sheweth a Table Square full of holes, and many things creeping out of it. This square is within a rownd

A voyce O Lux Deus nr̄

Hamuthz Gethog

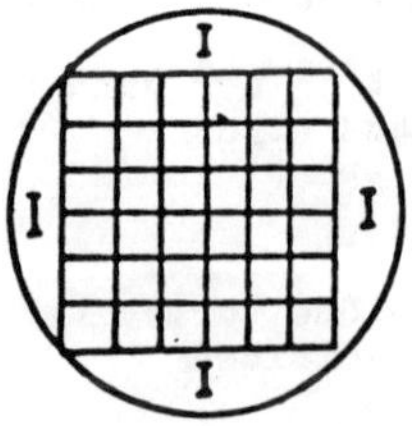

E T. Then stept out an other woman hauing a sword in her hand. She toke a thing oute of the dark

(a bright thing) and cut it in twayn and

the one parte she cut <u>into two vnaequall</u> partes: and the other half, she

cutteth into a thowsand (or innumerable) partes. Then she toke all the partes

vp into her skyrt. She hath a Table, and it hangeth on her shulders

She stept before the other woman, <u>whose hed standeth</u> in the dark.

This woman her Table is fowresquare. She is very bewtifull:

she sayd Lumina sunt haec Intelligentiae tuae

She sayd Fere nulli Credendus est hic numerus.

This woman taketh the little peces, and casteth them vp, and they become

little Sparks of light: and of the things she cast, There were two

great rownd things. And they were allso cast vp to the white Transpa=

rent Globe. And she went away into the Dark: which was, now, very

much lessened:

Then the other woman, (who <u>was forestept</u>) thrust oute her hed

who had the <u>rownd</u> conteyning the <u>Square</u>, with 36 places.

She crymbleth clay, and it turneth to <u>byrds</u>. She seameth to be

like a witch. Into the bosse of her Table, she put her hand

and that bosse, was in the Dark: and oute of the bosse, she

seemed to fatch that Clay . she sayd

Ad vsum tuum Multiplicati sunt.

E T She went into the Dark.

[flourish]

E T. A voyce,

Marginal notes:

line 16: Note this / stepping / before [with a line connecting 'stepping' with 'forestept' (line 26)]

line 21: The sterrs / Sonne and / Mone / Created

Lines join 'Square' (line 5) to 'Square' (line 27), and also 'rownd' (line 6) to 'rownd' (line 27).

[35a]

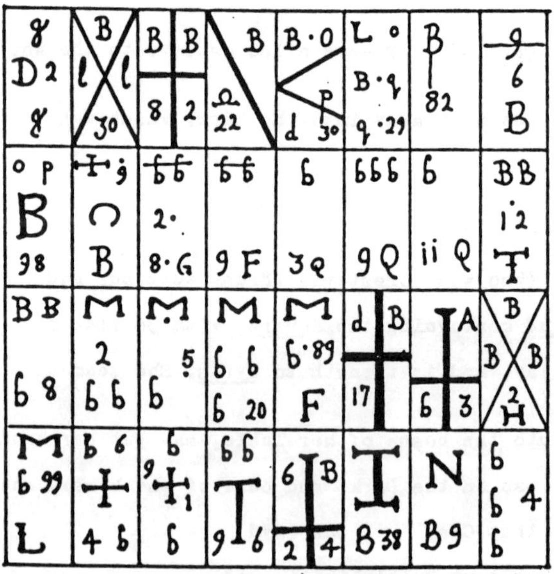

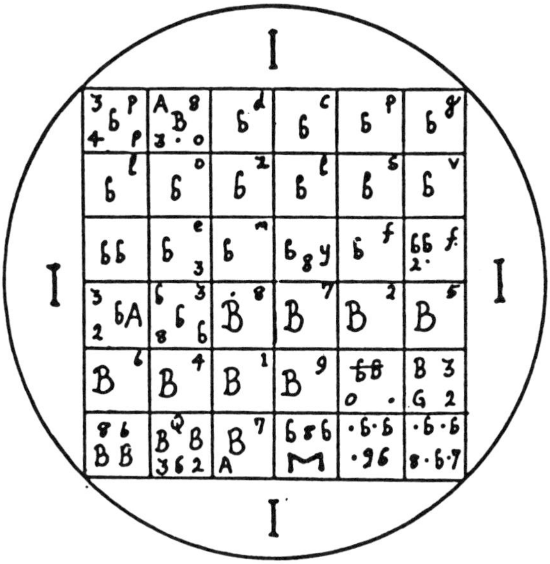

Marginal note:

bottom line of first Table: Note / the Cross / with the two / bees, the 4 and / the 6, is one of / the Notes annexed / to the second Table / of the 4 of Enochs / Tables: And the T of Enochs / Tables semeth to answer / vnto the T first in / the Seale of AEmeth / and the cross allso / 

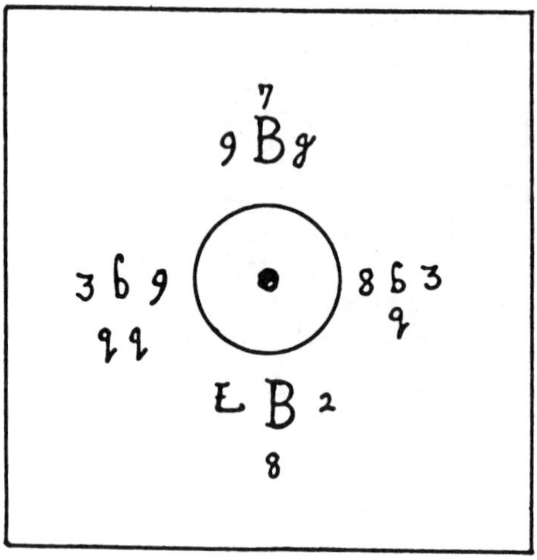

[36a]

E.T: A voyce is hard saying

Omnia gaudent fine

E.T: There commeth oute a woman, out of the Dark. She plucketh at the dark, and casteth it on the grownd: and it turneth to herbes, and plants becomming like a garden. and they grow vp very fast: she sayd

Opus est.

E T. She hath a fowre square Table before her.

Then cam one, all in white, <u>and taketh the Darknes, and wrappeth it vp</u> <u>and casteth it into the myddle of the Erthen Globe</u>, on which appeared

Trees and Plants.

E.T: Then appered Michael, his Chayre, and Table agayne manifestly, which all this while, were not seen.

Mi Obumbrabit vestigia v̄r̄a veritatis Luce

The Actor, The Actor, The Actor:

One Disposer; he, which is one in all; and All in all:

bless you from the wickednes of Deceyte: Create you

new vessels: To whome I commyt you.

E.T: he holdeth his sword over vs, in manner, out of the stone.

Mi Fare Well. Serue God. Be patient

Hate vayne glorie. Liue iustly. Amen.

Δ What spede shall I make for the yard square Table, the Wax, the Seale, and the Character? Mi. As thow ar motioned, so do.

Δ Gloria P̄r̄i et F et SS. S.e.i.p.e.n.e./s.e^{c}./i,ss. amen,

[flourish]

Note, All the Tables before were by E T, letter by letter noted out of the stone standing before him all the while: and [so wer] the [my] Tables following wer written by me as he repeted them orderly out of the stone.

[flourish]

Marginal notes:

line 4: hearbs / &c

line 8: <...> Centre
<D>arknes.

Aprilis 29: Sonday: Nocte hora 8½.

E.T. Two appeare Michael and Vriel.

Mi. Et posuit illos in ministerium eius.

Quid desideratis?

Δ Sapientiam et Scientiam nobis necessariā, et in Dei servito potentem
ad eius gloriam.

Mi Sapere, a Deo: Scire a Creatura et ex creaturis est.

▲ Vr. Venite filiae

E.T: Seuen women appeare bewtifull and fayre

Mi. This work is of wisdome (Δ sayd Michael, and stode vp).

E T, sayd to me (Δ), He putteth oute his sword and willeth me to sweare, to
that, that he willeth me: and to follow his cownsayle.

Mi. Wilt thow Δ Then with much ado, E T sayd as followeth

E T. I promise, in the name of God the Father, God the sonne and God
the holy ghost, to pforme that you shall will me, so far as it
shall lye in my powre.

E.T. Now they two seeme to confer to gither

Mi. Now you towche the world, and the doings vppon earth.
Now we shew vnto you the lower world: The Gouernors that
work and rule vnder God: By whome you may haue
powre

Marginal notes:

line 36: (Δ) I am not sure / if it wer Mi. / or Vr, that / <c>alled
for thē

line 42: <E>.T. his / <p>romise

line 48: <Pr>actise. / The lower world

[36b]

powre to work such things, as shalbe to god his glorie, profit all
your Cuntrie, and the knowledge of his Creatures
What I do wish to do, thow shalt here /know7 (c), before thow go.
We procede to One GOD, one knowledge, one Operation.
Venite filiae
Behold these Tables: Herein lye theyr names that work vnder
/vnder7 (c) God vppon earth: not of the wicked, but of Angels of
<Light>
/Light7 (c) The Whole Gouernment, doth consist in the hands of 49:
(<in>
(in God his Powre, Strength, Mercy, and Justice) whose nam<es>
Names are here euident, excellent, and glorious
Mark these Tables: Mark them. Record them to your <.....>
This is the first knowledge. Here shall you hau<e>
haue Wisdome Halleluyah.
Mighty and Omnipotent art thow, O God, God, God,
God, amongst thy Creatures. Thow fillest all thing<s>
things with thy excellent foresight: Thy Glorie be
be amongst vs, for euer. Δ Amen.
E.T. All the 7 (which here appeare) ioyne theyr Tables in One:
One, Which, before they held apart. And they be of this
Forme all to gither. The myddelmost is a great Square
and on eche side of it, One, as big as it, ioyning close to it
And ouer it ioyned two, which both togither wer aequall
to it: and vnder it, wer such other two, as may appe<are>

in this little pattern. Being thus ioyned, a bright Circle did cumpas and enclose them all, thus: but nothing was in the Circle.

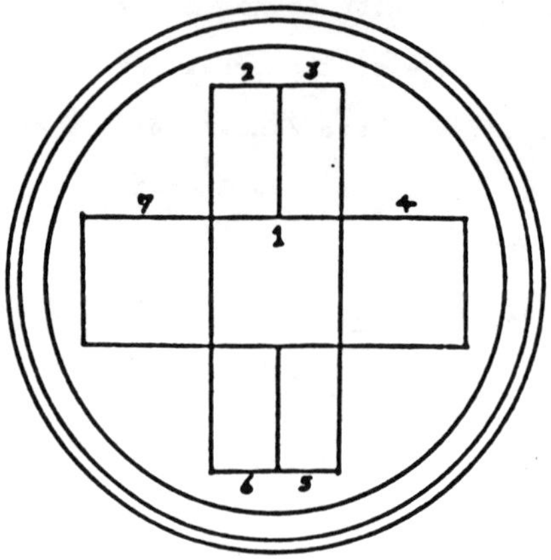

E T: one

Marginal notes:

line 3: To E T. he / spake

line 5: Filiae

line 7: .49. good / Angels / Governors.

line 1 : The / first / know= /ledg

[37a]

[blank]

[38b]

⟨blank⟩

[39a]

E.T: one stept furth, and sayde,

⟨1⟩ Wilt thow haue witt, and wisdome

Here, it is. (△ pointing to the middle table)

⟨2⟩ An other sayd, the Exaltation and Gouernment of Princis, is in my hand. (△ pointing to that on the left hand of the two vppermost)

⟨3⟩ In Cownsayle and Nobilitie, I prevayle (△ pointing to the other of the two vppermost: which is on the right hand)

⟨4⟩ The Gayne and Trade of Merchandise, is in my hand: Lo, here it is.

△ he pointed to the great table on the right side of the myddle Table

that I meane which is opposite to our right hand while we behold those 7 Tables.

⟨5⟩ The Qualitie of the Earth and waters, is my knowledge and I know them: and here, it is: (△ pointing to that on the right hand of the two lowermost.

6: The motion of the Ayre, and those that moue in it, are all known to me. Lo here they are. (△ pointing to the other Table below, on the left hand.

7. I signifie wisdome: In fire is my Gouernmēt. I was in the be-gynning, and shalbe to the ende (△ pointing to the great table on the left hand of the Middle Table.

Mi. Marke these Mysteries: For, this knowne, the State of the whole earth is known, and all that is thereon. Mighty is God, yea mighty is he, who hath Composed for euer. Giue diligent eye. Be wise, mery, and pleasant in the Lorde; in Whose Name, NOTE,

Begynne the Myddle Table etc △ I wrote oute of the stone the whole 7 Tables (as you see them here with theyr numbers and letters) while E.T. did vew them in the stone, and orderly express them.

△ As concerning 39 V. 47 L in the second Table, where are 7 places: and there but 6 numbers and letters, and yet euery place semeth to haue a letter, in the iudgemēt of E T his sight. Which is the Number and letter wanting, and where must it be placed?

Mi. Non potestis hoc videre sine ratione.

△ The Next day, as I was loking on the Tables being finished, and ioyned all to gither in One Compownd Figure: [and] E T, cam to me, and stode by me, and his ey was on the forsayd place which I was forced to leaue empty, in the 7th and last. And behold he saw houering and hopping in the ayre /̄.˙.7 (c) ouer the sayd place, and the next before it: And that, which I had placed the sixth, was to be put in the seuenth place, and that which was wanting, was to be set in the sixth place being 30.N.

E.T. Euery of the 7 Tables, as they wer written out of the stone do seme afterward to burn all in fyre: and to stand in fyre

E.T: After all the Tables wer written, eche toke [her] his Table aparte agayn and stode in theyr order.

E.T. Note moreouer, The First, had Bokes in hi[r]s hand

Kings ———————— The Second, a Crown in hi[r]s hand

Nobilitie —————— The Third, Robes

Merchants—Δ—A^{a}_{q} —The fowrth, aīal quadrupes viuū oīm colorū

Terra—The fifth, Herbes

Aer——The sixth, a fanne

Ignis-The seventh, a Flame of fyre in his hand

(Vr. Decedite

Marginal notes:

line 12: <Δ> I mar= / <v>ayle that the / <Ea>rth and waters are / <her>e ascribed to one.

line 34: Δ / This I enter= / sert now; / thowgh it wer / not at the / first Noting

line 38: < /.$\overset{c}{\cdot}$.7 t> wo numbers and / < t>wo letters supplied / to them.

A line joins 'wisdome' (line 2) and 'wisdome' (line 19).

[39c]

Decedite in noīe eius, qui vos huc misit.

E.T:—Vriel opened a boke in his own hand, and sayde

Vr. —— The Fontayne of wisdome is opened. Natura shalb<e> knowne: Earth with her secrets disclosed. The Elements with theyr powres iudged Loke, if thow canst (in the name of God) vnderstand /these/ Tables. Δ No: Not yet.

Vr. Beholde, I teache. There are .49. Angels glorious and <excellent> /excellent/ appointed for the governmēt of all earthly actions. Which 4<9 doe> do work and dispose the will of the Creator: limited from t<he>

the beginning in strength, powre, and glorie:

These shalbe Subject vnto you, In the Name, and by Inv<o>

Invo= cating vppon the Name of GOD, which doth lighten, dispose a<nd>

and Cumfort you

By them shall you work in the quieting of the estates, In lerning

learning of wisdome: pacifying the Nobilitie; iudgement in the

the rest, aswell in the depth of waters, Secrets of the Ayre, as in t<he>

as in the bowells and entralls of the Earth,

Vr. Theyr Names are comprehended within these Tables. Lo, he /teaches/ teacheth

he teacheth. Lo he instructeth, which is holy, and most highest

Take hede, thow abvse not the Excellency, nor overshadow it with

with Vanitie. But stick firmely, absolutely, and perfectly, in the Love

Love of God (for his honor) to gither

Be mery in him: Prayse his name. Honor him in his Saincts. Behold

=hold him in wisdome: And shew him in vnderstanding.

Glorie be to him; To the ô Lord, whose name perseth through the earth

Earth, Glorie be to the, for euer. Δ. Amen, Amen, Amen.

Vr Lo, I will breifly teache the: you shall Know the Mysteries in him:

him, and by him, which is a Mysterie in all things.

The letters are standing vppon 7 equall numbers. The Number before

before them is signifying, teaching and instructing (frō the first Table

Table to the last,) which are the letters that shalbe ioyned togither:

begynning all, with B, according to the disposition of the number

c
/number/ vntyll the 29 /49/ generall names be known. The first 29 are more

more excellent than the rest. Euery Name doth consist vppon the quantitie

tity of the place: Eucrie place with addition bringeth furth his name,

name which are 49.———— I haue sayde————

Δ I pray you to tell me the first Name. Vr. The first name is BALI/GON/GON

Mi I haue to say to the, and so haue I done

Δ Now he spake to E T, of the matter he sware him to, at the beginning of

of this last Instruction: and he told me after ward what Michael had willed

willed and moved him vnto. Wherat he seamed very sore disqu[illegible] and sayd this to me

to me E.T: He sayd that I must betake my self to the world, and forsake the

world. That is that I shold marry. Which thing to do, I haue no na=

naturall Inclination: neyther with a safe Conscience may I do it, contrary

ry to my vow and profession. Wherefore I think and hope, there is

is some other meaning in these theyr wordes.

Mi Thow must of force kepe it:

Thow knowest our mynde.

Δ Deo opt. Max^{o} oīs honor laus et gloria

in saecula saeculorum. Amen.

Ended hora noctis, 11½^{a} circiter.

/flourish/

Marginal notes:

line 2: a boke

line 9: Erthly Actions

line 12: Practise

line 23: We two / to gither

line 31: °Δ / Vide īpam / Tabulam ho= / rū 49 nōlm / Collectā, pa= / gina sequente

line 34: The first 29

line 39: °he ment / to E T.

line 44: E.T must / marry

[40a]

Tabula Collecta: 49 Angelorū Bonorū, Nōia continens ⊏ per Δ

1	BALIGON
2	BORNOGO
3	Bapnido
4	Besgeme
5	Blumapo
6	Bmamgal
7	Basledf
8	BOBOGEL
9	BEFAFES
10	Basmelo
11	Bernole
12	Branglo
13	Brisfli
14	Bnagole
15	BABALEL

16	BVTMONO
17	Bazpama
18	Blintom
19	Bragiop
20	Bermale
21	Bonefon
22	BYNEPOR
23	BLISDON
24	Balceor
25	Belmara
26	Benpagi
27	Barnafa
28	Bmilges
29	BNASPOL
30	BRORGES
31	Baspalo
32	Binodab
33	Bariges
34	Binofo[s]n
35	Baldago
36	BNAPSEN
37	BRALGES
38	Bormila
39	Buscnab
40	Bminpol
41	Bartiro
42	Bliigan
43	BLVMAZA
44	BAGENOL
45	Bablibo

46	Busduna
47	Blingef
48	Barfort
49	Bamnode

[40a]

[blank]

[41a]

Coordinatio Angeloru bonoru 49,

per Jo. Dee, ita disposita:

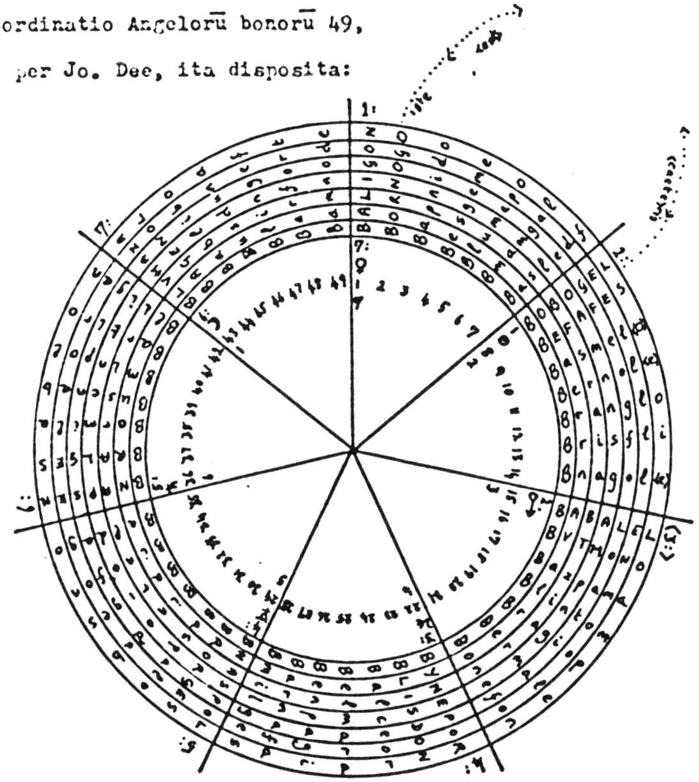

[blank]

[42a]

Liber <4.>

<1582.> Fryday Maij 4. hor 2½ a meridie

Δ E.T: wold not willingly now deale with the former Creatures: vtterly <m>islik<ing>

and discrediting them, bycause they willed him to marry. Neyther wold

he put of his hat in any prayer to god, for the Action with them: where=

vppon I went into my Oratorie, and called vnto God, for his diuine help

for the vnderstanding of his laws and vertues [knowing and vnderstan[d ing]]

which he hath established in and amongst his Creatures, for the

benefyt of mankinde, in his seruice, and for his glorie etc

And commyng to the Stone, E,T. saw there those two, whom

hitherto, we wer instructed to be Michael and Vriel.

E,T: Michael and Vriel, both kneled holding vp theyr hands: and Michael

seamed to sweat water abundantly, somwhat reddish or bluddish.

There cam 7 Bundells down, (like faggots) from heven ward. And Michael

taketh them kneeling. And Vriel taketh a thing like a superaltare

and layeth it vppon the Table: and with a thing like a Senser doth make

perfume at the fowre corners of the Table: the smoke ascending vp:

and the senser, at the last, being set on the Table it seemed to fall throwgh

the Table

VRIEL semeth to be all in a white long robe tucked vp: his garment full of plightes and seemed now to haue wyngs (which, hitherto, from the begynning of these kinde of Actions he did not) and on his hed a bewtifull crown, with a white Cross ouer the Crown.

Vriel taketh the .7. Bundells from Michael: and with reuerence layeth them on the forsayd Superaltare.

Δ:T. there commeth a man, as thowgh he were all of perfect pure glistring gold: somtyme seeming to haue One eye, and somtyme Three.

From vnder the Table commeth a great smoke, and the place semeth to shake.

Vriel lieth now prostrate on his face: and Michael contynually prayed sweating

The Glorious man seemed to open the Covering of the 7 bundells (being of diuerse cullored sylk,) and there it appered, that these Bundells seemed to haue in them, of all Creatures sōme, in most glorious shew.

The glorious man seemed to stand vppon a little hill of flaming fyre

He taketh of, of one of the Bundells a thing like a little byrd; and it hoouerth affore him as thowgh it had life: and than it rested vppon the thing like a superaltare

This glorious man seemeth to be open before, and his brest somwhat spotted with blud. He hath a berd forked of brownish cullour. his heare of his hed, long, hanging down to his sholders: but his face, for beutifull glittring, can not be discerned. His heares do shake, as thowgh the wynde carryed them.

This man blesseth the bird, making a Cross ouer it: and, so he did three

tymes. He looketh vp to heven.

Now the byrd, which, before, seamed to be but as byg as a sparrow,

seameth to be as great as a swanne: very beutifull: but of many cullours.

Now looketh Michael vp, and held vp his hands to heven, and sayeth

Sic, Sic, Sic, Deus noster.

Vriel, (sayd)——Multiplicabit omnia, benedictione sua.

The former Bewtifull man taketh this fowle, setteth it on the bundell, and

on the place, from whence it was taken: And, now, the place

where

Marginal notes:

line 4: E.T. is to / marry

line 20: Vriel his / manner / of appari- / tion

line 26: A Glorious / man.

line 35: All Creatures.

line 41: A / A description of / of the glorious / man.

line 49: Many / Many cullours in all / all his garmēts are / ar shewed in se- / sequentibus libris

line 53: Δ 

[42b]

where this byrd stode before, seameth allso, to be (proportionally) sa<xen>

as big, as the byrd, (thus enlarged).

this man taketh an other byrd, and putteth the wyng of it, beh<ind>

the wing of the first (as thowgh he yoked them

This second byrd, at this his first taking, was as byg, as the <first .....>

was become, (encreased, as it shewed), and it was allso a very bew< tifull....>

E.T: All is suddenly dark, and nothing to be seen, neyther Chayre, < nor>

any thing els.

E.T: A voyce was hard, like Michael his voyce, saying,

It was a byrd, and it is a byrd, absent there is nothing

but Quantitie

Δ A voyce. Beleue. The world is of Necessitie: His Necessit< y >

is gouerned by supernaturall Wisdome

Necessarily you fall: and of Necessitie shall rise ag< ain>

Follow me, Loue me: embrace me: behold, I, AM.

E.T: Now all the Darknes vanished, the man is gone. Vriel standeth at

the Table: and Michael sitteth now in his Chayre: and sayd

Mi. This doth GOD work for your vnderstanding

It is in vayne to stryve: All Government is in his hands

What will you els, what will you els?

Δ Progressum et profectum in virtute et veritate ad Dei honorē et gloriam.

Mi This hath answered all our Cauillations

Δ What hath answered all our Cavillations?

Mi Thow hast written

One thing you shall see more, as a persuasion to the Infirmitie.

E.T: The two byrds, which were there, before, [are] and gon out of sight, now

are shewed agayn: but none of the bundells appere

They seme to grow to a huge bigness, as byg as mowntaynes: Incredibly byg: and they seeme to hover vp in the ayre, and to fly vp toward heuen, and with [theyr wing] theyr wings to towch the sky: And one of them with his bill seemeth to take sterrs into it: and the other /bird/ to

~~to~~ take them from the same byrd, and to place them agayn in the Skye.

And this they did very often: and in diuerse places of the heuen with great celeritie.

After this they semed to fly ouer Cities, and townes, and to break the clowdes in peces, as they passed: and to cause all dust to flye from all walls, and towres, as they passed, and so to make them clene:

[illegible] And in the streetes, as these two Byrds flew, seemed diuerse brave fellows, like bisshops, and Princis and Kings, to pass: and by the wyngs of these byrds, they were striken down. But Simple Sely ones, like beggers, lame and halt, Childern, and old aged men, and women, seemed to pass quietly, vntowched and vnouerthrown of these two Byrds.

And than they seemed to come to a place, where they lifted vp, With [theyr wyngs] the endes of theyr wyngs, fowre Carkasses of dead men (owte of the growнde) with crownes on theyr heads: wherof one seemed to be a Childe

First

Marginal notes:

line 3: <The Yoa>king / <or cup>pling of / <the> two byrds

line 12: Δ / E.T: sayd the / Voyce to be / like Michael / his voyce.

line 14: Necessitie.

line 19: Vayne to / strive.

line 22: Δ / fortè your

line 30: The byrds towch / the sky and / sterrs

[43a]

First these 4, seemed leane, and deade: Then they seemed qui<ck> [thick] and in good liking: And they being raysed vp: parted eche fro<m> other, and went into 4 sundry wayes, Est, West, North and Sowth.

Now these two fowles hauing theyr wings ioyned togither, light vppo<n> a great hill: and there the First fowle gryped the erth mightily and there appeared diuerse Metalls, and the [caret] Fowle 'spurned them away still,

Then appeared an old mans hed, heare and all on. very much wythered. They tossed it betwene them, with theyr feete: And they brake it: And in the hed appeared (in steede of the braynes) a stone, rownd, of the bignes of a Tennez ball of 4, cullours, White, black, red, and greene

One of them (he that brake the Skull) putteth that rownd stone to the others mowth or byll.

The other eateth or nybbleth on it, and so doth the other allso

¶ Now these two byrds, are turned into men: And eche of
them haue two Crownes like paper crownes, white and
bright, but seeme not to be syluer. Theyr teeth are gold.
and so likewise theyr hands, feete, tung, eyes, and eares
likewise

All gold

On eche of these two men, ar 26 Crownes of Gold, on theyr
right sholders, euery of them, greater then other

They haue, by theyr sides, Sachels, like palmers bags, full of gold.
and they take it oute, and seemed to sow it, as corne, going
or stepping forward, like Seedmen.

E.T: Then sayd Michael, This, is the ende.

E.T: The two men be vanished away.

Mi. Learne the Mysterie hereof.

Δ Teache vs (ô ye spirituall Creatures). than sayd Michael,

Mi.—Joye and helth giue vnto the riche:
Open strong locks:
Be Mercifull to the wicked:
Pluck vp the poore:
Read vnto the Ignorant:

I haue satisfyed the: Vnderstand:

Read them ouer: God shall giue the some light in them. I haue
satisfyed the: Both, How you shalbe ioyned,
By whome,
To what Intent, and purpose:
what you are,
what you were,
What you shalbe, (videlicet) in Deo.

Lok vp this Mysterie:

*Forget not our Cownsayle:

Ô GOD

Marginal notes:

Lines 3-5: [Some faint marks remain on damaged margin]

Line 6: <Great> hill

Line 22: 26. / Crownes

Line 45: *to E T:

[43b]

O GOD, thow openest all things: Secret are thy Mysteries and holy is thy name, for euer

The Vertue of his presence, here left, be amongst you.

Δ Amen

Δ What am I to do, with the wax, the Table, the ring or the Lamine? etc

Mi. When the things be ready, then thow shalt know, how to vse Y.

Δ How shall I do for the grauing of the ring: May not a n o.. man do it, thowgh, E.T, graue it not?

Mi. Cause them to be made vp, (according to Instruction) by any honest

Δ What say you as concerning the Chamber, for our practise. May my furdermost little chamber, serue, yf the bed be taken d<owne>

*. Mi At the next Call for the Chamber, you shall know what to do to doe. Δ Benedictus Deus in donis suis:

et sanctus in omnibus operibus [suis] eius.

Amen. ended hor. 4½.

⁄flourish⁄

[44a]

Quartus Liber Mysterioru̅ [Tertius]

⁄flourish⁄ A° 1582

Δ Nouēbris 15.

Post reconciliationē Kellianam ∵ ⁄flourish⁄

Miserere n̄ri Deus

Dimitte nobis, sicut et nos dimittimus

Liber.5us

[44b]

⁄blank⁄

Δ Note. For, of Hagonel Δ Carmara, otherwise Baligo<n. Vide.....>

we never had any thing before.

<On>e (of the 7 which was by him) he who stode before him, wth his face fro<ward> him, now turned his face to him ward.

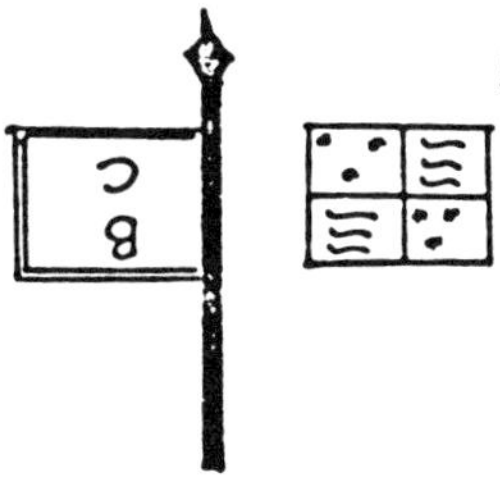

<♛—> Regnat potestas tua in filiis

Ecce signū Operis.

Δ There appeared these two letters, euersed and aversed, in a white flag: and a woman standing by, whose armes did not appere

<♛> Note. my name is Carmara.

<Δ—> On the other side of the flag, appeared the armes of England. The flag /seemed old/ [sem<ed>] //o<ld>/

Adhuc duo, et tempus non est, (Δ, sayd the man which stode before Carmara. and lifted vp his hand and avaunced his body: and the other 6 gaue him place. he spred his armes abroad: and so turned rownd toward all the multitude (appering within the Globe:) as if he wold require audience. he sayd than thus.

The Sonnes of men, and theyr sonnes are subiect vnto my comaundemēt This is a mystery. I haue spoken of it. Note it throwghly. They ar my seruants. By them thow shalt work mervayles. I gouern for a tyme: My tyme is yet to come The Operation of the Earth is subiect to my powre: And I am the first of the twelve: my seale is called Barees: and here it is ⊙ (Δ This he held in the palm of his hand: as thowgh it had byn a ring, hanging also over his mydd-

dle fingers. with a great voyce he sayd Come ô ye people of the erth:

.1. (△ Then there came a great Number of onely Kings from amongst the

rest of the multitude within the Globe. They kneele down; and sōme

kyssed his seale and sōme did stand frowning at it. These kings

that kissed it, had, each of them, a sword in one hand, and a payre of

Ballance in the other: the balances being euen, and cownterpeysed. But

the other had also ballances, which hong vneven, the one scale lower then

the other. The euen balanced kings were of glad cheare: but

the other wer of sowre and hevy cowntynance

It is, and shalbe so: And the workmanship of this, is to this ende.

Then cam noble men: (△ and he held vp his hand, and they

parted them selues into two Cumpanyes. and ouer the heds of them, appered

.2. these two wordes Vera, over one Cumpany:and Impuria over the other

....
....
.... etc .... etc

Verus cum veris, et Impurus cum Impuris

Come ô ye Princes of Nature. (△ Then cam in Auncient and grim

.3. Cowntenanced men in black gownes: of all manner of sortes Diuerse of

them had bokes: and some had stiks like measures: and they parted

into two Cumpanies. Eyther Cumpany had his principall. One of

these Cumpanies fell at debate among them selues. The other Cumpany

stode still. There appeared before eche of these Cumpanyes a great boke

Vppon the bokes was written: on the one, Lucem; and on the other,

Mundi tenebras. The Forman [(or Principall)] spred his hands ouer them, and they all fell down: and the boke with Lucem on it waxed bright

---

Marginal notes:

line 16: ⌊P⌋agenol

line 17: Filij Filij & Filij / Filij Filiorū supra / sup libro 2°.

line 20: Kings / <Kin>gs of the erth / etc

line 21: Earth

line 22: :12.

line 23: Barees

line 24: ☉

line 25: All people / of the Erth.

line 26: Kings

lines 29-30: ⌊part of a sketch of a pair of evenly balanced scales and a sketch of a sword⌋

lines 31-32: ⌊part of a sketch of a pair of scales unevenly balanced in favour of the right hand side⌋

line 35: Nom / Noble men

line 42: Philosophers

line 21, over 'a tyme': △ gouerns

line 21, over 'my tyme': △ particular or my governmet lasteth not

line 44, over 'measures': △ Geometrae

At the foot of the page: △ / He hath recyted the offices of [three] ⌊two⌋ Kings, as of Blumaza and Bobogel / And then he sayeth, Gather by these few spriggs etc: which Bobogel is over the Nobility and written of / < Wisdome of Metalls, & all Nature >

lines join: 'Δ' (line 1) to 'I haue spoken' (line 19),
'Regnat' (line 6) to 'Philosophers' (MN 42),
'in filijs' (line 6) to 'the Sonnes' (line 18),
'Carmara' (line 11) to 'twelve' (line 22) and
thence to 'Ͻ' in the diagram (lines 5-9),
'the man' (line 13) to 'first' (line 22),
'come' (line 21) to '.3.' (line 43).

[45b]

waxed bright: and they which attended on that boke (Lucem) <departed>

Gather by these few spriggs the Cumpas of the whole le field.

Δ I demaunded of him, what his name was: and he answered

I am Primus et Quartus Hagonel

Δ This Pri: Quar, shewed his /the7 seal ⊙ to the Multitudes and th<ey> they.....

1 it, and of them some florish: som stand, and some fall.

Δ Then he sayd ⊐ The first were /the7 Kings of the earth: which t<ell> tell the

priks of the last  , take place, are, and shall be.

In this thow mayst lern science. Note a mysterie.

Take a place, is as much, as, Ende with place.

Δ Then he threw down a great many of them before him

Here is his name, (pointing to Ho (⊏ Δ × Car[a]mara) ⊐ on the ye Vpper

part of the Globe) Notwithstanding I am his Minister —— 

There are kings, fals and vniust, whose powre as I haue uc augme...

and destroyed, So shalt thow.

Thow seest the weapons. The Secret is not great.

Δ I know not what the weapons are.

Pri. Quar sayd. Write, and I will tell the. Δ The three, of eche side did syt down: while Pri Quar did thus speake.

I am the first of the fowrth Hagonel.

Δ I had thought that ye [sad] sayd before, you had byn the first and the Fowrth of Hagonel.

Pri. Quar. ⊐ I am HAGONEL, and govern HAGONEL. There is Hagonel the first, Hagonel the second, and Hagonel the third, I am the one that govern the three. Therfore I am the first and the last of them.

Note Δ In the meane space of the former multitude some were fallen downe, of some theyr mowthes drawn a wry: of some theyr legs broken.

And then, pointing to Ho (Δ Carmara) he sayd.

In his name with my name, by my character and the rest of my Ministers, are these things browght to pass.

These things that lye here, are lyers, witches, enchanters, Periurers, Blasphemers: and finally all they that Vse NATVRE, with abvse: and dishonor him which rayneth for euer

The second assembly were the Gouernors of the Earth, whose glory, yf they be good, the weapons which we haue towght the, will augment: and Consequently, if they be euill, pervert

The third assembly are those which taste of Gods mysteries, and drinke of the Iuyce of Nature, whose myndes are diuided, some with [eyse] eyes looking toward heaven, the rest to the center of the Earth. Vbi non Gloria, nec Bonitas nec bonum est. It is wrowght, I say, it is wrowght (for thy vnderstanding) by the seuen of the seuen which wer the sonnes of sempiternitie, whose names thow hast written and recorded to Gods Glory Δ Then he held vp his hands, and seemed to speak but was not herd (of E.[T]K.) as he told me: and thervppon Pri quer: sayd Neyther shalt thow heare, for it is Vox hominibus non digna Illi autem cum filijs suis laudauerunt Deum. Benedictus est qui filius est vnicus, et Gloria Mundi.

E K. saw like a black cloth come in and cover all the forepart of

the

Marginal notes:

line 1: <Hagonel.>

line 5: < The Foreman / with the short / .... >

line 7: <Ki>ngs / Kings

line 12: Carmara his / Minister: forte / Prince, / Hagonel

line 14 RH: Δ / in < generall > / pa<rticularly> / B<lumaza >

line 16: Weapons where= / with to destroy

line 25: Note this First, / and Last, / bycause of / Baligon ali / Carmara. his / <prince> & tables.

line 29: Practise, w[th] / spirituall wea= / pons

line 31: Liers / Witches / Enchanters

line 34: Gouernors

line 42: Note / :: Practise / lib°. 2° Filij filioru /

E.. ——— 1.		These 7 are na= med in the great Circle following
A.. ——— 2.		
Ave ——— 3.		
Liba ——— 4.		
Rocle ——— 5.		
Hagonel ——— 6.		
Ilemese ——— 7.		

line 48: The black cloth / of silence, and / staying

At the foot of the page: Note: how he governeth Three / and Carmara (his King) hath also a Triple crown

Lines join: 'et' (line 4) to 'first of' (line 20),
'shewed' (line 5) to 'seest' (line 16),
'threw down' (line 11) to 'destroyed' (line 15),
'Fowrth' (line 21) to 'filius' (line 47),
'Ministers' (line 30) to 'seuen of the seuen' (line 41),
'the weapons' (line 35) to 'weapons' (MN29),
the second 'seuen' (line 41) to 'Illi' (line 46),
'whose names' (line 42) to 'Illi' (line 46).

[46a]

In the first leafe were the Offices of the two Kings Blumaza & Bobogel recited, as appeares by the Note at the bottome of the 2^{d} page: /ũ also 5: ^{c}May 1583.7 ꝑhaps this first leafe was lost bifore he drew vp his Booke of de Bonorū Angelorū invitatiōib^{us} because I find a Blank where Blumaza is placed.

 This Character seemes to stand for Carmara, as apꝑs from sev~all places in .fol. 2.a. & b. & many other.

It apꝑs by a note of D^{r} Δ: (de Heptarchia &c: Cap. 1.) That Michaell & Uriel were ꝓsent at the beginning of these revealed Misteries & gaue authority to Carmara to order the whole Heptarchicall Revelacōn

phaps this authority was entred in the first lost leafe of this /5.7 4th booke (though Dr Δ: calls it [here] the 2d Booke in this Note.) see Chap: 2. at ye begining. By a marginall note at the begining of the first Chapter, it should seeme, yt the Dr meanes by the first [chapter] Booke the Action only of the 16 of Nov: 1582. & by the 2d Booke the Actions of the 17 [&] 19 /+ 20c7 of Nov. 1582. but his marginal Note of 19 should be 20 of Nov, for so it apps by ye Actions entred. The 21 of Nov: vizt: the action of yt day he calls the Appendice of the 2d chapter.

[46b]

This is the writing
of Elias Ashmole.

FM

[47a]

the stone, so that nothing appeared in the stone: then was hard a voyce

saying. Loke for vs no more at this tyme: This Δ shalbe a token, (from this tyme furth) to leaue.

Δ Laus et Honor sit Deo Immortali et Oipotenti nunc et semp. A<m>en

/flourish7

Marginal note:

line 2: <The To>ken / <to le>aue of, by a black / <shad>dowing all /inc7 ŷ stone.

<158>2 Die ♀. A meridie: hora 5. Nouemb. 16

Δ He with the triple Crown on his hed, in the long purple robe, had now onely that part of the rod in his hand, which was clere red: the other two parts being vanished awaye. He shoke the rod, and the Globe vnder him did quake. then he sayde Ille enim est Deus, Venite Δ. All the 7 did bow at his speche

He holdeth vp the flag, with the picture of a woman [in it] paynted on it, with the

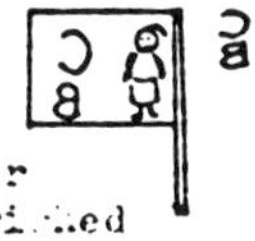

(as before was noted) on the right side of her. And on the other side of the flag, were the Armes of England. He florished with the flag very [muche] muche, and went as thowgh he <did> marche, in warlike manner vppon the vpper & vtterparte of the Globe.

He pointed vp to the Flag and sayde There is two to come, there is no more, All the people in the Globe seamed to be glad and reioyce

Now he setteth down the Flag, and sayd, Come, Come, Come; And the 7 cam all before him. they held vp all togither Heptagonum stellare, seeming to be Copper.

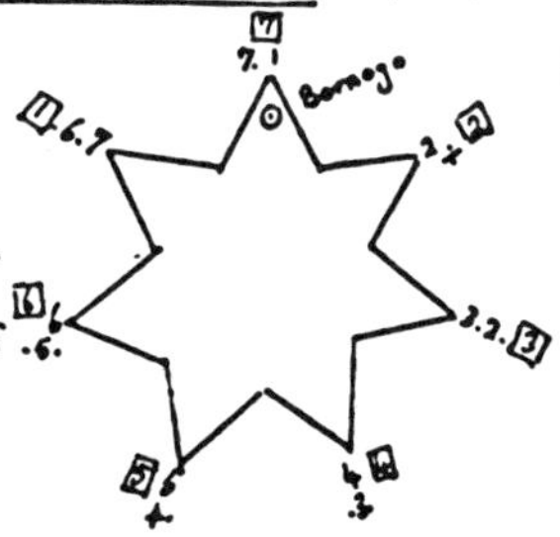

.1: The first Holder, sayd, Ille nosti and so pulled his hand of frō the Heptagonū.

2: The second of the .7. taketh his hand of and doth reverence and sayd I am he which haue powre to alter the Incorruption of NATVRE. with my seale, I seale her and she is becōme perfect. I prevayle in Metalls: in the knowledge of them. I haue byn in Powre with many but Actually with few. I am of the first of the twelue the Second of the Seuen. wilt thow know my name Δ full gladly. I am BORNOGO: this is my seale: [what thow desyrest] This is my true Character. what thow desyrest in me, shalbe fullfilled. Glory to God. Δ. He kneled down, and held vp his hands toward the Heptagonum.

3: The next (or third,) sayd, I am Prince of the Seas: My powre is vppon the waters. I drowned Pharao: and haue destroyed the wicked. I gaue life vnto the seas: and by me the Waters move. My name was known to Moyses. I liued in Israel. Beholde the tyme of Gods visitation. I haue measured, and it is .8. This is a mysterie. God be mercifull to his people. Behold, Behold

Lo, Behold

Marginal notes:

line 13: [There is a marginal drawing of the arms of England in Sloane MS. 3677, similar to that at 45a,6]

line 15: [There is an illegible marginal note which has been erased]

line 18: Δ so he sayd / in latin, in / the forpart of / the leaf before.

line 20: Δ — Note. / Copper apperteyneth / to ♀

line 21: Δ / Hagonel [with line to 'Holder' (line 21)]

line 22: Δ Forte / Bagenol / Hagonel, if H be for B / Than B[a]gonel/<conteyned> Ba / genol

line 27: Metalls

line 29: One of the / first of the / Twelue.

line 31: Prince / Bornogo

line 35: The Seas

line 39: 8 / Gods visitation / And it is 8: may be 8 yeres / added to this tyme, and that maketh 1590. Novēb. 16. That 8, or 88, I know not yet [with line to '8' (line 39)]

lines join: 'Ille' (line 10) to MN18,
'Flag' (line 16) to 'There' (line 17).

[47b]

Lo behold, my mighty powr consisteth in this. lern wisdome by my <words.>

This is wrowght for thy erudition, what I enstruct the from God: Look<e>

[vnto thy] Charge truely. Thow art yet deade: Thow shalt be raysed. But <oh,>

Glorie God truely. The blessing that God giueth, I will bestow Vp on the by per<mission>

O, how mighty is our god, which walked on the waters: which healed me w<ith>

his name. whose Glory is without ende. Thow hast written me, yet dos<t>

not Know me. Vse me in the name of God. I shall at the tyme appointed be ready

I will manifest the works of the seas, and the miracles of the depe shal<be>

knowne. I was Glorified in God. I Skurged the world. Oh oh oh, how they do

repent. Misery is theyr ende, and Calamitie theyr meat. Behold my name is pr<int......>

for euer: behold it Δ he opened his bosom and seamed leane: and [semed to] haue feathers vnder his robes: He had a golden gyrdel: and on it, written, B<EFAFES> [BEFAFES]

Than he sayd. Blessed be thow Ô God, God, God, for euer. I haue [said]

Δ He toke his hand of frō the Heptagonum.

Δ The black Cloth was drawn. which is now appointed to be <our>

token from them, that we must leave of for that instant

Δ. Deo soli, ōīs honor, et Gloria. Amen

[flourish]

Marginal notes:

line 1: Δ

line 2: Δ / My charge

line 8: The seas

line 12: Prince / Befafes / wth feathers / vnder his robes.

Friday After drinking at night circiter hora 8[a]

Δ On the left side of Ho (sitting in the Chayre) appeared yet three

holding vp the Heptagonum. [and] [on] one and the other side below. He sat with his

his face from E K toward me. I stode and my face southward. E K he

sat at the same table, with his face Northward.

4. The Fowrth (holding below) Cryed. Earth, Earth, Earth.

E.K. he speaketh Hollow, so that I vnderstand nothing. Δ than he

answered They are the wordes of my Creation, which you are not

not worthy to vnderstand. My Powre is in Erth: and I kepe the bodies

of the Dead. Theyr members are in my bokes. I haue the key of Dis=
solution. Behold Behold, All things, yea /bis/ All things, haue theyr
there workmanchip with me For I am the ende of Working. E K
He falleth down prostrate, and speaketh I know not [what] what; Δ
than he sayd I haue the Light of his anger, and I will destroy it. O,
^O, Behold, It is in a light left within the bottomles pit. It is the ende
and the Last. O blessed shall thy name be, Blessed shall thy name
be for euer. Behold this is my seale  Behold, the bowels
B wells of the earth are at my opening Δ Then I requested
/hed/ him to help me with some portion of Threasor hid, to pay my detts withal
/withall/ and to buy things necessarie etc. He answered O Wordling
thow shalt be satisfyed with welth of this world. Behold Behold
Behold Lo lo Behold, vehemētly I say Behold I haue, horded vp
Threasor, for the Sonne of perdition, the first Instrument
of his destruction. But, Lo these Cauerns Δ he
shewed to E K the Cavernes of the earth, and secret places therof
thereof and afterward sayd: Mark this, All spirits, inhabiting within
the earth; where, their habitation is, of force, not of will, (except
/except/ the myddest of my self, which I know not), are subiect to the
powre hereof. Δ Pointing to his Seale. With this you

shall

Marginal notes:

line 21, over 'and the other': <u>and one on the other side below</u>

line 27: In earth. /

line 28: The Dead mens / bodyes.

line 32: The Light of / his anger. [with a hand]

line 37: Threasure hid / requested.

line 41: ·Δ·/ Antichrist

line 46: How can the / middest of a / <s>pirituall crea / ture be ima= / <g>ined? / my dowt to ax / <He meant the middest or > / Center of the Earth. The middest of his <charge> [with a hand]

lines join: 'his' (line 21) and 'ende' (line 30), the diagram of the seal (line 35) and 'this' (line 44).

[48a]

shall govern, with this you shall vnlok: with this (in his name <u>who rayneth</u>) <u>you shall discouer her entrayles</u>. How say you now? Can you do it? Ar not your Magiciens acquaynted with me Yt greueth me to regester <u>the bones of the Wicked</u>. Prayse him Butmono, Prayse him Butmono, prayse him. Δ Is that your name, I pray you tell me. he answered Yea it is my name. It is the <u>ende</u> of all things. E K. now he sitteth down.

⟨5.⟩ Δ Now the Fifth turned his face toward .E.K. (who [E K] sat before me, and opposite vnto me) and stepped furth and sayd: <u>I am life and breath</u> [of all things] <u>in Liuing Creatures</u>. All things liue by me, <u>The Image of One excepted</u>. Behold the face of the Earth E K. There appeareth all [Creatures] /Kindes7 of brute beastes, fowles, Dragons, and other Δ He Clapt his hands to gither and /they7 all, vanished away /at7 ones: they cam agayn: and went then away and retorned no more. But the people within the Globe remayned still as from the begynning: he sayd while the beastes were yet in sight Lo, all these, do I endue with life: my seale is theyr Glory. Of God am I sanctifyed: I reioyce: the Liuing, The ende, and beginning of these things, are known vnto me: and by sufferance I do dispose them vntyll my Violl be run E K. he taketh out of his bosom a bottle vyol glass. and there seameth to be fiue or six sponefulls of oyle in it. Δ He answered and sayd. That it is: and it is a mysterie. Δ I spake somwhat of this oyle, and he answered me, and sayd Thow sayst true. In token of God his Powre and Glory, write down BLISDON.

E K. he taketh his hand of from the Heptagonū The sixth pulleth open his Clothes and red apparell, and there yssueth mighty fyre oute of his sides [Δ Note, the cote of the first of these seuen is shorter then any of his fellows coats are.] The sight of the fyre is very owgly, grisely, terrible, and skarsly of mans eye can be beholden. At length he pluckt his coates to gither, and sayd to E,K. Ô I wold shew the, but flesh and blud cannot see. write shortly, (it is enowgh) Noui Januam Mortis. Δ than sayd he to me in an ernest muse, Ô, Muse not, My words ar dark, but with those that see, light enowgh. Et per cussit Gloria Dei, Impiorum parietes. Dixi. Δ In mervaylous raging fyre, this word BRORGES did appeare, tossed to and fro in the furious flames thereof, so abundantly streaming out, as yf all the world had byn on fyre. so that E K, could not endure, (without great annoyance to his ey sight) to behold the same and finally he sayd Mysteria $\overset{c}{[in]}$ animis vestris imprimite. and so the fyre vanished away:

E K

Marginal notes:

line 1: <P>ractise

line 2: [hand]

line 5: <Pr>ince / <Butm>ono

line 10, over 'Liuing Creatures': ·Δ· In Animantibus oratis

line 11, over 'Image of': (Δ x man)

line 17, written vertically: Δ A great dowt <........> / me yet the <di> / uersity of t<he 4th> / and fifth offi<cers,> / and officis as they are here a<nd in the> Repetition ensuing

line 18: Virtus officij / sui

line 21: A little Viol / of oyle

line 25: Prince / Prin[ce] Blis= / Blisdon

line 29: Short Coat. / The first.

line 37: Prince Bo= / Prin[ce] Brorges:

lines join: 'endo' (line 6) to MN17, 'Liuing Creatures' (line 10) to 'all these' (line 17).

E K. The stone semeth all Blew: and onely One now [beholdeth]
the Heptagonū: all the rest being set down: who semed now
[to extend] theyr hands one toward an other, as thowgh they playd, now being
[rid] of theyr work. Now the last putteth his hand to the Heptagonon
and turned his face to E K. hauing his face (all the while before)
turned toward Δ, he sayd The Creatures liuing in my
7. Dominion, ar subiect to my powre. Behold I am BRALGES
The powres vnder my subiection, are Invisible. Lo what...
are. E K. All the world semed to be in brightnes or w...
fire: and therein appered Diuerse little things like little smokes...
without any forme. he sayd. This is the seale of my Go=
uernment. Behold I am come, I will teache the Names
without Numbers. The Creatures subiect vnto me shalbe known
vnto you. ☾ Beware of wauering Blot out suspition of us
for we are Gods Creatures, that haue rayned, do rayne & shall
raigne for euer. All our Mysteries shalbe known vnto you.

E K. All the 7 vanished away. onely Ho remayning
who sayd (being stand vp and leaning vppon his Chayre, and turned
to E K Behold, these things, and theyr mysteries shalbe
known vnto you, reseruing the Secrets of him
which raigneth for euer: [E K The voyce of a mul=
titude, answered singing,] Whose name is Great for
euer. Ho Open your eyes, and you shall see from the
Highest to the Lowest. The Peace of God be vppon you.
Δ Amen. E K. The black Cloth was drawn before

all the things conteyned in the stone: which was the Token of Ceasing for that tyme.

Δ sanctus sanctus sanctus D̄n̄s Deus n̄r̄

[flourish]

Δ BLVMAZA Rex est sup Reges Terrae /

et illius sunt primus

princeps, et illius Ministri vt coījcio

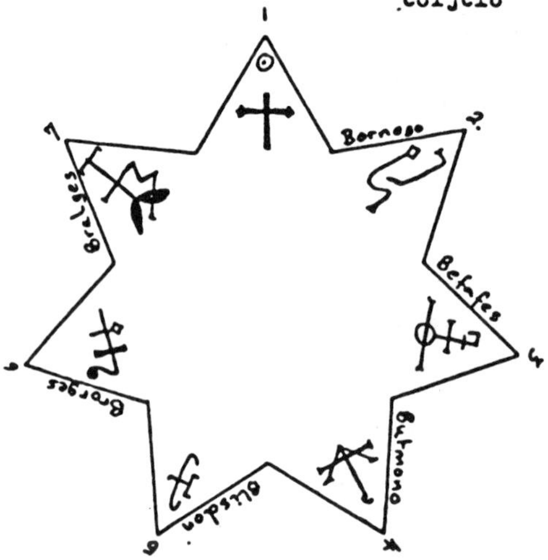

Marginal notes:

line 6, written vertically: But Baligon, <āls> / Carmara, in the endo of this boke / sayeth it to be his / office. Consider well

line 7, over 'Dominion': Δ forte, in Aēre

line 7: Prince / Bralges / hath Blumaza / his king

line 11: The seale.

line 14: Exchue / Wauering or / suspition

line 16: All Mysteries / shalbe known / to vs

line 20: Secreta / Dei, non / sūt hōibus / reuelanda.

line 24: Δ / Note Highest / and Lowest / to be vnderstode / ꝑhaps in Ta= / bula collecta.

LH of Heptagon: Hanc partem primā / vocat Ho vnum / Librum in / quinta pagina se= / quente, ad hanc / Notam

RH of Heptagon: Δ / It shold seme that this / character shold be onely / a circle and a pryck / fol. 6.b. I haue forgotten / how I cam by this Crosse / annexed to it

RH next to 'Befafes': alr / Remēber / Obelison his promise to m< e > / of knowing and vsing

RH at bottom of page:

Words	9 9 9 7 11	45

[49a]

An: 1582: Saterday Die 17. Noūeb: A meridie hora circiter 1ā

Δ—The Cloth remayned drawn, a prety while after we had done our prayers to God

and so was all the things in the stone kept from sight.

Δ—The Man with the Crowne, (he onely) appeared first, and the transparent Globe

with the people of the world in it, as before. The Diaphanitie, or (as it wer) the Shell

of the forsaid Globe, was very glystring bright. The man shaked his hand toward me

and the bak of the Chayre was toward E.K. On this globe apeared a trace

like a seame, of two things ioyned to gither, or rather a very narrow path: which began

below on the Convex superficies of this globe and went vpward to the verticall point or
(as it wer) the zenith prik of it: but frō the lower part of the same to the place where
the chayre stode, it seamed broder, and more worn, than from the chayre vp to the vertex
or top prik: for that part (which semed to be about the eigth part of the whole
did appere very smalle, and vnworne, or vnoccupyed.

Δ—He turning his face toward E K, spake this. I haue declared things
past and present: And now I speak of things to come. The
Whole shalbe manifest. Nam ipse vnus et Indiuisibilis est.
Gloria Gloria Gloria Creatori n̄ro
Two partes are yet to cōme, the rest are finished allready Δ He shewed the
rownd table with letters and numbers which master Kelly sent me: and than
he toke it away agayn. then he sayd:

Venite gradatim repetamus opera Dei.

Δ The first of the .7. which had yesterday appeared, did now appere w/th/ the short
robe, as he did before. Than Ho sayd smylingly (being turned to E K)

Haec sunt documenta tua, quae nondum intelligis

Δ Than the man with the short robe, the Forman of the 7 (yesterday appearing) sayd

Vnus est Deus, et vnum est opus n̄rm

Δ Then cam very many vppon the Globe his convex superficies and they sayd,

Parati sumus seruire Deo nostro.

Δ Eche of these had somwhat in theyr hands. som had crownes, some garmēts, etc

The number of them was: 42. and stode in this order.

and sayd embracing (as it wer) the whole

number of this Cumpany

Et nomen meum, numerus est totus

Nec est crimen in numero nostro

Moyses nos nominauit

Potestas istorū, quàm istarum, quamvis non vna, tamen in vno sunt.

Δ I sayd that I thowght there wanted at the begynning of this sentence, this word Tam.

he answered, [it] might be vnderstode by his pointing to them there standing, and sayd

furder in respect of this my dowt: Quatenus est haec vanitas vestrorū?

Tu nosti numeros hos esse in Deo, in Mundo, et in minori mundo.

In Deo, id est, Nobiscum. In Mundo, quantū apud vos: In minori Mundo, quantū in vobis.

(Combinatur animus tuus cognitatione)

Dimeritur apud Phos, idq maximè.) de NATVRA, quae non vobiscum, sed nobiscum (ah, ah, ah,) et nra potestate est.

Videbis Deum. Vidisti opera nra, Opera (inquā) manuū suarū:

Digito Dei mouebimur. A Deo venit. Homo et cū hominibus fuit: est enim cū illis. Illius namq potestas vim, virtutem, et esse dat,

non nobis solum modo, sed operibus nris

Inhumata tibi anima tua, quid quaerit? Δ I vnderstand you not he answered

Ab humo, homine; Ab homine dictum est. I axed the, what thow desyrest.

Δ Wisdom, and Veritie, I answered: | then, he, answered,

Ho Thow shalt. Δ there cam in a smyling fellow: and they pluckt

Δ ☾ Note this to be a REPETITION of the Heptagonon \ him / this little Treatise affore. Lern to reconcile the 4/th/ and the <5th>

Marginal notes:

line 4: Carmara / al: Baligon

line 7: /there is evidently a note missing/

line 15: past / present / to come

line 18: <Δ hā ....bis / dext... Adhuc / duo, et tempus / non est.>

line 18, over 'partes are yet': Δ forte, of this work.

line 19: The rownd / Table.

line 22: Short Coat.

line 24: Δ I think he / ment by the / rownd table / shewed, which / Mr K. had sent / me etc. bycaus / the names cam / out of that / Table

line 29, over 'garmets': Vide lib^o. 3°.

line 31: Δ / I dowt it shold / be short / coat holding / or ēbracing all / the Table with / his hands, and not Ho.

line 36: Δ / Note Istorū / Istarū / as if it were / filios et filias etc

line 40: Numeri

line 44: Natura

line 48: Dei / potestas.

lines join: 'repetamus' (line 21) to note at line 55, 'Nobiscum' (line 41) to 'Deum' (line 46).

pluckt him, and towsed him. He cryed he wold tell Newes: and they answered, that

there was none for him to tell and he skaped from them, or they let him slyp wit<h>

with all his clothes torn of: and he semed to crepe or get away vnder the globe, an<d>

and (as it wer) to get behinde the Diaphanous Globe.

Δ These 42 had all of them somwhat in theyr hands: as eyther whole Crownes or $\frac{1}{2}$

of Crownes, or robes etc. Six of them semed more glorious than the rest

and theyr Coates longer: and had cerclets (abowt theyr hed) of Gold: and they

had pfect Crowns in theyr hands. The second six had thre quarters of Cr<ownes> /Crownes/

The Third six, haue clothes in theyr hands. All the rest semed to haue balls <of>

of gold: which they toss from one to an other: but at the catching they sem<ed>

seamed empty wynde balls: for they gripe them, closing theyr hand [closing theyr]

as yf they wer not solid, but empty, like a bladder.

Δ The first six sayde. Our names cannot be expressed neyt<her>

can the names of these that follow.

Δ The first six made cursy to the man with the short robe: the

second six made cursy to the first, and the Third to the second

and they all, and the short robed man, made cursy to Ho.

Our workmanship is all one Δ sayd the short robed man

Ho The whole day is diuided into 6 partes: Euery part occupyeth a

part of them here (pointing to the 42 standing ther. Therfore yf

thow wilt work with Kings (thow knowest my meaning) finally

what soeuer thow wilt do in theyr estate; Cast thyne eye vnto the first place. In all good causes thow shalt work by six in generall.

The rest are for Depriuation: I meane the next six. The residue all do serue to the entents and purposes apperteyning vnto Kings.

But bycause thow shalt not be ignorant, what they are, in name, they shall shew forth theyr Tables

Δ Than they, spedyly (eche of them vppon the place of theyr standing, made a square table: and euery table had but one Letter. The first of the first first six did go away, and in his table appeared an O. etc and so of the second six, orderly theyr letters appeared in theyr tables: but the Third six, they cowred down [vppon] theyr letters, and were loath to shew them: but at length, did. etc. and at the last of euery row, they all cam to= gither etc.

♛ 40 Remember, how they stode, when they wer secondly disposed vnto thee: They stode first in six rowes, and next They wer turned into .7. I speak of the greater number and not of the less. In speaking of the greater, I haue comprehended the lesser.

	Δ
O F S N G L E	4 howres
A V Z N I L N	4 howres
Y L L M A F S	4 howres
N R S O G O O	4 howres
N R R C P R N	4 howres
L A B D G R E	4 howres

Δ They went euer away toward the ..... hand

The third row went of lamenting: being commaũded: by the Short Robed man. All parted in fire, falling into the Globe

The fifth now did synk into the Globe, euery one in a sundry fyre by him self.

The sixth fell with smoke down into the Globe.

E K. Now remayneth onely the man with the Crown Ho: he made shew with his hands, beckning toward E K and sayd, I haue told the, that theyr workmanship is to gither.

Theyr names are vppon these tables.

The first letter, is the Second letter of the first name of the Table

Δ How can Bobogel Thow be accownted the first name?

Marginal notes:

line 7: Note this / reckening / by Six and / six

line 13: Names.

line 15: Short coat.

line 18: So he sayd pagina / precedēte, vnū / est opus nrm̄.

line 19: The diuision / of the Daye

line 23: Practise

line 25: Kings.

line 29: The first 6

line 30: The second 6.

line 32: The Third six [with line to 'The third' (line 45)]

line 40: In sexto et / 7° sunt oīa / fol. 10.

line 52: • Δ. Now he / meaneth at / Bobogel in / that table / collected frō /  made before:

lines join: 'six of' (line 6) and 'six' (line 24), 'names cannot' (line 13) and 'in name' (line 26).

<Note>

The Table  to be conferred with the rown<d  >

Thow hast 49 names in those Tables. Those names thow hast in former Tables,

by the written: in that of 7 tymes 7. Confer it with the rownd Table

The first letter from the point of his sword, is B. That B signifieth the

number of the Bees, begynning the 49 names, environing that Circle

In the former Tables thow shalt fynde B.1. B.2. B.3. B.4. etc and so to B.49

Those Bees begynne the names of all the powres that haue governed.

do gouern, and shall gouern 

The next letter hath his circle and members going rownd abowt it: which

thow shalt fynde in the former Tables.

The Letter standeth in the myddest of euery square, of euery Circle: though

some be turned vpside down: Which onely signifyeth that they are

Spirits of Destruction, wrath and Indignation in Gods Judgement.

There are two numbers: that, on the right hand, over the letter, is the nuber

pertayning to that Letter.

O in the Circumference is the ninthe letter

Gather the former Tables to gither, which thow hast made before, conteyning

49, depending onely on B. Where thow shalt finde BOBOGEL, a

name consisting on 7 letters, and so the rest.

Reade my instructions as concerning those Tables, and thow shalt fynde

the truth of them.—————————————I haue sayd.

Mighty is thy name, o [Lord] God of Hostes:

Blessed is thy name, Ô Lord, for euer.

Δ Amen.

[flourish]

Marginal notes:

line 5, over 'the first letter': sent to me by E.K.

line 8: Note

line 9, RH: # a sword in the mans hand / within the Circle [refers to line 57]

line 17: O in this Table. [(in this Table] / <O>FS etc) is of / <th>e eighth name / <the> second letter / <but> the ninth / <here> in respect / <of> the circle of / numbers.

line 21: Note who / <s>ayeth this.

line 22: Δ / Note the like phrase / fol. 2. of Hagonel / who sayd he had spoken of / it. wheras we had receyued / nothing of him before.

a line joins 'my' (line 21) to 'I' (line 30) and also to MN22.

After 7 of the clok at night. die ♄.

Ho Lo, here I byd them do, and they do: I haue appointed them, and they are contented,. My Charge is not of my self, neyther do I speak darkly obscurely or without truth, in affirming that I towght the those Tables: For they are frō him, which made and created all things: I am from them in powre and message, vnder whome I here rule and shall do, tyll the ende of all things be: Ô Great and bowntifull is his liberall mercy. The mercy of him, whome we prayse and laude and sing vnto, with Joy for euer.

Behold thow desyrest, and art syk with desire. I am the disposer though not the Composer of Gods medicines. Thow desirest to be cumforted and strengthened in thy labors. I mynister vnto [the^{c}] The Strength of God.

What I say, is not of my self, neyther that which is sayd to me, is of them selues, but it is sayd of him which Liueth for euer.

These Mysteries hath God Lastly, and of his great mercyes, granted vnto the

I haue answered thy dowting mynde.

Thow shalt be glutted, yea filled, yea thow shalt swell and be puffed vp with the perfect knowledge of Gods Mysteries, in his mercyes. Abuse them not: Be faithfull. Vse mercy. God shall enriche the

Banish wrath: yt was the first, and is the greatest Commaundemēt

I rayng in him, and liue by him which rayngeth and liueth for euer.

Δ I pray you make sōme of these last instructions more playne, and euidēt.

Marginal notes:

line 31, over 'them': Δ him

line 32: <Ba>ligons rule / [a]nd governmēt

line 32, over 'tyll the ende': sūp fol. 1. b.2.

line 32: < t>he / ende / <of> all / <t>hings

line 35: Δ / <D>ce his / <l>anguishing / <d>esire

line 39: /hand7

line 40: <God> graunt.

line 45: < Δ I > vnderstode / <not> this to / <be> so: tyll he / <ca>lled to my / <re>mēbrance / and made me / <tu>rne my bokes / <to> that Parcell which he called the Prologe declared by Annael: whan Saul skryed. etc

line 45, over 'greatest Commaundemet': Δ ∻ hardest, for me, in respect of my Imperfect<ions>

lines join: 'them' (line 31) to 'them' (line 38), 'art syk' (line 35) to 'medicines' (line 36).

[50b]

<Those as he> semed <to>

Embrace them <fo. 5.>

Ho I haue shewed the perfectly. Behold I teache the agayn O how mercifull is God that revealeth so great secrets to flesh and blud? Thow hast 42 letters. Thy Tables, last, conteyn so many. Euery letter is [a name] the name particular by him self of the generall actions, being, and doing of these 42, which appeared with theyr workmanship. The first wa<s> theyr Prince: and he gouerneth onely the estate condition and being, <limited> by God vnto Kings of the earth. The 7 next him, are those that are <Messagers> /Messagers7 of God his good gifts to those that beleue him, and faithfully serue him: wherof few <re......> and rayng now frutefull in his sight.

Regnat Regnat, Regnat ô regnat Iniquitas super faciem totius terrae

Cor hōis impletum est malitia, et nequicijs

Incipit, incipit enim noua illorū potestas, illis non sine re dedita, nec dis..

Vide quaeso. △ He pointed down to the people, in the Globe, all bei<ng....>

sore and diseased of some sore, vlcer, botch, etc

Ho All the residue of the Angels, (for so they are in dede) ar ministers of God h<is>

wrath and indignation vppon the Faythless: whose mysterie is most lamenta<ble.>

7 onely, haue 7 letters comprehending the dignitie of theyr vocation: The rest

are particular, not onely in powr, but allso in theyr vocation. Like leaves

they spring and grow from one branche.

These words which thow seest in the last Table, some of them vnhable to be

pronownced, are notwithstanding the names of those 7 which held the fayr

and bewtifull Crownes. which names (as I sayd before) do comprehend not

onely the powre, but allso the Being of the rest.

The whole Composition is the truth of the words. I will ones more teach.

There were 42 that appeared, besides him, which was theyr prince.

The first 7, are called by these names, that thow seest, as OFS etc.

△ and so of AVZNILN etc Ho Thow hast sayde

There are but .6. names, that are in Subiection. I teache breifly

Doost thow not remember the Circle and the prik in the myddest: which was on

the right hand of him, that was theyr Prince?

That onely representeth 7 in number. Which being added vnto the rest maketh .49. Read the letters. Δ I red OF etc and he willed me to strike them out.

Ho That is the name of those of the first of the 7, which held the Crown< es > in theyr hands

The second line, is the name of the second, and so to the ende of the table.

42, letters: 42 names: 42 persons.

The first where his fote stode, is both his Name and Character. And so of the second, Third etc.

Notwithstanding, Generally these are the names, the first 7, the One presupposed, the rest being six in order.

This is the truth, and some of the Tables. Yt is easy to be vnderstode and perfect

Whan thow wilt work for any thing apperteyning vnto the estate of a good King: Thow must first call vppon him which is theyr prince. Secondly the ministers of his powre are Six: whose names conteyne 7 letters apece: as they Tables do manifest: by whome generally, or by any one of them, in particularitie, thow shalt work for any Intent or purpose.

As concerning the letters particularly, they do concern the Names of 42

which

Marginal notes:

line 5: 42 letters.

line 8: The Prince.

line 9: Kings of / the erth.

line 11: The Prince and / his first 7

line 14: Istorum / Noua potes= / tas incipit

line 14. over 'dedita': X data

line 18: Angels, minis= / ters of Gods / wrath.

line 19: Consider / the recke= / ning here by 7 / but below he / had a reckening / by .6. [with hand]

line 23: The Powre and / being of the / rest.

line 24 RH: △ There were but 6. holding / bewtifull Crownes

line 27: NOTE / The Prince

line 28: Now by 7

line 30: Six names / in subiection

line 30, over 'but six names': △ each of .7. letters.

line 32: ⊙ on the / right hand

line 36, over 'of the first of the 7': △ forte of the first 7. / △Videlicet

line 38, over 'The second line': △: of the six lines

line 39: NOTE

line 40: Note, Name / and Character.

line 47: Praxis / Call.

line 48: Prince .1. / Ministers .6. [with hand]

line 52: 42

lines join: 'Those' (line 1) to 'next him' (line 9),
'first' (line 7) to 'him' (line 27) and to 'theyr prince' (line 28),
'The 7 next him' (line 9) to 'onely in powr' (line 20),
'those 7' (line 23) to 'first' (line 36),
'7' (line 23) to '△' (MN24 RH) and to '7' (line 36),
'Crownes' (line 24) to 'Crown<es>' (line 36),

'The first 7' (line 28) to '7 letters' (line 49),

'onely' (line 33) to 'One' (line 43),

'vnderstode' (line 44) to 'powre' (line 48),

The first '42' (line 39) to 'the Names of 42' (line 52).

[51a]

<w>hich 42, in generally, or one of them do and can work the destruction

hindrance or annoyance of the estate, Condition or degree, as well for body

as government of any Wicked or yll Liuing Prince.

In outward sense, my words are true. I speak now of the vse of

one of the first, that I spake of, or manifested yesterday

Sayd I not, and shewed I not, which had the gouernment of Princis?

For, as it is a Mystery to a farder matter, so is it a purpose to a present

vse. Yf it rule worldly princis, how much more shall it work

with the Princis of Creation?

Thow desyrest Vse, I teache Vse, and yet the Art is to the furder

Vnderstanding of all Sciences, that are past, present or [to come]

yet to come

Frute hath a furder vertue than onely in the eating: Gold his furder con=

dition, property, and qualitie, then in melting, or common vse.

Kings there are in Nature, With Nature, and above Nature.

Thow art Dignified.

Δ yf I wold haue the King of Spayne his hart to be enclined to the pur

pose I haue in hand; What shall I do?

Ho First Cast thyne ey vnto the Generall prince, Gouernor or Angel that is principal in this world [△ as yet, is BALIGON or Carmara.

Secondly consider the circumstances of thy Instruction

Thirdly place my △ name, whome thow hast all ready

Fowrthly, of him, which was shewed the yesterday, whose garmets were short, and of purple.

Firstly, his powre, with, the rest of his six perfect Ministers

With those thow shalt work to a good ende. All the rest thow [maist]

mayst vse to Gods Glorie. For euery of them shall minister to

thy necessities

Moreouer, when thow workest. Thy feete must be placed vppon those tables

which thow seest written last comprehending 42 letters, and names.

But with this Consideration, that the first Character, which is

the first of the 7, in thy former boke, be placed vppon the top of the

△ Table, which thow [was commaunded] wast, and art, and shalbe

commaunded to haue, and Vse.

Last of all, the Ring, which was appointed the: with the

Lamine comprehending the forme of thy own name: which

is to be made in perfect gold, as is affore sayd.

Euen as God is iust, his iudgements true, his mercies vnspeakable

so are we the true messagers of God: and our words are

true in his mercy for euer.

Glory, ô Glory, be to the, ô most high God.

E K. Now commeth Michael and heaveth his hand out of the stone

and sayth GOD Bless you.

Ho As concerning the vse of these Tables, this is but the first step.

Neyther shalt thow practise them in vayne.

And whereas thow dost vse a demaunde, as concerning thy doings

to a good

I shall not practise these Tables

in Vayne

Marginal notes:

line 2: Destruction / or hurt.

line 7: [there appears to be a note missing]

line 7, over 'Princis': Δ ℵ Kings

line 12: <... Scienc>es / <past prese>nt / <or to co>me

line 16: Diuers <kin>gs

line 17: Dignificam / tion

line 20: Δ who is that?

line 21: Practise.

line 21 RH: Δ Is it not / Annael wth / whome I began? [with line to 'Generall prince' (line 20)]

line 23: ·Δ̇· — Ergo it / shuld seme / to be his office / to deale with / Kings: but / in the ende / he declareth / his office to / be of all A8= / reall actions

line 24, over 'of him': Δ the name

line 24, over 'whose garmēts': Δ. Hagonel

line 26, over 'powre, with': Δ Character

line 26, over 'perfect Ministers': of 7 letters a pece

line 30: The placing / of my fete / in practise [with hand]

line 33: ☉ † Note former boke

line 34: Δ / The Table / of practise / of a yard square / libro: 1°.

line 36: The Ring.

line 37: The Lamine.

line 38: The stone was / not yet browght

line 40: Truth.

line 43: Mich.

lines join: 'my name' (line 23) to MN23,
'perfect' (line 26) to MN40,
'them' (line 46) to 'I shall' (line 49).

[51b]

to a good intent and purpose: and for the prayse and advancem^t: of Gods Glorie, with Philip the Spanish King: I answer ẏ^t what=soeuer thow shalt speak do or work, shalbe profitable & accepted And the ende of it shalbe good.

Moreouer wheras thow vrgest the absence of thy frende, as an excuse for the ring. No excuse can preuayle: Neyther canst thou shew the frutes of a iust mynde, but of a faynting stomack wth ẏ excuse God hath retorned him, and wilbe mercifull vnto you both.

Thy Chargis in worldly affayres, are not so great, that God cannot Minister help to theyr necessities. Thow shalt be conforted. But Respect the world to cōme; (wherevnto thow art provided) and for what [2] ende: and that, in [3] what tyme.

Serue God truely: Serue him iustly

Great Care is to be had with those that meddle with Princes /affaires/

Much more Consideration, with whome thow shalt medle or vse any practise. But God hath shaddowed the frō destruct<ion> ation. He preserueth his faithfull, and shaddoweth the iust with a shi<eld>

shield of honor.

None shall enter into the knowledge of these mysteries with th<ee> but this Worker

Thy estate with the Prince (now raynging) shall shortly be /amended7 [am<ended>]

Her fauor encreased, with the good wills of diuerse, that are now, deceyuers

Thy hand, shall shortly be theyr help: and thow shalt do wunder =full and many benefits (to the augmenting of Gods Glorie) for <thy> thy Cuntry.

Finally God doth enriche the with Knowledge: and of thy self, <hath> hath giuen the vnderstanding of these worldly vanities He is [w..] [derfull] Mercifull: and we his good Creatures, neyther haue, <do> do, nor will forget the. God doth blesse you both: who<se> Mercy, Goodness, and Grace, I pronownce and vtter vppo<n> you. I haue sayd:

Δ Laus, honor, Gloria, virtus et Imperium,

Deo Opt°. Max°.

Amen

Ho yf you will stay one half howre, I will say furder vnto you.

Δ We will: by gods leave.

/flourish7

Δ After that half howre passed, (being 10½ Noctis ♄.) he sayd

Ho Venito BOBOGEL Rex et princeps Nobilitatis

Venito cū ministris: venito (inquam) Venito cum

satellitibus tuis munitus

△ I fele: and (by a great thundring noyce, thumming thuming in <myne>

myne eares) I perceyue the presence of some spirituall creature abowt me.

E K. And I here the thumming.

Ho Behold, Before this work be finished, (I meane the Manif<estation>

festation of these Mysteries) thow shalt be trubbled, with the Contrarie Powres

and bey<ond>

Marginal notes:

line 3: Dei Miseri= / cordia magna / ipi △ concessa

line 11: Respice / ista Tria

line 19: Secresy.

line 21: Dee,

line 24: God graunt.

line 28: Worldly vanity.

line 29: Good Angels

line 41: Noble / men

line 46: Note

At foot of page: F

[52a]

and beyond any accustomed manner. But take heade, they prouoke the not to

work agaynst our Commaundemēts. Both thy ey and hand shall be ma=

nifest witnes of it: well, this is true.

E K, They that now cōme in are ioly fellows, all trymmed after the manner of Nobi=

litie now a dayes: with gylt rapers, curled heare: and they bragged vp and down.

BOBOGEL standeth in a blak veluct coat; and his hose close, round hose of vel=
uet vpperstoks: ouer layd with gold lace: he hath a veluet hat-cap, with a blak
feather in it: with a cape on one of his sholders his purse hanging at his neck
and so put vnder his gyrdell. his berd long: he had pantofells and pynsons.

Of these, in Company, are 42. 7 of them, are apparayled like BOBOGEL:
sagely and gravely: All the rest are ruffyn like. Some, are like to be men and women:
for, in the foreparte they semed women, and in the bak part, men, by theyr apparayle.
and these were the last 7. They daunsed, lepe and kissed

E K. The stone is brighter, where the sage and graue 7 do stand and where the other do stand
the stone is more dark

E K. Now they come to a circle, the sage and the rest, but the sage stand all to gither

Δ The first of the sage, lyft vp his hand a loft, and sayde:

Faciamus secundū voluntatē Dei: Ille Deus n̄r est verè nobilis
& aeternus. he pluckt vp his right fote, and vnder it appeared,
an L. L
Then the Second moved his fote, and ——— E ——— appeared.
Vnder the third, likewise E
etc. N
A
R
B

Then the last, B. and immediately they grew all to gither in a flame of fyre

	and so sonk down into the former Globe		
	Of the rest the first pluckt vp his fote		
	and there appeared an L. etc	L	
2.		N	
		A	
		N	
		A	
	At the last, they fell down like	E	
	drosse of metall.	B	
	Then whipped out fowr in a cumpany	R	
3.		O	
		E	L E E N A R B
		M	
		N	L N A N A E B
	They clasp togither, and fall down	A	
	in a thick smoke ————	B	R O E M N A B
4.		L	
		E	L E A O R I B
		A	
		O	N E I C I A B
		R	
	They ioyne to gither and vanish	I	A O I D I A B
	like drops of water. ————	B	
5.		N	
		E	

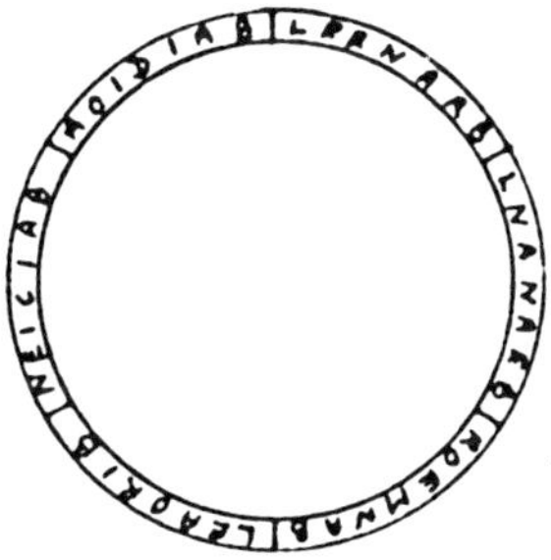

I

C

I

They fall down like a storme A

of hayle. B

Marginal notes:

line 1: <Ca>ve

line 4, over 'ioly': Jolly

line 6: BOBO / <BOBO>GEL his / <a>pparayle

line 16: Circle [part of this note is missing]

line 38 RH, over the table of letters: Δ This I fashioned thus after / my first dictata penning / of my own fantasie.

[52b]

A

O

I

D

I

A

The last vanished away. B

Δ then he sayd Well, I will shew the more of these things at the next time.

God be with you: God bless you both.

Δ Amen.

Δ When shall that next tyme be? a voyce spake, on monday.

Δ Deo soli omnis Honor et Gloria. Amen.

/flourish7

Monday. Nouembris 19. Circiter 1^{a} horā a meridie

△ Long after our comming to the stone (abowt half a quarter of an hower

the Cloth of sylence [was] /remayned7 drawn: and nothing appeared: but E K heard

as a far off very pleasant Musik the while

Ho He seamed to take the cloth away with his hands. After that (abowt 6 mi=

.6. minutes, Nothing altered or shewed, other than the standing furniture, vsually

of late appearing ther.

E K. Now come in 7 men with Musicall Instrumēts and before them cam one

with a veluet Coate, and a hat Cap, with a sword by his syde, and a Cloke or

or Cape hanging on one sholder: and a blak feather in his hat. etc.

Afterward cam 42. more, seeming to be very far behynde the first 7. Their

Melody sownded very swetely and pleasantly all the while frō the begynning

The forme of theyr Musicall Instrumēt

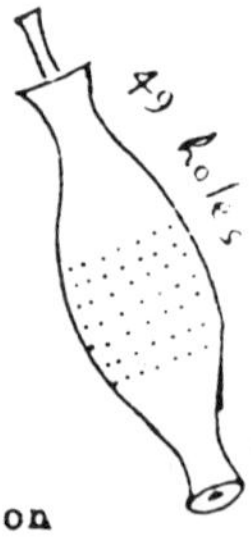

These Musiciens play, one with an other, iestingly

they bobbed one an other, and than played agayn.

The 42, which semed a far off, cam nerer and nerer, and

seamed to bring a rownd thing, like a table in theyr hands

The 7 Pipers went away: and the Man w^{th} /the[c]7 Cape hanging on

one of his sholders (somwhat like a Nobleman) remayned.

Then wer they come at hand, the 42 with the rownd table.

These seamed to be of two sortes. Of which, the last 7: on the forepart to behold seamed rather wemen, with fardingales very much sprowting out

but theyr face had no peculier attyre of wemen.

The 42 held the circle (or rownd Table) vp, over theyr hed, flatwise.

Then they layd the Circle down, and stode rownd abowt it

Ho sayd. Tam mali, quam boni, laudant te,

Deus, Deus, Deus noster.

Δ The letters appeared to E K, and he told me them, and I began to write

L E E N A R B

Ho Thow writest in vayne. Thow hast written them allready

Δ It is true: I see them now last below noted down.

Ho Loke the eight /[Ho ninth] 7 name in the Tables [Δ ☉ of 49, collected]

Loke to his Character in [[the Heptagono,]] /Δ the great Circle/ [the the Table w/th/ 7 Angles.]

Loke the second name in the Table wth 7 angles.

Δ That I finde to be Bornogo.

E K. He with the cape on his one sholder; sayth, Nomen meū est Bobogel.

And he that is my subiect, is Governor of the second Angle of the 7

Bobogel——— Rex

Bornogo——— Princeps

Marginal notes:

line 22: BOBOGEL / Rex,

line 30: a rownd / Table

line 31: The .7. pipers / went away

line 35: women like

line 37: The Circle

line 45 RH: Δ /eight/ that is Bobogel.

line 46: Charac- / ter

line 49: Bob.

line 52 RH: Δ / in Heptagono /with line to 'of the 7' (line 50)/

line joins 'far' (line 24) to 'far' (line 29).

[53a]

Bob: I weare these robes, not in respect of my self, but of my Governmēt.

I am the Prince, Chief, [E K. he falleth down on his knees and speaketh

wordes which I vnderstand not] Yea the onely distributer, giver, and

bestower of Wisdome and Science.

I weare this apparayle, for that in dede, being a Prince I am a Cownsaylor

to estate and dignitie. All Dignitie and gouernmēt that is not cownsayled

by me, and my subiects, is frustrate, voyde, and cleane without

firm grownd.

Those which thow sawest (being pipers) [wh] signifie praters, with

vnaccustomed, and not vsuall Instruments: which allwayes seame to sownd

that, which None but I my self, with my subiects, (yea not all of them,

but the fewest) can performe

But I am true Philosophie. I am true vnderstanding. Oh

my descending from him which rayngeth, is euen vncomprehensible

of the Angells. Neyther do I know, my self: But what I

think, I vtter, and What I measure, I am.

he sayd. Ordinationem Infinitae potestatis eleuate

E K. Now come Three out of the 42, and layd theyr fingers vppon the the three first letters. and

The first sayd. O Vnitas in Natura et in Deo

The second sayd O AEqualitas Dei et Naturae. Deus in Deo Natura a Deo et se.

The Third sayd. Concentus eius, est sine numero: Tamen nobiscum est in Vno, Fons et Caput Naturae

E K. They ioyne them selues to gither and become, <u>all One Man</u>, most beaw= tifull to behold: Whose hed and to the brest, seamed to be neare to heven. His brest and myddle part, in the ayre: His feete seamed to stand on the earth. There cam like a Fire, out of the Crown of his hed, and to enter into the heven, hard, by it: This great high and fayre man sayde <u>Veritas quaesitas</u>, nr̄a est.

E K. His apparayle is diuided, into two halfes: frō the Crown of his hed to his fete. The one half seemed to be most fresh florishing herbes: The other half seemed to be of diuerse metalls: and his right fote seamed <u>to be Leade.</u> he sayd (with an Aposiopesis) thus

Beatus est qui Lumen capitis mei etc.

E K; The rest, all, quake. he sayd furder

Vnus in Capite, vnus in pectore, vnus in pedibus

E K. Then stept oute 9, at ones

E K. Then the great man, returned, or was restored to his former estate of three particular men agayn: and they three leaned to the Jentlemā with the Cape on his sholder. x BOBOGEL. who sayde

Dee, Dee, Dee, at length, but not to late.

E K. In the place of the former first thre, appeared LEE

E K. of the 9, which stept out, they of the first Ternarie

sayd eche thus orderly

1 Volumus

2 Possumus

3 Quid non

This Ternarie sayd, Faciamus, quae fecerunt, nam nos Tres, sumus Adam, societate.

E K. They become one man, as the other before, but a slender and a weak one

neyther so high as the first, euer laboring or striving wth it self to stand vp

right, but still it bended, bowed, and inclined downward, as thowgh it wold

fall for feeblenes [of ..] The Body of this Compownd man, seamed to be

of Gold

Marginal notes:

line 4: Wisdom / & Science : / true No-/bility.

line 5: <Councell>

line 9: Pipers.

line 13: philo- / sophie

line 19: .1. / ^LEE

line 32: Vegetible, / Minerall.

line 34: ♄

line 42: Dee

line 44: 2 / NAR

line 49: Adam

[53b]

Of Gold glittring. When they retorned to theyr distinct shape: they semed /naked/ nake<d>

and to be sorry, and lament: and Bobogel did put them frō him, [wi<th>]

with his sworde, skabbard and all, as it hanged by his side:

Theyr letters were NAR

E K Then cam the Ternarie — BLN, and orderly they sayd thus

1 Ab illo
2 Per illum
3 Cum illo

Bob. Qui caret hijs tribus, [E K: he whispereth to the first Three lea<ni...>

to him and with all, seeing me muse at the Aposiopesis, h<e...>

No No , Thow shalt not dowt [pointing to me.]

In ecclesia Dei, laborabit in Vanum.

E K. This Ternarie of men becam to haue one onely hed, and three <b....>

and that one head was in good proportion

E K. The side of the Diaphanous Globe opened, and this Transformed Tern<arie.....>

point into it, toward the multitude: and the people had theyr brests nak<ed:>

and semed to wepe: and to wipe theyr breasts, and where they wiped the place

becam fayre.

E K. This Ternary did seme to stand vppon a triangular stone, and to turn

(as a horsmyll doth, abowt one axeltree) orderly agaynst, and by, the hole of the Globe so opened. and euery of the three bodyes, in theyr turning, as they

cam agaynst the open place of the Globe, they extended, and stretch out theyr

hands toward the people: The first seamed to hold a rownd ball in his hand

.1. being very little, but fayre white.

2 The second body, his hand had in it, a little sword flamming wth fyre.

3. The third had a thing like a hatt band of lawn, of many cullours, which

ever as his turne cam to be agaynst the opened hole, he seamed to cast tow=

ard the people, and the people did seme to be drawn to him ward, by the

casting of it toward them.

These three bodyes, thowgh they turned contynually, yet did the face

or Cowntenance of that one Compownd hed, stedyly and immoveably

regard or loke into the Globe at the forsayd hole therof.

Ho A wonder to behold the heuen, much more this.

E K. Now this Ternarie separated it self, and the hole or Clyft in the Globe

did shut to. These three did sit down by Bobogel.

Ho ———— Sunt semper, et Cibus illorum est vnus.

Δ Note. The first Ternarie, they seemed to stand leaning to Bobogel

The Third Ternarie was set orderly and vicissim, close by

Bobogel his feete, one of these betwene two of the first, euer

so that orderly one of the first, and one of the Third ternarie:

one of the first and one of the third; one of the first and one

of the third.

E K. Then cam the Ternarie ANA

They sayd, orderly thus. 1. Ab illo sed

2 Cum illo sed, looking on his own belly

△ Then I demaunded of theyr [Appr]

Apparayle: and E K sayd that

these were brauer than the former

Ternary. Bobogel sayd, Aliqui a dignitate, Caeteri talia quia non

sunt Digni. this he sayd pointing to theyr appa=

Then the third sayd. 3. Per illum, Per illū, Per illū ‖rayle

with a frowning cowntenance thrusting furth his hand.

E K. They ioyne to gither into one hed and three bodyes.

The Hole of the Globe opened very wyde now

This one

Marginal notes:

line 5: .3. / BLN

line 17: Penitence

line 19: 

line43: 4 / ANA

[54a]

This one Compownd Hed had many eyes, many noses, many mowthes, as thowgh it were a Cahos of Faces, in one hed, but three bodyes. One of this bodyes had in his hand a little Ball, like the other before, [but] very white, but with twynkling brightnes in it.

The other two bodyes, theyr hands were emptie.

E K. They turn in order agaynst the Hole of the Globe. But the People regarded them not: but at the comming of the hand with the Ball, against the hole, the people loked a little vp at it.

Bob. sayd. Et quia carebant in ardentibus ignis

E K. These, being dissolved into theyr former state, go and sit (with hevy chere) by them that sat affar of from BOBOGEL. Theyr apparaill semed to be simple: theyr good apparayles was gone.

Δ. Here I fownd a certayn error in my writing of the first Notes: which I since amended in the writing of this: But while that error did trubble me, the spirituall creature sayd these wordes Bob —— The Fawt is in E K his remembrance, and not in his will. Note this,

LEE ar the Three that stand with me
NAR are the Three that I reiect
BLN are the Thre which are enterlincked with me
ANA are the Three that are reiected.

Bob. sayd. Omnes naturam ad, Sed, Nôn in illo.

E K. The 30 remayning, cam all away, and satt betwene Bobogel and the reiected Cumpany. and frõ that Cumpany cam onely 7 to the Circle agayn. Euery of these 7, sett theyr feete, eche vppon a letter of the Circle, which letters are these,

AOIDIAB

E K. They say, In vse, we are perfect; Misvsed, we are Monsters.

Sumus septem Januae Naturae, et sui ipsius qui novit Deum.

E K. These 7, seme to vanish into wynde, or white smoke, and to fall into the Globe. And the six reiected, turn into a black smoke: and the rest

of the 30 seemed also converted into black smoke, and to fall into the Globe.

Bob. sayd In sexto et septimo sunt omnia.

E K The six that were next him, semed to clyng hard and close to Bobogel

(Bob. Behold.) E K They be ioyned all into One body, and becam like

the sonne, into the forme of a bowle or Globe: and so moved vp [the] or rowled

vp the small narrow race, or line vnworne, which remayned higher then the

chayre, toward the top of the. Diaphanous Globe, as before is declared.

So that this Princely [Jen] Noble man, and his six adherents, in this manner

went out of sight

Ho Formator horum, secundus est in Heptagono:

They are diuided into the day, as the other wer before: But wheras

the other are chiefly vppon that day which you call Monday, so

are these to be Vsed onely on the Sabaoth day.

Theyr Vse, is onely thus (obseruing the former order) with the

Circle vppon the grownd. The first six, [△ of the six orders] with theyr King

and the seale of theyr Prince, taketh place in the whole body of the

day: The other being 6 tymes six, are diuided into the partes of the

day as before.

The Letters onely where they stode, are theyr names and Characters

What doth the heven behold or the earth conteyne, that is

·Δ· not

Note the Circle vppon the grownde.

Marginal notes:

line 22: Δ There re= / mayned 10 / tymes Three

line 23, over second 'Cumpany': Δ of 30

line 27: Note by theyr sitting / that they are / indifferent: and so / they say:

line 27: Δ They se= / med therfore / to sit betwene / the perfect / and the re= / iected: as / indifferēt.

line 31, over 'the 30 seemed': Δ beside AOIDIAB

line 32: [6, 7.]

line 36: NOTE / the narrow / path, above / the chayr.

line 38, over 'adherents': LEE. BLN

line 40: Δ / Bornogo.

line 42: Monday

line 43: Sonday:

line 44: Note former. ergo / There is also a /·Δ· circle on the grownd

line 47: Practise. / by .6.

line 49: Names and Cha= / racters

line 52 RH: vide ante 3 folia, of my fete placed vppon the / Tables: Ergo they shold seme to be on the grownd

line connects 'ANA' (line 20) to 'six' (line 30)

[54b]

is not (or may be) subdued, formed and made by these.

What lerning, grownded vppon wisdome, with the excellencies of Nature, cannot they manifest?

One in heuen they know
One and all in men, they Know.
One and all in erth, they know.

Measure heuen by a parte, (my meaning is, by these few)

Let God be Glorifyed: His name praysed.
His Creation well taken: and his Creatures, well vsed.

Δ I craued for some playner Instruction, as concerning the vse of the...

and he answered:

Ho Behold: Are thy eyes so blynde? Dost thow see and wilt not see. Thy mynde telleth the. Thy Vnderstanding [furdeth the] furthereth and thy Judgemēt doth establish it: That as thow sawest a Body in three places, and of Three Compositions: Thowgh but two in [forme]

So shall this work haue relation, to tyme[1] present & present vse, to Mysteries[2] far exceding it. And Finally[3] to a purpose and intent, Wherby the Maiestie, and Name of Go<d,> shall and may, and of force must appeare, with the Apparit<ion> of his wonders, and mervayles, yet vnhard of.

Dixi.

Δ Than Immediately after he began agayne as followeth.

Ho Venito, Veni (inquam) adesto. Veni Rex.
O Rex, Rex, Rex Aquarum, Venito, venito inqu<am.>
Magna est tua, maior autem mea potestas
Deus n̄r, restat, regnat, et est, Quod, et sicut fuit

E K. Then cam one and sayd

———— Parati sumus nomen eius Creatoris $\overline{nri}$, nomen, nomen laud<are>

Nomen (inquam) Vnius nunc et viuentis.

Obscura sunt haec $\overline{ais}$ obscuris. Vera et manifesta Veris et perfectis.

Ecce adsunt E K. he that sayd this, is as thowgh h<e> were a king, with a Crown on his hed: His apparayle was a long robe whitish: But his left arme was very white, and his righ<t> arme, black.

E K There cam after this King a Cumpany of 42: and [euery] e<very> one of them had a letter in his forhed, and they were 7 in a row and six, downward.

The King had written in his forhed

BABALEL

The first 7, (begynning frō E K his left hand toward his right) had these letters, and the second, Thirdth etc had these letters as here appeare.

·	·	·	·	·	·	·
·	·	·	·	·	·	·
·	·	·	·	·	·	·
·	·	·	·	·	·	·
·	·	·	·	·	·	·
·	·	·	·	·	·	·

E	I	L	O	M	F	O
N	E	O	T	P	T	A
S	A	G	A	C	I	Y
O	N	E	D	P	O	N
N [A]	O	O	N	M	A	N
E	T	E	V	L	G	L

Ho At the next tyme, more.

Δ $\overline{Oe}$ quod viuit Laudet $\overline{Deu}$

Vnum et $\overline{trinu}$, in $\overline{oe}$ aenum

E K The cloth draws. Amen

[flourish]

Marginal notes:

line 1: Theyr off<ice>

line 2: Wisdome.

line 8: Δ / This boke is / sometimes / called liber / Creationis / & sometimes / Tabulae / Creationis

line 16: A Threfold / Vce of this / Doctrine

line 25: Rex Aquarū

line 34: Note this / Kings appa= / rayle, and / shew.

line 40: King / BABALEL

[55a]

Nouēb. 20. Tuesday, a meridie circa 2ª.

Δ After a great half howre attending, and diuerse tymes our prayers to god

The black Cloth was pulled vpward: and so vanished away.

♔ He appeared sitting in his chayre, and his face toward me: and so looking

abowt he paused awhile half a quarter of an howr.

In the meane space cam one skypping lightly, a little boy, in a grene coate

and sayd, He is here, at an ynche Than he sayd, Hark. To

me he sayd, Ha Sir ha. Δ what wilt thow say to me? [Grene

Coate] I am Multin his minister, wilt thow any thing with me? I

cannot tarry. Δ Then this skipiak espyed a spirituall creature comming, and

sayd: Ha, ar you there? Δ and so went out of sight

Δ This was King BABALEL, with a crown of Gold on his hed, his gar=

ment whitish, and his right [ar] sleue [of] on his arme, blak: and the left sleve very

white. He seamed to stand vppon water

The other 42 cam likewise and stode

Bab. Veni princeps 7 principū qui sunt Aquarū Principes.

Ego sum Rex potens et mirabilis in aquis: cuius potestas est [in aquarū Visceribus.

Princeps iste (△ pointing to a Prince, new cōme to sight which had a red long robe, and a cerclet of gold on his hed) est Tertius principium in Heptagonon. △ I sayd Heptagono: he replyed Heptagonu, [ad] and sayd: verè, planè; et perspicuè dixi.

Bab Mensurasti aquas? Befafes answered, Factum est.

△ I seemed to dowt of some matter here, and [Bab] /Befafes/ sayd, Thow shalt be answered in any dowt. I am thy frende: I haue fauored the in many things. Phērs haue imagined vaynely of my name. For thy loue towards me, Thow shalt know my name.

I was with Salomon; I was also (vnknown) with Scotus. I was in respect of my powr: vnknown, in respect of my name. He called me Mares. Since I was not with any. And I preserued the from the powre of the wicked, when I told the things of truth to come. When I rid thy house of wycked ones, and was with the in extremities. I was with the. Behold: I was with the throwghly.

△ Then he bad E K Ax me, yf I knew Obelison. △ I had to do with Obelison, but by reasons of my Skryers nawghtynes, I was in dowt what I might credit.

Bef. Thow shalt know this for a most manifest truth hereafter.

I am Obelison, the fifth of the Seuenth which haue the skowrging of Obelison the wicked: but not wicked for euer, neyther accursed to the ende. We Angels haue tymes, and our faultes are amended.

△ shall I Note your name, by Befafes. he answered, my

name is so,. in dede: The AEgyptians called me [so] Obelison in respect of my nature. △ I pray you what is the Etymologie of Obelison? Bef. A pleasant deliuerer

E K The former 7, haue Crownes: Theyr letters stand betwene theyr feete. EILOMFO etc

Bef. Thow hast receyued these letters allready.

E K. The water seameth, contynually to pass ouer these letters.

Bab. I Gouern vppon Tuesday

E K the first seuen take the water and throw it vp, and it becomethh

∴△ The fifth of the seventh

I vnderstand not this yet Vide lib. 5. A° 1583 Maij <.1.>

Marginal notes:

line 9: Multin / his Mini / ster

line 12: <Babalel.>

line 16: <He calleth / Befafes.>

line 19: Befafes.

line 20: The Prince his / apparayle.

line 24: Prince / Befafes / my old frende / vnknown of me

line 30: Mares

line 34: OBELISON

line 39: NOTE of / Wicked spirits / some restitution / to favor

line 46: or Cerclets / <p>haps.

line 50: Tuesday.

line connects 'principū' (line 16) and '7' (line 46).

---

it becommeth clowdes.

The second throweth it vp, and it becommeth hayle and snow.

One of the first 7. sayde, Behold, Behold, Behold:

All the motion of the waters, and saltnes thereof is aequally <mea>
sured by vs: we giue good success in battayles, reduce ships, &
all manner of vessells that flote vppon the seas: our might <is>
is great. Muse not For whan the seas are trubbled, with <the>
the wickednes or vprore of man, our Authoritie giueth victor<y,> <from>
from him that is most Victorious. Fishes and Monsters <of the>
of the sea, yea all that liueth therein, are well known with ...
Behold we are (generally) the Distributers of Gods Judgm<ents>
ents vppon the waters that couer the earth.

E K Than stept furth all the rest

The Third seuen sayd, some of vs conduct the waters throwgh the
.3. earthe. Other of vs, do beawtify Nature in her Composition.
The rest of vs are distributers and Deliuerers of the Threasures
and the vnknown substances of the seas

Bab. Praysed be God which hath created vs, from the begynning with
with Glory. His Glory be augmented.

E K. Now the 42 diue into the Water and so vanish away: and
Befafes, and Babalel also wer suddaynly gon.

Ho. standing vp sayd, Lo, Thus thow seest the glory of Gods crea=
tures: Whome thow mayst vse, with the consideration of the
day, theyr king, theyr Prince, and his Character.
The King and prince gouern for the whole daye: The rest according

| to the six partes of the day

Vse them, to the glory, prayse, and honor of him, which created them to the Laude and prayse of his Maiestie.

A day is 24 howres. △ But whan doth that Day begyn?

Ho Thow shalt be towght the rest.

Ho, proceded, and sayd { Vitam dedit Deus omnibus Creaturis Venite. Veni Ignis, veni Vita mortalium (inquam) Venito. Adesdum. Regnat Deus

Ô Venite. Nam vnus ille Regnat, et est Vita Viuentium.

E K. Now there commeth a King, and hath a Prince next him and after them 42, like ghostes or smokes, wit<hout> all forme; hauing euery of them a little glittring spark of fire in the myddest of them.

The first 7, are red, as blud The second 7, not so red The Third 7 like whitish smoke	The sparks of these were greater then of the rest.

△ Whereas in the former Treatise, ther was a dowt of Butmono The fowrth and Blisdon theyr offices, being assigned here clere contrary: The dowt may <be answer>ed by <the> notes A° 1582 Maij <.5.> of the Table and my character.

Marginal notes:

line 4: Theyr officis

line 7: △

line 14: The Third 7.

line 16: Threasors in / the seas.

line 23: Practise

line 25: King and Prince / <g>overn the whole / day.

line 27: Vse

line 29: A Day:

line 33: Ignis

line 46: Therefore I suspēt / < some Intruder / to have first ....>

[56a]

The fowrth 7
The fifth
The sixth } are diuerse cullours: All had firie sparks in theyr middle.

Euery spark had a letter in it.

Verè beatus (sayd this King	B B A R N F L
that now cam)	B B A I G A O
Δ I pray you to tell me yor name.	B B A L P A E P
I am the fowrth in <u>the Table</u>	B B A N I F G
and the two$^{\triangle}$ and twentyth	B B O S N I A
Δ I vnderstand in the Table of the	B B A S N O D

names collected frō the 7 Tables

of 49. And in those tables taking of the first septenarie Baligon

for the first /King^{c}/, and in the second septenarie Bobogel for the second King,

and in the third septenarie, taking Babalel, so accownted the third

and in the fowrth septenarie, the first of septenarie is Bynepor, and

so accownted the fowrth: but accownting euery one from Baligon

he is the 22th: and so the fowrth and the two and twentith.

E K. a Voyce I here, saying, you shall begynne to work agayn, at 6 of the clok next.

△ Oīm bonorū largitori, laus perennis et immensa, Amen.

[flourish]

Marginal notes:

line 8: <..... / .... or / King.>

line 8, over 'fowrth': △: King

line 12: < △ Butmono / his Pri> nce

△ Abowt half a quarter of an howre after 6: we retorned to the work and the cloth was drawn away. Ho sitting in the chayre.

E k. There appeared a little ronning water very clere chrystalline: and on this side the 42 last specifyed.

Bynepor sayd: Lo, (and than he kneled down, and semed to pray, a prety while) The generall state and condition of all things resteth, onely and dependeth vppon the distribution, and participation of my exalted most especiall and glorified powr. My sanctification, glory, and renowne, all thowgh it had begynning, cannot, shall not nor will haue ending. He that Measureth, sayd, and I was the ende of his workmanship. I am like him, and of him, yet not as partaking nor adherent, but distant in One degree. The Fire that holdeth, or is, the first Principle of all things in generally, /generaltye/ hath his [workmanship of my creation] vniversall and vnmeasurable powre in the workmanship of my Creation: Visible and Invisible, were not, withoute my record. when he cam I was magnified by his comming, and I am sanctifyed, world Without ende:

Vita suprema,
Vita superior,
et Infirma, sunt meis mensurata manib[us]

Notwithstanding, I am not of my self, Neyther is my powre myne owne, Magnified by his name: Behold I dubble life from One, vnto a thowsand of Thowsands: and one thowsand of thowsands, to a

number

Marginal notes:

line 25: △ Note this Chrys= / talline water.

line 32: Ipse dixit.

line 35: Fire, one of / the 4 Elemēts

line 38: Ipse

[56b]

number, exceeding cownt: I speak in respect of mans Capacitie. I am <in all> and all hath some being by me: yet my powre is nothing in respe<ct of> his powre, which hath sent me. Write this reuerently. note it with Submission: What I speak hath not byn reuealed <no> /noc t/ in these last tymes, of the second last world.

But I begynne new worldes, new peoples, new kings, < & new> knowledge of a new Gouernment. To be short,

Vitam [dedit] tradidit, deditq mihi pot<estatem>
mtem esse, Viuere, et in perpetuum, glorific<....>
omnibus et vbiq.
As these cannot be comprehended, what they are, with m<or....>
So cannot any thing be browght to pas in me, without a <living>
sight, and a perfect mynde.
I Gouern vppon Thursday. For Instruction, the rest as befo<re.>
Thow shalt work mervaylously, by my workmans<hip>
in the highest. To whome (with overshaddow<ing>
thy light, with life, and blessing you both, in his name
of whome I am the Image,) I prayse God.

E K. Now he descendeth into the Globe, and it becam very bright there among
the people: which, allso, at his comming, seamed to be more cherefull.

Ho stode vp and moved his hand, aboue his hed, cumpassing with it
a loft.
After that cam a Cumpany, with a King, and after him a prince
The king had a red robe on, and a crown on his hed.
The Prince had a robe of many cullours, and in his hed a Cerclet.
The Cumpany seemed to stand rownd abowt a little hill of Claye
Behynde this Cumpany seamed to stand an innumerable multitude of
Vgly people [a far of:] Those which seeme to stand rownd abowt the little
hill seme to haue in the palmes of theyr hands, letters, in order
as here appereth.
[BINEPOR sayd]

△ The King spake. Beholde, All the Earth with her bowells and secrets what soeuer, are deliuered vnto me. And what I am there thow mayst know. I am great, But he in whome I am, is greater then I. Vnto my Prince, (my subiect) are deliuered the keyes of the Mysteries of the earth. All these [hand] are Angells that gouern vnder him whose Gouernment is diuided, as before, Vse them, they are and shalbe at thy cōmaundement. Those that stand afarr of are the

vide lib^o 5: 1583. Martij 26 / Vide de istis in libro Craco= vie<nsi Junij> 26.

Marginal notes:

line 5: Note second / last world.

line 6: Ecce oīa / Noua.

line 12: Note.

line 14: Thursday

line 16: *△ I dowt, / I did not here / p̄fectly at / this writing / down.

line 25: The king

line 26: The prince

line 27, over 'Cumpany': 42

line 28: An Innume= / rable Cum= / pany of vgly / Creatures, a / far of.

line 33: Δ / Bnaspol

line 35: Wensday

line 40: Δ / Bliadon

line 43: Angells.

line 45: Vse them.

[57a]

are the spirits of perdition, which kepe earth with her Threasor, for him etc. and so furth. I haue sayd.

Δ Ho, standing vp, sayd, His name is the fifth and the 29th: and his Prince his name, ye fifth, and the 23th. Δ The first name, I vnderstand in Tabula collecta, The second name I vnderstand, for the fifth to be in Heptagono and the 23th to be so fownd the same, in Tabula collecta.

Ho: Venite, vbi nulla quies, Sed stridor dentium

E K. Then cam the man agayn, with vgly fyrie flames out of his sides, which was here before, the last day. Ho beckened with his hand vnto him, [and] and his coates went to gither, and so couered that horrible sight.

E K. There appeareth a rownd Table, which 42 hold, and toss, all in fyrie flames.

Ho: Write quickly, thow [E K] canst not behold it

E K. The first seameth to be a King with a crown on his hed, and the etc

Lo I Gouern (as I haue sayd before) All enchanters, Coniurers, witches,

& Wicked spirites that are hated of God, and included for euer, in owteward darknes (except a few which remayn in a second payne, which gape and grone for the mercies of God, and haue tyme of Joye, whose measure I haue, and kepe accownt of) are all my governmēt.

By me thow shalt cast oute the powre of all wicked spirits

By me thow shalt know the doings and practises of euill men, and more then may be spoken or vttred to man.

Blessed be his name, whose Glory is euerlasting, fode to the Just, and sempiternall .˙. to the Wicked.

Ho The 36[the] name, is the King his name, And his Prince his name is the last written in the Heptagonon.

Δ Brorges.

Ho Venite vos qui sub mea estis potestate.

E K. Then cam bright People 42: And besides these, all the fyre swarmeth with creatures.

Theyr letters are in theyr forheds: these stand in a circle: they take the letters

c
from theyr forheds, and set /them/ in a Circle

Ho Of these, I am Gouernor my self.

Behold I am of tyme present. I am of the last Ternarie.

Loke what may be wrowght, in all aëriall Actions, I can distribute and

bestow at my pleasure: my tyme and day is Friday

The day of the last before, is Saterday

The day of the Fifth is Wensday

Beholde,

Marginal notes:

line 1: <Treasure hid in> earth, kept by wycked spirites.

line 3: <Bnaspol>
Bl<is>don

line 14: The King

line 15: Mark who sayd so / before

line 17: Note a great / Secret of / spirits in payn / expecting / release.

line 23: Saterday

line 25: somwhat / was not hard / of me, or for= / got —— phaps Terror

line 26, over 'King his name': .Δ. Bnapsen

line 27: Δ saue one

line 27 RH: this I considered / Note & 1583. Maij In dede after a sort / Brorges may be cownted the last, for the begyning secretly / was with Bralges

line 30: Bralges / sayd his govern= / ment was of / such sup fol / 4.b.

line 34: The Circle / of letters.

line 36: The last Ternarie

line 36 RH: That is expownded lib° / 5. Martij 5

line 38: Friday

[57b]

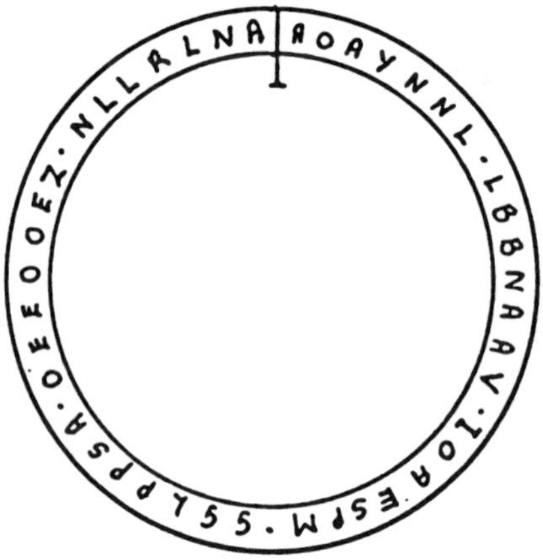

Ho Behold

I haue towght the. His name be blessed who raigneth and liueth [for] /< for>7<e>ue<r>

Δ Amen, Amen, Amen.

Ho. I will answer the of all Dowtes herein (being demaunded of me) to /morrow7 [morrow]

For, so I call it, for thy sake: Not, for that, it is so to me.

Δ so he went away.

Δ Then cam VRIEL, and MICHAEL, and an other (I think RAPHAE<L)>

and the chayre and table appered, as in the first boke hath byn shewed: And

also Ho had his peculier chayre, at his tymes of teaching me.

MICHAEL (sayd) Mercifull is our God, and glorious is his name

Which chuseth his creatures, according to his own Secret Judgement

and good pleasure.

This Arte is <u>the first part of</u> a Three<u>fold Art</u>, ioyning Man

(with the Knowledge <u>of the</u>[1] <u>WORLDE</u>, the GOVERNMENT[2]

of his Creatures, and the SIGHT[3] <u>of</u> his Maiestie):

Vnto him: (Ô, I say) vnto him; which is

Strength, Medicine, and Mercie

to those that feare him:

Amen.

Δ Gloria, laus, honor, et perennis Jubilatio,

sit Deo nr̄o Omnipotenti,

Optimo, Maximoq̧.

Amen.

[flourish]

Δ Note, Remēber, and enquire what it meaneth, that no Mention is made of Bralges the Prince,—Nor of Blumaza his king. in this Treatise, being a certayn Repetition of the Heptagonum stellare, going next before.

Marginal notes:

line 10: Note a pe= / culier chayre

line 14: Prima / pars Artis / Triplicis. / he termeth / this afterward / of three pro= / portions in / Esse: Consider / theyr three / principall points / here.

line 18 RH: Annael

line 26: 1588. on twelfth / day at night / as I reconsidered / the Method of this / boke, this cam / to my mynde.

line joins 'the WORLDE' (line 15) to 'proportions' (58a, line 37).

[58a]

Wensday. Noueb̄. 21: hora 7. a meridie

Δ There appered the first table, covered with a cloth of silk changeable
cullour red and grene: with a little cloth vnder it: all hanging very
low. The first Chayre allso: wherin Michael vsed to sit.
And Ho did appere likewise, and his peculier chayre: and he standing by it.
But the Diaphanous Globe, and the people or world in it, did not now appere.
and, bycause no voyce or word cam from these spirituall creatures, yet:
I declared that I did attend theyr pleasure first, as a scholer comming in the
presence of his Master; and whan they had sayd those things which were
for vs first, (at this instant) to lerne, that then, I wold move some dowtes
of the premisses, as I was yesterday advised to do:

Ho, he held vp his rod, (which had two portions or partes of it black and
one red: and sayde.

Ô quanta est hoīs infirmitas et Corruptio, qui Angelis, idq suis
bonis, fidem autem Deo, vix habet?
Oīa mundana, faeces: Mundi Corruptiones in se habent:
Deus n̄r, Deus n̄r, Deus [n̄r], (inquam) ille n̄r Verus, cum
Veris suis angelis, eiq /Idq/ inseruientibus Semper verus est,
Pete quae vis? Dixi: et quod dixi, obumbralū

est veritate, iusticia et perfectione
Ecce, (Δ holding vp the rod)
Hic (Δ pointing to the ende of the rod)
Per hoc (Δ pointing to the middle of it)
Et a Mensurae fine, nos nostramq mensurabis potestatē.
Age (inquam) Quid vis?

Δ I, than, of the premisses vsed a little discourse: how they might para=
bolically, betoken after more profownd matter, and litterally other:
yet what sense so euer the premisses had, that theyr first rudiments
and Text was to be made somwhat playner to me, then yet they
were: bycause I dowted as well of the vnderstanding of some of
that, I had written, as allso of mys writing: eyther throwgh
E.K. his mys reporting to me [his] matter shewed to him, or by
my mys hering or negligēt writing etc. To some part therof he
sayd these words ensuing

Ho In vmbra mortis non est aequalitas.
Obscurum enim nihil est quod per illū /E K/ recepisti. Age.

Ho Thow hast a work of three proportions in esse; of 7 in
forme: which is of it self diuided by a number septenarie, of
the course, estate and determination of things aboue, things next,
and things below: which, of it self is pure perfect and without
blemish. Notwithstanding I will answer the thus
The 7 Kings are orderly conteyned in the first of the Seuens
diuided in generall numbers: whose names are expressed, published
and perfectly formed within the first grownd and fowndacion of
this threefold work. The kings I meane with
theyr Characters, and the names of theyr .7. liuing and

semper adherent Ministers: Whose names thow mayst see

An Aue: Rocle Liba   not onely

Marginal notes:

line 2: Note. / The Colour / red & grene / of ye Table of / Covenant.

line 5: Two Chaires.

line 21: Note of this Rod.

line 37: A Three= / fold work.

line 45: Threfold / Work

line 48: The Kings with / their Characters.

line 48, central at foot of page: I vnderstand of Il, An, Aue &c / in the characters of the 7 kings.

[58b]

Δ. Filij filiorū ——— An, Aue &c

not onely there written, but openly, and most playnely, truely, and sincerely spoken of before: as, by due examination of thy bokes thow shalt manif<estly> perceyue. Notwithstanding, as euery king, in his Maiestie, <doth> comprehend the dignitie of his [hol] whole seat and estate, So I of my self being the First, haue the gouernment of my self perfectly, as a mysterie known [to] /vnto7 my self: which is a thing vnlawfull to be published vnto man and lawfull in respect of the charge committed vnto vs: and the slender Dignification of manns frayle estate, Which thow mayst see in the H<ep>tagonon: where there wanteth a name: The rest of the S..

the vtter Circumference of the Globe, are the six Kings <or> ...
following: according as they are written in the Mysteries of the ...
which do begynne the Powres, with theyr Prince, and th<e> ...
Characters orderly taken, by and vppon the Heptagonon. ...
Ô God, how easy is this first vnderstanding.
Thow hast byn told perfectly, playnely and absolutely, not onely the
Condition, dignitie, and estate of all things that God hath fra-
med: But allso withall, thow wart deliuered the most perfect forme
and Vse of them.
But this will I tell the, (to the intent thow shalt know: and forby cause
I wold not, thow sholdest be ignorant in true Wisdome) that those
Six Names in and vppon the Heptagonum are Collected, do growe
and are gathered from the names in generally affore sayd.
Take the Names, I will teache the to know them, which els, by
direction thow canst not fynde.
Loke thy First Table: I am called BALIGON
with men. Thow hast Noted my name (which is secret)
among the Angels, begynning with this letter M, consisting of
7 letters, the last being an A.
I am called MARMARA: but otherwise CARMARA: but
that letter M, shall not be expressed. etc.
Thow seest, next BOBOGEL; He it is that is the Second King
Thow seest the name BORNOGO, to be the first vppon the Heptagonū:
it is his Prince. And therfore I did Note him with a Coronet,
and not with a Crown: nay rather, but with a Cerclet abowt his
hed. etc

△ I concluded (of his instruction) the Kings and theyr Princes, theyr names to be thus lerned out of the Table Collected of 49 names, it is to weete

1 —△— 44 ·△· ·△·

·△· {
8 ——— 2
15 ——— 9
22 ——— 16
29 ——— 23 } modo retro=
36 ——— 30 grado quasi
43 —△— 37

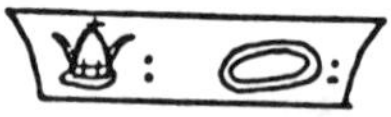

then Rex. Princeps

[△ He allowed of my Coniecture for these .6. but of his Prince

and farder he sayd, The Characters

△ I than sayd nothing: tyll at the fayr writing hereof, this, here added, cam into my mynde. How well I know not yet: Novēb. 23.]

Marginal notes:

line 3: Examination / to be made / of these bokes

line 5: The First King

line 6: A Mysterie.

line 8: △ / fortè, Vnlawfull / and was myshard.

line 11: The Globe.

line 13: △ / forte their

line 13, over 'Prince': princis

line 16: △ / Liber Creationis

line 17: Note, what hath/ bin tawght in / this boke.

line 20: Δ as may apper, / by the 49 names / Collected

line 24, over 'els, by': wth out

line 25: Δ / I suspect / this to be / an imp̃fect / phrase.

line 26: [hand]

line 27: Name / among / Angels

line 30: MARMARA / CARMARA.

line 31: M

line 32: Bobogel }
Bornogo }

line 33, over 'first vppon': Δ ⁖ name expressed.

line 35: Note Attire.

line 40, between '·Δ·' and figures: Addendo 7 — / fit hic processus. / Ergo addendo 7, / numero 43, pro= / ueniet 50: numerus : / maior [41] quā 49, / per .1. qui respi= / cere p̄t illum [44]; primū Re- / gem Baligon.

line 41, under central '·Δ·': Addendo 7, fit processus hic. g° / Si 7 addantur numero / 37: inde emerget 44. / pro proximo principe

line 46, under above note: [Δ / It is not Baginol, / but Bagenol / with e not i. / and therefore con / sider]

line 46, RH of above note: 44° / .l.

line 41, under RH '·Δ·': ·Δ·As far as I remēber, he / sayd, <u>My Prince is in my</u> / <u>self: which is a mysterie</u>

line 44, under above note: [·Δ· My Coniecture (herevppon, and / vppon this retrograde respect / to finde the princis among the / 49 names in Tabula Collecta)/ is, that <u>Baginol</u> is the Prince / vnder <u>BALIGON</u>: by cause the /

Letters are all one: but the order / of theyr places diuerse: and so / is his prince conteyned in him self.]

line joins 'Δ' (line 1) to 'before' (line 3)

[59a]

Δ Note that he calleth that, contynually a Globe:

vppon such a globe Naluage shewed out all the Calls

The Characters of Kings, are in the Globe, and of the Princis in the Heptagonon

Δ Note, frō the  on the left side, vntyll these words finished, he was out of sight. and /whan/ [what] he had ended these words, he cam in sight agayn: and browght a thing in his hand like a stere ∴  : or Heptagonū

Ho Beholde. Euery one of these Princis hath his peculier Table. Thow hast Noted the First Table which begynneth, as I will tell the.

/1./ 2: In BOBOGEL, that O, (the second [the] letter) is the first of the Table OF/E/SNGLE. and the second of Befafes,is the second, and the thirdth of the third: and the fowrth of the fowrth and the fifth of the fifth, and the sixth of the sixth, and E, in the seuenth, [Bag] Bnagole is the seuenth and last of this first seuen of this first Table: [so] accownted the first CAVZNILN The second seuen by like order is gathered of Babalel, and the rest of his Septenarie. And so furth to the ende downward as thow didst before. etc.

2. 3: In the second Table; L (the first letter therof), is out of Bobogel

his last letter, the second letter, is the sixth of Befafes: the third

is the fifth of Basmelo etc and so you haue LEENARB.

for the rest kepe that order downward to the ende of the last

name Bamnode. trauersi, quasi retrograde.

3. 4: In the Third, begyn at the lower letter of the latter worde of the last

of the second seven: and so vpward, toward the right hand: △ the

last word is of second seven is Bnagole: the last letter therof

is e: which is the first of this Third Table and the i, in

Brisfli, is the second, and l in Branglo the thirdth, and than so

furth, vpward, overthwart, toward the [left rig] left hand till ye

come to Bobogel, his second letter being O. Then to n in Bonefon: e in Ber

male: o in Bragnop. etc.

4. 5: For the Fowrth, loke, Bobogel. Than loke to this fowrth Table

The first B of the table is the first B of Bobogel

The second B of this Table, is the B of Befafes,

The third letter is [a] the second letter of Basmelo.

The fowrth letter, [R] is the thirdth of Bernole

The fifth is the fowrth of Branglo.

The sixth is the fifth of Brisfli

The seuenth is the sixth of Bnagole // ble.

And so in to the next sevens downward orderly for the rest of the Ta=

.5. 6: The Fifth begynneth from Bnagole vpward: begynning at the last letter

being e: and then vpward crosswise: exactly tyll the B of Bobogel

And so of the next seuen, for the next: begynning at the n of

Bonefon, and so furth.

6. 7: In the sixth, (the Infernall Table) The first is B of Bobogel.

the second is A of the 15th: The third is N of the 22th: the

fowrth, is the fowrth of the 29: the fifth of the 36: the sixth

of the 43: and the seuenth of the 49: being E in Bamnode

two letters being taken in that last septenarie.

The second septenarie begynneth at the first of the 15th, the second at the

second of the 22th, (being Y), the third at the thirdth of the 29/th/. then the

4th of the 36th,: the $5^{th[e]}$ of the 43th.

Marginal notes:

line 3: Characters

line 9: <...> peculier / <...> of Princis

line 12: <...> king / <..... fir>st, / [BOBO] / answering / to Blumaza, / as I perceyued / 1583 Maij .5. manè / by meditation: and / of Necessity must be: / yf that last be for Baligon.

line 21: Δ / The next L is the last / letter of Babalel / and then transversim / as before etc.

line 26, over 'lower': last

line 26, over 'latter': last

line 27, over 'right': left

7. 1: The Seuenth: the first A, is the A, of Baligon, and so downward all

the second letters of the 7 kings. Then all the third letters, then all y/e/

fowrth letters, Then all fifth letters, then all the sixth letters only, &

finally the seventh, and last letters of the first names of the 7.

tenaries.

Δ Note, this Table is made all of Kingly substance. etc.

Δ Now I trust I vnderstand (meterly well,) the making of the 7.

Tables: I wold gladly here some instruction of the great

Circular table (which you call the Globe): which hath the Ki...

with theyr Characters, and so within, 7 tymes 7, seuen tymes..

7 tymes 6, seuentymes furnished with Letters and numbers....

sorts

Ho That doth appertayn to an other tyme.

E K The Cloth was lett down; and the stone did <y>eild

voice but nothing visible but the forsayd blak cloth.

Ho One thing is yet wanting. a mete receptacle etc

there is yet wanting a stone etc

One there is, most excellent, hid in the secret of the depth etc

In the vttermost part of the Roman Possession

Ho Write. All lawd, Glorie and honor be vnto him, which raygneth for

euer. Amen. Be of good Cumfort

Lo, the mighty hand of God is vppon the

Thow shalt haue it. Thow shalt haue it, Thow shalt haue it

Dost thow see, loke and styr not frō thy place ∴E K pointed toward it

Δ I see it not

Ho It is sanctified, blessed, and ..^Δ...........

In the vse of his Creatures.

Thow shalt preuayle with it, with Kings, and with all Creatures of the world: whose beauty (in vertue) shall be more worth then /the^c/ Kingdomes of the earth.

Loke, if thow seest: But styr not, for the Angel of his powre is present.

E K loked toward my west wyndow, and saw there first vppon the matta by my bokes a thing, (to his thinking) as big as an egg: most bright, clere, and glorious: and an angel of the heyth of a little chylde holding vp the same thing in his hand toward me: and that angel had a fyrey sword in his hand etc.

Ho Go toward it; and take it vp.

Δ I went toward the place, which E K pointed to: and tyll I cam within two fote of it, I saw nothing: and then I saw like a shaddow, [of the bignes of] on the grownd or matts hard by my bokes vnder the west window. The shaddow was rowndysh and less then the palm of my hand. I put my hand down vppon it, and I felt a thing cold and hard: which (taking /vp^c/ <v>p I) perceyued to be the stone before mentioned.

Ho Kepe it sincerely.

Veritas in veritate: Deus in Deo, Vnus in vno est.

Let no mortall hand towche it, but thine owne.

Prayse God.

Δ Illi qui venturus est Iudicare Saeculū ꝑ ignē

sit ōīs honor, laus, et gloria, in sempiterna saecula. Amen.

Marginal notes:

line 9: The Vse of / The Circular / Table, (here / before, often, / called a globe) / at another tyme

line 15: A voyce

line 27: Δ / I omitted / a word, and our memories / could not yeld / it, <then> perhaps / Dignifyed

line 36: An Angel hol= / ding vp the / stone.

line 49: Caue [with hand]

[60a]

Liber Mysteriorū Quintus

[flourish]

1583 Martij 23.

[flourish]

Liber 6us

Liber .7us.

[60b]

[blank]

Jesus. ✝ .

<An:>^{o} 1583. Martij 23. Saterday. a meridie.

Δ E K being cōme, with M^{r} /John/ Husey of Blokley. (on the 22 day of marche

and E K being desirous to vnderstand somwhat of our spirituall friendes

as concerning such matter as had falln out very strange to him and M/r/

Husey: abowt a certayne moniment of a boke and a skroll fownd in

Northwik hill by the direction and leading of [some] such a spirituall

Creature, as when they had gotten the same, and they endeuored by art to

haue some exposition of the skroll, written in strange characters, they wer

willed to repayre to me, and there they shold be answered: etc: which thing

now they did.

Being therfore now ready to receyue instructions of our frendes, there appered

[first] in the stone One, in a foles cote, going abowt a clowde, which

appered first in the stone. I charged him if he were the enemy of God

to depart. He [tore] /tore/ his clothes all, and appeared all hery vnder. and

sayd Penetrasti Vim iniusticiae meae

Δ Glorifie God and depart. [Fe] he sayd Feci, Nam decedo.

He went away as it had byn a brush of fethers pulled in peces.

The Clowd wexed bigger, and went all to the right hand

At length the Table appeared, But the Chayre seamed not to be /of/ the same

sort it was, but more Glorious.

Then appeared three, of which, two went away, and one tarryed behynde.

he sayd———————— Auete

Verum est, et incredibile he kneeled to the Chayre and spake, but his words could not be discerned

Via, veritas et [wirtus] virtus, vnum sunt: et multiplex et admirabilis est eius magnitudo: Et venit ab ore tuo flatus, (et vitam habet) quo viuunt oia, nutu, et illuminatione tua.

Aue Verbum, Aue rerum formatrix et mensura eorum quae fuerunt, sunt, et erunt: Illuminasti oculos creaturarum monimentis et admonitionibus planis: Vita bonis, mors autem impijs, et a consideratione tua abiectis. Quanta et innumerabilia sunt, (Justitia) dona tua? O remiges varpax Kyrie eleyson.

Δ All this he sayd Kneeling to the chayre; and then he rose; and I sayde O beata Trinitas, mitte lucem et veritatē tuam, vt ir< a > me ducant ad montem sanctum, et ad tabernacula tua.

e. Vbi, non increduli.

Δ Nos non sumus increduli: sed spes nra viuit aeterna et Omnipotens est Veritas, fons vitae

Adduxi vobis aquam ex eodem riuulo. Medicina verò est imperfectionibus et necessitatibus vris. Intelligite nunc et quis sum, et quibus ornatus. Bibite, et accipite Ossibus vris pinguidinem. Multae namq sunt mortaliū imperfectiones. habeo, et habebitis: Adduxi, et videbitis. Verbum est

Lumen

Marginal notes:

line 6: The Book.

line 7: The boke fownd in / Northwik / hill

line 15: Pilosus / Pilo[sus]

line 29: Justi= / Justitia

line 41: Aqua. <A>qua.

[61b]

Lumen illud quo ōīs imperfectio [falletur] aboletur. Credentes introibu<...>
in Sanctum eius. vbi potio, et Medicina sempiterna.
Cogitasti verè. sum, etiam, et Credas. Nam veritate
et iustitia, vera et perfecta sunt verba et disciplina eius.
What willt thow?

Δ Recte sapere. Me: Thow hast it.

Δ I perceyue it not: otherwise, then that I beleue, it may be the decree
of the highest.

Δ He shewed a Tree, and a great deale of water at the roote or botom
of it: and he sayd [Me] Hath this Tree, now, any frute?

Δ I see it not. But the skryer may say.

E K The water commeth vp the tree, and it swelleth, and it hath
frute, great, fayre, and red

Me. Lo ¶ eate of it my self, and it lighteth the harte of those that
are chosen [he semeth to eate]. So is it in the.

Δ Ecce seruus Domini, fiat Decretum eius in me (iuxta misericor=
diam eius), de me pronunciatum.

Me. Go and thow shallt receyue. Tary, and you shall receyue
slepe, and you shall [see] see, But watch, and your eyes shall be fully
opened

One thing, which is the grownd and element of thy desyre, is all redy perfyted
yt seemeth that you beleue not. But I haue sayd, as he hath sayd and his worde shall endure for euer.
For he shall, and will performe it, for he liueth for euer.
Oute of Seuen thow hast byn instructed most perfectly
of the lesser part, the rest I haue browght you, in
this my vessell; A medicine sufficient to extinguish
and quenche oute the enemy to our felicitie:
Muse not, thowgh I say ours: for we all liue in tasting of
this liquor. His hed is a marble stone: His hart is
the blud of a dragon. his leggs are the tops of the Northen
Mowntaynes. His eyes are bright, and his face of many
Cullours, eche substance amongst the turmoyle and trubble
of nothing. For as then, they were Nothing: Had a forme
applyable and necessary according to theyr quantitie and secret
qualitie. The heuens are lightened by his two eyes: wherof
the one sight is brighter then the other. Aboue and in him self
which is by him self, and in no other, is this great and | vertuous
fowntayne: In nature Intellectuall he hath watred the plants

Marginal notes:

line 3: Δ <Loquitur de> / mea cogita= / tione quod / <esset> Raphaël

line 23: Increduli

line 26: Seuen

line 31: A parable.

line 35: Nothing.

[62a]

plantes of her beauty, and stroked vp the garments of her felicitie. In her darkest members entreth in the taste and sauour of this percing Medicine, reviving and recalling all things past present and to come, vnto theyr lively and dignified perfection. My words ar sentences. My sentences, wisdome; My wisdome the ende in my message of all things: Mighty and glorious is the Vertue of it, whose springs do endure, and are clere for euer: whose name be blessed

Δ Amen. I respect the time: God be with you.

[flourish]

Martij 24: Sonday: morning abowt 8.

Δ The Table appeared, and the Chayre: and he who appeared yester=day: kneeling or rather lying prostrate on his face, as if he were a slepe: he lay a long while

A thing like a lambs hed did seeme to lik him: and then he rose and wiped his face, as thowgh [w] he had wept.

Me he sayd. <u>Signa sunt haec vobis, humilitatis et paenitentiae; quae facio omnia, vra, [sunt] non mea sunt.</u> Laudetur verbum eius in Caelo, Laudetur etiam et in terris: Investigate potentiā in humilitate loquelae eius, et videbitis gloria frontis eius. Misericors namq et omnipotens est gloria virtutis eius. Vana sunt corruptionibus suis; Necessaria vero Necessitatibus vestris. Nam fecit oīa ad laudem [eius] eius: et opera manuum suarum (Ecce) collaudant lumen vultus eius. <u>Ad invicem diligite,</u> Humilitate viuite. Medicina vero mea (quae eius est) <u>omnia resanabit.</u>

The feldes wither without the drops of his Mercie

Mans Memorie is dull, vnleast it taste of the sprinkling of this vessell

[E K. He hath a great thing vnder his gown.]

Nature and reason haue disputed profowndly and truely by the fauour hereof: it perceth therfore depely. But vnderstanding and reason haue eleuated and lifted vp the dignitie and worthynes of Mans Memorie, by taste hereof. The Immeasurable and vnspeakable begynnings (yea with the begynner and [Principall] Principle therof), are exactly (after a sort) and perfectly known of them. Yt hath towght from the earth vnto the heauens: from the heven, vnto his seat: from his seate, into his Diuinitie. From his Diuinitie, a Capable measuring of his vnmeasurable mercies. It is true, most true, and true shalbe for euer. That from the lowest grass to the highest tree, [from] the smallest Valley, to the greatest mowntayn; yea euen in the distinction, betwixt light and darknes: the measure whereof is the deapest: yea (I say) it hath towght a Judgment. When he axed

Wisdome

Marginal notes:

line 14: A lambs hed.

line 16: Note hereby to / consider theyr / actions, gestures / and other cir= / cumstances.

line 29: Nature ∴/ Reason ∴

[62b]

wisdome, and forsoke the world, he receyued it and it measured the things of the world. Great are the inward eyes, and greater are the meanes, which deliuer things subiect or obiect vnto them. Finally it procedeth from him, that procedeth: Wherevnto the first was formed, after, and not like. Whose fote slipping hath dasshed his hed in peces, and it becam dark: vntyll agayn, the Medicine which I haue browght, revived his slombring. Hereby, he, not onely knew all things, but the measure and true vse therof. Yf the body haue no inward fyre, it presently falleth. Euery Organ is voyde of qua= litie, vnleast a meane be adiected. So, is all that thow hast before, more wonderfull, then, as yet, profitable, vnleast thow be directed and led in vnto the true vse and order of the same. Great are my words; and great is thy thowght: Greater shalbe the ende of [God] these Gods Mercies New worlds, shall spring of these New manners: strange men: The true light, and thorny path, openly seen. All things in one, and yet this is but a Vision. Wonderfull and great are the purposes of him, whose Medicine I carry. I haue sayde.

Δ he lay down agayn, a good while. and at length he rose: after my long prayer and confession made to god, and my discourse to him. etc.

E K. He plucketh out a boke: all the leaves are, as thowgh they were gold, and it semeth written with blud, not dry.

Δ he sayd, Cownt, Δ he turned ouer the leaves. but E K could not well cownt them: wherevppon he sayd: I will raze out thy dulnes, and at length, make the clere

E K. There are 48 leaves

Me. Et finis est. One is one, neyther is, was or

shalbe known: And yet there are iust so many.

These haue so many names, of the so many Mysteries, that went

before

This is the second and the Third: The Third and the last.

This is the measure of the whole.

Ô what is man, that is worthy to know these Secrets? Heavy are

his Wickednesses, Mighty is his synne.

These shalt thow know: These shall you vse. The one is a

Master, the other is a Minister. The One, is a hand, the other is a

finger: Grutch not. Neyther let wickednes tempt you: loue to gither.

Be contented with your calling: For, all beasts see not a like: yet

are they all Creatures. Vessels, not of one bignes, yet are they all full.

Both, most sufficient; but according to fayth, and vnderstanding of Consci=

ence. Yet must there be a third; whō, God doth not yet chuse

The tyme shalbe short: the matter great, the ende greater.

Ask now what thow wilt and he shall answer the

E K. There appered one like my self laying his two armes; one, on E K his

sholder: and the other on a man his sholder vnknown to vs, but somwhat

like to Mr Adrian Gilbert. etc.

Marginal notes:

line 7: *Note / *Adam, before / his fall, knew / all things

line 10: NOTE

line 12: The true vse / and order / of the premisses

line 15: New worlds

line 16: The Thorny Path:

line 17: A Vision.

line 22: A boke

line 27: 48: leaves

line 29: 48 1 / 49

line 30: Mysteries before.

line 32: Note of this / boke

line 36: J Dee, and / E K

line 42: A Third to / be chosen

line 47: A.G.

[63a]

Δ ys it your will to procede in this matter, you now haue begonne withall:

or will you of these characters, and places of Threasor hid (here portray=

ed by picture), say any thing?

Me: As thow wilt. Δ As the will of God is, so will I. the will of God you know, better then I.

Me The aeternall liquor be vppon you. Ones more, what wilt thow?

Δ I. do prefer the heuenly liquor, before all things, and do desire to be bedewed with the supercaelestiall dew thereof.

Me. Consider the former tree.

Δ The tre with the water at the fote?

Me Thow hast sayd. His growing powre, bringeth furth Act Remember the Prince and Subiects, which haue powre (as is told the) of Erthly Bowels (The thing there, whose /which you/ desire of me, is no parte of my charge,) Call him: It is his office: for by his ministers it hath byn shewed. God doth impart his mercy, to those he loueth, in all necessitie: whether of the one, or of the other, where it is dew. I leave it: his Office is to speak it. Notwithstanding liue in truth and humilitie: Vse God his Creatures, to his glorie, and thy Necessitie, the profitt of thy own lymms, and cutting /out/ of all Canker and rotten flesh. Thow vnderstandest: For thy eyes shalbe opened. Amen.

E K. he spreddeth his hands abroade, and goeth away, and putteth his boke in his bosom as he goeth.

Δ Gloria p̄ri. etc. Amen.

/flourish/

Marginal notes:

line 11: Potentia / Actus.

line 14: Δ Blisdon is the / prince vnder / Baaspol the / king vide s̄up / lib. 4. / A° 1587. Circa / Maiū: Quidam Ben, / (spiritualis Creatura) / dixit ip̄i E K, / se custodiuisse [et] / [permisisse] illū / puluerē et librū / Dunstani. &c.

Martij 26. Tuesday hor. 10: ante Meridiē.

First, appered a clowd: and that vanished away: Three cam in, they made Cursy to the chayre: and two went away. Then the third which remayned, lay down of the grownd as before. There cam like a lambs hed, and licked him. he sayd then, as followeth: being stand vp:

Magna sunt, Alla, quae dixisti, making cursy to the chayre. There was a sword hard before. after a while he sayd.

Me Thy Kingdome is established in aeternitie

Thy hands are invisible, and no man can distinguish thy mercies.

I attend your desire.

Δ As concerning the Characters, and shew of the ten places, we are desirous to know whyther we may require now Baaspol, or other vnder him, to say vnto vs, that, which may conten vs, for the Case as it standeth with vs.

Me. The buylder of the Temple was riche, before it was adorned. With Wisdome, cam the Instruments necessarie for mans worldly vse. He hideth no light from those he loveth: neyther shutteth vp his tents from such as seke him. If one be great, ô how small is the other? How small therfore is the mynde, and how much weakened that desireth those trifles? But as the smallest thing is feetest to the smallest

---

Marginal notes:

line 30: Δ / A lambs hed, / may be a token / of our humilitie / required etc.

line 37: Bnaspol.

[63b]

the smallest vse, so is the existinction of things of light accownt, necessary

for the lightnes and vanitie of this world. A part (Notwithstanding)

may beawtify the whole: and a small thing, may cure a great infirmitie.

I told the before, that my fete are not placed vppon such brittle and crakling

sand, [nay] neyther are my lipps occupyed with the vanitie of nothing.

I will not manifest, in any point, the thing which thow desyrest, neyther

is it any part of my charge.

I haue byn thy Scholemaster and director to the Sterne, to rule the

reason therof, with those, which can reache the Judgment therof.

All those before spoken of, are subiect to thy call.

This vessell at all tymes they greatly accept: yet haue they times

and seasons: when order breaketh in her self, the labor is in vayne.

Euery thing is for and to an ende.

Of frendeship at any time, thow mayst see them, and Know what

thow willt.

But One thing differeth, the Ende, and the Begynning.

That onely, is the El, rod, or measure which all ready is deliuered

The stroke of which, bringeth all things, in theyr degree, to an ende:

as far as the seven (magnificencie of euery Seuen) stretcheth out

it self.

Euery one (to be short) shall at all times and seasons, shew the direction in any thing. But, SO, thow canst not vse them, in the determination, and full ende of euery practise.

It is one thing to affectionate; and an other thing to effect.

What thow seest, is true, and to a former [∴ furder] commoditie: For, with Furderance, euery thing in Nature is ayded

Δ ———

Reade ouer that, which now, lastly, I declared: Then see, if you be not answered

Δ ———

Therfore mayst thow know, what that is, all thowgh thow do not, yet, or presently, put it in practise, by him, whose Charge it is, to deliuer it.

Δ Of your so greatly commended liquor I cam desirous to haue farder Vnderstanding.

Me. What liquor is more liuely then the dew of Truth, proceding frō a fowntayn most swete and delectable? euen that veritie which thy mowth hath preached of. What water recreateth more, or cooleth ignorance deeper than the knowledg of our Caelestiall speche? your voyces are but fayned: shadows of the wordes and voyces that substantially do comprehend euery substance in his kinde. The things which you do loke on, bycause you see them not in dede, you allso do name them anyase: you are confownded, for your offenses: and dispersed for your punishments: But we are all one, and are fully vnderstanding. We open the eare, and the passage thereof, from the sonne in the morning to the sonne at night.

Distance is nothing with vs, vnleast it be the distance, which separateth the wicked from his mercy. Secrets there are none, but that buried are in the shaddow of mans Sowle.

We see all things: and Nothing is hid from vs: respecting our Creation.

The Waters shall stand, if they here theyr own speche.

The heuens shall move, and shew them selues, when they know theyr thunder.

Hell shall tremble, whan they know what is spoken to them.

The first

Marginal notes:

line 1: Note. / All tymes / Speciall tymes [connected by a line to the beginning of line 11]

line 6: Note ——

line 10: NOTE.

line 14: Of frendship, / at any tyme.

line 21: Note.

line 32: NOTE / Whose charge / it is to deliuer / it.

line 35: Veritas

line 37: Lingua et / Vox Ange= / lica

line 46: The Powre / of the primitiue / diuine [spech] / or Angelicall / specke.

[64a]

The first excepted, No man euer was, is, or shall be (excepted where I except) that euer shall vnderstand, hath, or doth know the least part (∂ it is incompre= hensible) of this Vessel. He named all things, (which knew it): and they are so in dede, and shallbe so for euer.

Thow shallt speak with vs; and we will be spoken with, of the.

Three they are excepted, which taken from amongst you, as they were, do yet speak with vs, which are provided in the three laws to destroy that Monstre

They are fed with caelestiall fode, and they, talking, speak all vnderstanding.

This it is, I take God, (onely him that created me) to recorde.

It is determined: els wold I not: And may be vndetermined, yf you break his Commaundemēts.

A Stone it is that perceth down all things before it; and kepeth them vnder him, as the heuens do a clowde. What art thow, (O God,) and how mighty ar the drops of thy mercy, that preparedst [mai] man before to examin thy Mysteries?

The plagues of those that plagued them selues, shall fall vppon you, yf you transgress one iote of your eye sight.

For, What you desire, is graunted: and if you loue him, you shall endure for euer.

I am not as a clowde, sheuered with the wynde: nor as a garment, that waxeth olde, and torn in peces: But I am for euer (bycause my message is such) and my truthe shall endure for euer.

Beholde, Beholde, yea let heven and earth behold: For with this, they were created: and it is the voyce and speche of him, which proceded from the first, and is the first; whose glorious name be exalted in his own horn of honor. LO, this it is. [E K. he sheweth a boke, as he did before all gold] And it is truth; Whose truth shall endure for euer.

E.K. The leaues of the boke, are all lyned: full of square places, and those square places haue characters in them, some more then other: and they all written with cullour, like blud, not yet dry. 49 square spaces, euery way, were on euery leaf. which made in all .2401. square places

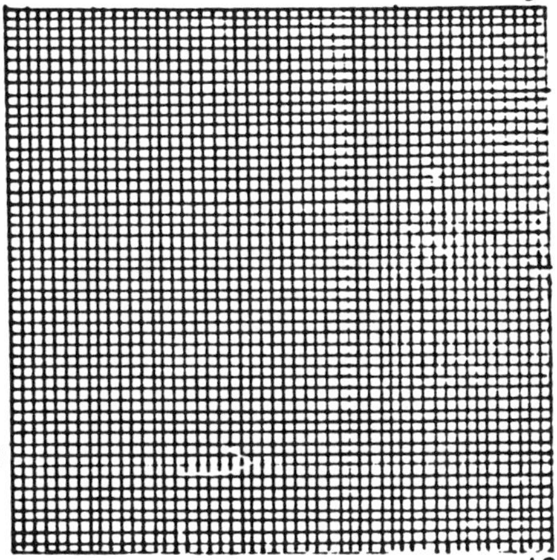

He wiped his finger on the top of the Table, and there cam out aboue the Table certayn Characters enclosed in no lines: but standing by them selues, and points betwene them

He pointed orderly to them with his finger, and loked toward the skryer at euery pointing

Me. Note what they are.

Δ They are Noted.

E K. He toke from vnder the Table, a thing like a great globe, and set that in the chayre and vppon that Globe, layd the boke. He pointeth to the characters: and cownteth them with his finger, being 21: and begynning from the right hand, toward the left.

He putteth of the Crown of gold, from his hed: and layeth it, on the Table. His here appereth yellow. He maketh curay: and <u>from vnder the Table taketh a rod of</u> gold in his hand, being diuided into three distinctions. He putteth the ende of the rod on the first of

the

Marginal notes:

line 2: <u>ADAM</u>

line 5: Angelorū Collo= / quia

line 6: Tres ab hoībus <u>in</u> / caelos rapti in / Angelis conversātes

line 8: Enoch / Elias / <Jo...> } fortè.

line 10: NOTE

line 13: Yf

line 13, over 'perceth': fortè / presseth

line 15: Note

line 21: The boke / The first / Language / of God Christ.

line 31: The cullor of the / Letters.

line 37: 21 Characters

line 47: Δ By his often taking / things from vnder / the table it shold / seme that there shold / be som shelf made / vnder our Table

---

[64b]

the Characters, and sayeth Pa

and there ⌈app^e^red⌉ in english, or latin letters, V—— Pa —— b

Pa: he sayd Veh: and there appered Veh in writing: then Ged: and after that he sayd Vnus Vnus Vnus, Magnus, Magnus, Magnus,. es. Then he pointed to an other, and sayd Gal, and there appeared Gal: then or. [the Voyce seemed Orh]. Then vn [the sownd semed vnd,] Then Graph: [The sownd Granpha, in the throte] Then Tal, [in sownd stall or xtall.] Then gon: then na [but in sownd Nach] as it were in the nose.] Then ur, [in sownd our or ourh] Then mals, [in sownd machls]. Then Ger, [in sownd gierh]. Then drux, [in sownd drovx]. Then Pal the p being sownded remissly. Then med. he sayd Magna est gloria eius. Ceph, sownded like Keph, But before that, was Don: Then Van, Fam, Then Gisg. Then he lay down before it: and there cam two lines and parted the 21 letters into 3 partes, eche being of 7. he said. Numerus ô perfectissimus, Vnus et Trinus. Gloria tibi, Amen.

Then he put on his crown, and pluckt a black veale before all in the Chayre he sayd. Remember to lerne those names without boke, and to know them.

Veh	c
ged	g
gal	d
or	f
un	a
graph	e
Tal	m
Gon	i
na	hath
vr	l
mals	p
ger	q
drux	n
Pal	x
med	o
don	r
Ceph	z
van	u
fam	s
Gisg	t

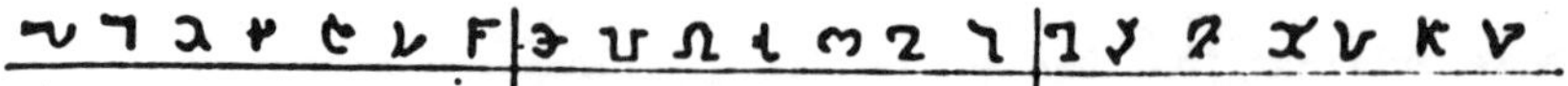

t s u z r o x | n q p l h i m | e a f d g c b

y

[flourish]

Marginal notes:

line 29: 

line 32 RH: , Δ. Thus I / deciphered / them after / a day or /

two or / three

Martij 26. a meridie  Tuesday hor. 5½

First there was a great noyce of harmony, hard

There appeared two great Armies fighting, and much blud shed on both sides.

One Captaine in red harness, the Contrary Captayn, in white and grene.

There appered Flags with a croked tree, or like a ragged staff, or cudgell, in

them: and they were on the red Capitayns side. He and his soldiers had the worse

and were putto flight, and they ran away.

The Captayn with the white and grene was Master of the felde: and assembled and gathered

ered his men to gather after the Victorie.

Now this Capteyn goeth to a town and semeth with his hand to heave vp the towne

being a big towne.

There was a voyce hard, saying thus ——— So shall it be, with 21 more

Δ Wyth what one and twenty?

A Voyce —— As yet, you can not know.

This will happen, before the sonne hath twise gon his course.

E K. Now the Capteyn appeared alone, on fote, in his harness. he holdeth vp his

hands to heven. He is now Vanished away. I meane the Capteyn in white and grene

greene

Now

Marginal notes:

line 36: [some indecipherable marks] ⁊ x /

line 38: A Battle / foreshewed.

line 50: Before two / yeres finished / Ergo before / A° 1585 /

Martij 26

[65a]

Now appeareth the red cloth before the chayre. There come in Three.

they all make cursy: and two of them went away.

Δ Our desyre is to know what we are to think of the Man which cam out

of my Oratory and layd the fyry Ball at Mr Adrian Gilbert his fete yesterday,

as he sat [by me] in my study with Mr Kelly and me. Whether it were any

Illusion, or the act of any seducer?

Me No wicked powre shall enter into this place. Neyther shall Iniquitie

range where the fyre of his percing Judgment and election doth light;

which shall quicken his deadness, and revive his courage to the auancement

of the name of him, which liueth now

He chose with fire and lightened theyr harts, and they immediately vnderstode

and felt the Illumination of his glory. What wilt thou?

Δ

To the performance of the glorie and encreasing of his name, which shortly maketh [and] an ende With for euer.

Δ This phrase, for euer, is somwhat dark

Me With this world, for euer. Δ This giveth some light.

E K. The stone is become very dark

Me As the Buylding is grownded and ended vppon Three, so must the mysteries hereof be practised With Three. The fowrth is the Boke, Which, Lo, is here present.

Δ Must Adrian Gilbert, be made priuie of these Mysteries?

Me. Thow hast sayd

Δ May I note to your name any peculier Character or syllable to distinguish your speches from ours or others?

Me. Medicina sum.

Δ I may then vse this syllable Me, to Note Medicina or Medicus Dei.

Me Behold, these things, shall God bring to pass by his hands whose mynde he hath now newly set on fyre. The corners and streights of the earth shall be measured to the depth: And strange shalbe the wonders that are Creeping in to new worldes. Tyme shalbe altred, with the difference of day and night. All things haue grown allmost to theyr fullness.

But beware of Pride. We teache duty, Humbleness, and submission

Shortly shall these things come to passe.

Δ Than, this Adrian Gilbert shall cary the name of Jesus among the Infidells to the great glory of god, and the recouery of those miserable people from the mowth of hell

into which, for many hundred yeres past, and yet cōtynually they do fall. etc.

Me Who made thy mowth to prophesy? or who opened the eyes of thy vnderstanding?

Who annoynted thy Jaws, or fed the with vnknown meate. Euen he^Δ it

is, that pricked these things forward, and shall vse you as his Instruments

to a mightie honor.

Δ May he require description of the Cuntryes, for his better instruction, etc.

Me Let darknes go behinde the, and tempt him not, that iudgeth. These things belong not

to my charge. Thow knowest them, which are sufficient, whan short time

shall serue, for the whole instruction. Greater nede were to enquire How

or by what meanes thow mayst be made worthy: and so, consequently, haue knowledge

for the knowing, hauing and vsing of this caelestiall medicine.

Forget not.

I instructed the before hand, and told the, that both of you must iointly lerne those

holy letters (For so, I may boldely call them) in memory: with theyr names: to the

intent, that the finger may point to the hed, and the hed to the vnderstanding of his charge.

for Discoveries making of the seas and theyr bownds.

Marginal notes:

line 1: Three.

line 4: A. Gilbert.

line 7: NOTE

line 8: Election

line 11: The Apostles on / Whitson Sonday.

line 19: Three.

line 20: Foure.

line 23: A. Gilbert / may be made / priuie, but he / is not to be / a Practiser.

line 28: A. Gilbert / his Task

line 31: Note a / prophesie.

line 33: Pride

line 35: Adrian Gilb.

line 38: ·Δ· / of god

line 42: Description / geographical.

line 44: Tenebrae post / dorsum.

line 46: Instruction requisite

line 47: Note

line 50: Both ioyntly / E K and / J <:D:>

lines join: 'name of Jesus' (line 35) to 'these things' (line 40); 'are' (line 45) to 'making' (line 53).
'he' (line 39) to 'pricked' (line 40) and to 'honor' (line 41)

[65b]

Δ You perceyue that I haue diuerse affayres which at this present do withdraw me

from peculier diligence vsing to these Characters and theyr names lerning by hart:

therfore, I trust, I shall not offend, if I bestow all the convenient leyser that I shall

get) abowt the lerning hereof

♔ Me Peace, Thow talkest, as though, thow vnderstodest not We know the, we see the in thy hart: Nor one thing shall not let an other

For short is the time, that shall bring these things to profe: wherein he

that liueth, shall approve him self aliue. Beautifull are the footesteps

of his comming, and great is the reuenge of the wicked

O Liber, Liber, Liber, bonis vita, malis vero mors ipsa

Magna sunt mirabilia in te inclusa: et magnus est nomen Sigilli tui

Lumen Medicinae meae, vobis

E K. he holdeth his hands abroad. He draweth the Curten.

Δ Gloria Laus et honor Deo prl et F. et ss. Amen

[flourish]

Marginal notes:

line 8: God will shew / him self aliue.

line 10: Liber

Martij 28 Thursday morning Mawndy Thursday

A voyce. Pereant omnes qui insidiantur virtuti nois mei: et qui

Lumen [as]absconderunt Justitia mea.

E K. Now the veale is pluckt away

Three appeare, as before time

All three sayd——— Multa nos, quia multa patitur ipe

E K. The two go away and the Third remayneth, who is like in all points to

him, who yesterday to me alone, in your absence had declared him self to be

an Illuder. Δ NOTE; for the better vnderstanding of this dayes Act it may be remembred that E Kelly, while, I, (John Dee) was at London, yester= day (being wensday) had vsed meanes to haue conference, with the good Crea= ture, with whome we haue dealing iointly: and that there appeared one very like vnto our good frende, Who toke apon him to be the same, and now semed to be constrayned by E K to tell the truth: and therfore his outward beautifull apparell semed to go of, and his body appered hery and he confessed that he was an Illuder etc Wherevppon E k. was in a great perplexitie of mynde, and was ready to haue gone his way. And at my comming home told me a long processe of this Tragicall Act. But I comforted him, and wold not yeld to his opinion, But did declare my confidence in the goodnes of God: for that we craved at his hands, things good and necessarie: and that therfore he wold not give his childern a stone for bred, or a scorpion for nedefull food required etc. And this morning the matter was propownded by me, and therevppon the former sayings wer vsed, and all the consequences of matter, which hereafter is recorded.

Δ The veritie I require of yesterdays doings with E K in my absence.

Camikas zure he sayd, holding his hands vp to heuen.

E K. he walketh vp and down and semeth angry: and beat his hands to gither

There commeth a little streame of fire whitish from aboue: and cam to his hed:

he kneleth down before the Chayre, and loketh vp and sayde

Me Oh how brittle are the works of thy hands [he looked vp] whose Imperfections are more innumerable then the sands of the sea: or clowds that were lifted vp since the begynning of the world. Darknes dare presume to place him self in Lightnes: yea dishonor, (o God) to dwell in place of glory: His lying lipps presume against Truth: whilest thow suffredst his old and withered face to be garnished with thy beawty. Heavines is his seat, yet are his lipps myrthfull: and little there

that

Marginal notes:

line 17: Insidiatores

line 30: Pilosus.

[66a]

that separateth him from the dignitie of honor: But his ponishment is sufficient, his dishonor vnspeakable, and his damnation for euer: which how bitter it is, great and vnspeakable, Thow, ô thow (I say) that liuest (which hast estranged him so far from thy glory) makest onely manifest But yet how long shall the sonnes of men puff vp them selues with bragging and boasting of that they see not? But (alas) All things are confownded, and are contrary to thy commaundemēts: some onely which differ, remayn with concordant myndes praysing the, and lifting vp thy name, as much as strength performeth. But herein is thy glory and long sufferance manifest, in that thow dost not onely with greif behold theyr synnes, but like a iust iudge, fauorably dost ponder the greatnes of theyr enemies, which infect theyr myndes, and blynde the light, which thow hast given /vnto/ [to] theyr vnderstanding, with inflammations bodyly, instigations worldly, and tentations innumerable. Great therfore and most great, and none greater can be, which deridest the Aduersarie, and healest the weak: whose smallnes of habilitie thow canst augment, wherein the mysteries of thy great glorie and might, is manifest. Thy seat yeld prayses, with incessant and dutifull obedience. Thy name be magnified, thy mercy published to thy glory: Holy Holy, yea great and most holy, is thy euerlasting kindenes for euer.

E K. Now he standeth vp, and sayd

Me As I haue all ready told, from whome I cam, so haue I not hydden, what I am, or what message I bring; why it is sent, it is allso written. How long shall I perswade /to/ stedfastnes? But the greater your measures are the greater shalbe the quantitie. These afflictions are necessary. For herin is a measure [is a measure] to distinguish ^ from falshode, light from darknes and honor from dishonor. The more they are like vs, or shew them selues so, (for, nothing can be more dislike) the more they are Judges of theyr own dam=

nation. Yea, if his strength had byn great, he wold haue devoured thy
sowle. [loking to E K] But whome God hath chosen, shall none over=
turne. Brag not: eyther Credyt my words by thyne owne reason. But
Consider that diuerse may be dishonored, yea thowgh they be in honor: yet
shallt nor thow neyther be ouerturned with the one wynde nor the other:
thowgh the afflictions that shall follow the, be great and hard.
In my words are no error: neyther haue you fownd my lipps vntrue.
Whan I kneeled, I spake for you. But I haue promised that No vnclean
thing shall prevayle within this place. Neyther am I a revenging spirit
nor of any such office. I quicken the deade, revive them that are falln
and cure or sow vp the wowndes, which they are permitted to work vppon
man, as tokens of God his Justice.
I call the same god, (whome I haue called before) to recorde, that these words
are true, my sayings iust, and his mercies more perfect. Whilest heven
endureth and earth lasteth, never shall be razed out the Memorie of these
Actions. Vse Humilitie: Reioyce whan the enemy is discomforted
in his traynes, and inventions: A ponishment so great, Et caetera.
Whan I yoked your* feathers to gither, I ioyned them not for a while.
your flying is to be considered in quantitie, qualitie and Relation.

Thank God: Be mercifull: forget your synnes: and prepare

your selues, For, great and wonderfull is the immediate powre

of him that illuminateth from aboue.

It shall light apon you: For those that are present with him, liued

with him, eat and drank with him, ⌐and¬ were instructed by him, Were

but

Marginal notes:

line 22: Raphaëlis / officium

line 26: *fortè, truth [with caret under 'truth']

line 34: Afflictions to / E K

line 37: This place

line 38: Raphaëlis / officium

line 43: Note the durance of / of these Memorialls

line 46: *Note of the / Vision which / was shewed / A° 1582.

[66b]

but hearers onely: At Length God was glorified, in one instant a<11>

things browght vnto theyr remembrance: yea some of them taken to

behold the heavens, and the earthly glory. I haue sayd

Δ

Me Behold. Veniat vindictum dei, et percutiat linguam mentientem

E K. he goeth his waye and taketh all with him, Table, Chayre, and Curten

and all. There cam in a great many with flaming swords, and bring in the

wicked spirit, who yesterday delt so diuilishly with E K.

One of them holding him by the arme, sayd, Speak now for your self, you

could speak yesterday: They all drew theyr swords: they sknorked fire. And then seamed a water to com in, but it went away again

A voyce ———— Dicat, nam nrm non est

E K. Now is the Skroll with the Characters browght in, which was fownd by

spirituall direction this [last] month, the 12 day, abowt 10½ after none.

by Mr Kelly and Master Husy

He semeth now [to] as like our good frende, as may be.

Our frende cam with a sponge and annoynted the wicked spirit his lipps

A voyce ———— Els could I not speak.

Δ Being now thow canst speak, answer me

The Wicked, sayd ——— Ask quickly.

Δ What is thy name? ———— The wicked answered Gargat.

Δ What is the sentence of that Skroll? ——— Gar. I know not.

Δ In the name of Jesus, I charge the to tell me the truth as concerning

That roll here shewed: ——— Gar. I haue cownterfeted this roll, and

browght it: for it is not the true roll.

Δ After [many] many words betwene him and me, and the more, bycause he denyed

that he knew of any Glorie belonging to God, I vrged him so, at length w/th/

short and euident argum̄t, that he answered, he must confess the powre

and glorie of god: and sayd, that he was damned for euer. and did

wish damnation to me: And I requested God to vse his Justice on him

for the glory of his name: then he entreated me somwhile, and somwhile

derided me, saying, Art thow so lusty? etc

Δ All the Cumpany fell on him, and hewed him in peces: and digged a hole in the earth, with theyr swords, and he fell in, and [there] after that was a myghty roaring hard

A voyce———————Sic soleo iniustis.

Δ The Cumpany went away. There cam a fire and seamed to burn all the howse.

A voyce———————Purifica Domine sanctum tuum, et dele iniquitatem inimicorum nostrorum.

Δ Then returned our frende Me, and all seemed light and bright agayn: likewise all the furniture, of Table, Chayre, Globe in the Chayre covered with a red covering etc.

Me. Visio vera, verè denotatur. Denotetur etiā ad gloriā Dei.

Δ Master Kelly, is your dowt of the spirit, now taken away?

E K. ye truely, I beseche God to forgive me.

Me. Dixisti, et factum.

Δ As concerning Adrian Gilbert, there might be some dowte in common externall Judgmēt, of his aptnes to the performance of the Voyage wth the appertenances, But the Secret of God his prouidence, I will not meddle with all: for he can make infants speak, and the dum to shew furth his glory etc.

Me. If God be mighty, acknowledge his powre. Who made the sonne of nothing?

Marginal notes:

line 14: The finding of / the skroll, of / the Threasors.

line 24: Cownterfeted / Roll.

line 25: ∅ vid. infra / pag 152. 153 &c.

line 43: Write

line 44: [hand]

line 47: A.G.

of nothing? or man, so brittle a substance? Nature thrusteth vp her sholders amongst trees and herbs, like a ientle fyre: In beasts and all the creatures of the fielde, waters, and earth, in a palpable imagination: Amongst the sonns of men, she walketh by her own qualitie, mixing the quantities, with her before iudged proportion. Amongst all these is some distinction, yet in all theyr kindes are perfectly and substantially norrished. Yf Nature haue such powre, What powre hath our God, and how great is his might[e] in those [he] in whome He kindleth a sowle, vnderstanding. The strength of body and inward man, with the strength of him that allso leadeth him, are augmented and diminished at his pleasure. Yf earth, in mixture become fyre, how much more shall he encrease, whom God hath strengthened: Yf he wold haue conquered with thowsands, he wold not haue sent back the dogged harted people. Yf riches or renowne were his felicitie, he wold haue kindled the twelue Lamps of his aeternall light, on a higher mowntayne: But he chose them in the Valleys, and from the watering places. I think this be sufficient to confirme your Vnderstanding.

Δ I trust, God be not offended with this matter propownded. etc

Me He is pleased: And it is enowgh. Eternitie is mighty and glorious to the righteous.

Δ Whan shall I make him priuie of these things?

Me Whan thow wilt. For euery thing is acceptable with those that are accepted.

See thow cownsayle him, and be his Father.

Δ As concerning John Dauis, we are to ax somwhat etc.

Me John Dauis, is not of my Kalendar. Lern of them, of whome it is necessary

Be not negligent, in lerning the things before prescribed.

God be amongst you.

E K. He hath drawn the curten of red.

Δ soli Deo sit oīs honor et gloria. Amen.

/flourish/

Marginal notes:

line 7: /hand/

line 8: Δ / Note Body / sowle / spirit

line 13: The 12 Apostles

line 20: A.G.

line 23: Jo. Dauis

line 25: Lern the / Alfabet.

Mawndy Thursday, after None. hor. 3½

Δ The Veale being drawn away after a quarter of an howre (almost) after the

first motion made by me. Three cam in, and made obedience to the chayre

Two went away, and the third remayned there, as before.

Δ As concerning the Kalendar to be reformed, I am grieved that her Ma/tie/ will not

reforme it in the best termes of Veritie

And as for the priuiledge for Mr Adrian Gilbert his Voyage, I think not well of it, that Royalties shold not be graunted

Therfore both these points, respecting her Matie, I wold gladly haue cownsayle, such

as in the Judgment of the highest might be most for my behofe, to follow.

Me In one gouernment there are sundry principall partes: Euery part in

subdiuision conteyneth many and sundry offices. Many Offices require many

disposers: yet hath euery disposition continually some partition in his qualitie.

All things, one thing: And one thing, something: some thing many

things, and many things, most innumerable

The heuens in proportion are gouerned vniversally of a few; particularly of

many: eche place possesseth his diuision: and euery thing diuided, his pro=

pertie.

Princis ar governors which move and stir them vp to work, as it is provided,

and to behold in speculation How euery particular Action shall haue due, perfect,

and

Marginal notes:

line 34: The reformatiō / of the Kalendar.

[67b]

and appropriated Locall being, motion and Condition

Subiects, (yea, the Highest,) are stirred vp, by theyr propre Angels:

The inferior sort do follow the disposition of theyr leaders

Vertue and Vice dwell euery where

Light and darknes, are allwayes intermedled

Consider, How I speak it.

The myndes of all that move, euen vnto the least qualitie in Nature, haue

of them selues propre vertues: and therfore propre Instigators.

I call to memory thy words, the manner of thy speche, and the secret purpose

or meaning, wherevnto it is vttred. I see thy Infirmities, and know

what thow desyrest.

But mark me, Whom God commonly choseth, shalbe whom the

Princis of the Erth do disdayn.

Consider, how the prophet that slew that Monstrous Gyant, had his

election.

God respecteth not princis, particularly, so much as the state of his whole

people. For in Princis mowthes, is there poyson, as well as proverbs.

And in one hart, more Synne, then a whole world can conteyn.

yt is not myne office to meddle with theyr vanities, neyther is it a part of

my pageant to towch anything that tasteth not of Medicine

But what? doth thy mynde reply? Dost thow think, that my cownsayle

herin, to a grieved mynde, is, (thowgh it can be) Medicinall?

Peraduenture thow thinkest I am not, in thy marrow: yej I haue byn

long in the highest part of thy body, and therfore ame somthing perswaded

of thy meaning

Δ In dede, I thowght that your good Cownsaile, was or might be a remedie

and a medicine to my afflicted mynde, for this vnseamely doing, in the

[the] two former points expressed.

Me Behold, wherunto thy earthly man wold seduce the. Dost thow think,

that if it pleas god, it shall not please the Prince? if it be ne=
cessarie, all ready prepared?

secretum duo

For all things are Limited, with a full mensuration, and vnsearchable
forsight: yea, I say, all ready, vnto the ende.
Be not discomforted. Quayle not at the blast of a small tempest:
For those that speak the fayre, haue dissembling harts, and priuilie do
they shote at the, with arrows of reproche.
Whan they shall haue nede of the: I meane, of the help of God,
throwgh the, (some shut vp, some entangled, some gad=
ding like masterles Dogges,) Than shall they gladly seke the
and desire to finde the. They shall smell oute thy fote steps,
and thow shallt not see them. The key of theyr Cares
shalt thow be Master of: and they them selues shall not vnlok
theyr own grievousness. yea they shall say, Oh let the earth devour vs.
But I am to long. I answer the, all thowgh it be not my office,
to declare that thow desirest: yet for that thow desyrest my Medicine,
I say, Thow shalt preuayle agaynst them, yea euen agaynst the Mightiest.
As thow wilt, so shall it be in God his blessings.

Beware of Vayne glory. Vse few wordes

Thy weapons, are small, but thy Conquest shalbe great.
Lo. Doth this satisfy the? Haue a firme faith:

It is

Marginal notes:

line 2: Angeli / proprij

line 8: Peculier and / propre Instiga= / tors

line 12: God hi's Elect.

line 20: Medicine

line 24: △ / Raphael long / tyme visiting / my hed

line 30: A secret

line 36: Lingua dolosa.

line 38: England,

line 40: Miserie to= / come

line 45: Note. eache in his / office.

line 47: Praevalescentia

line 50: Conquest.

line 51: A firm faith.

A line joins 'all ready' (line 31) to 'all ready' (line 34).

[68a]

It is the greatest lesson. Be it vnto the as thow hast deliuered
One thing, I answer the, for all Officis. Thow hast in
Subiection all Offices: Vse them when it pleas the,
And as thy Instruction hath byn.

I haue sayde.

△ As things be planted here, for preparation of Table, sigillum Dei etc which things are not portable with eas: so, bycause I think, that some seruices to be done in gods purposes by me, will require other places than this howse, so shall
c
diuerse my practises haue /(as I think)7 a more compendious manner, and redy to be executed in any place etc.

Me Truely thow hast sayd, and so shall it fall vnto the.

As I am here in this place, and yet in dede not, So, here:
so shall it fall oute, and follow in the Mysteries of your
Associated Operation.

The other shall be, but, as necessary help to the first Practises,
to plant the Tree: which being confirmed and strongly
rooted shall bring furth frute, most abundantly.

The Erth and the tree, can not be separated
This is the ende, and true it is.

Let him be record, whom I beare record of here,

And so, with the. Amen.

I must help the. Lerne ioyntly the Elements or grownds of this
heuenly doctrine; the ende and Consummation of all thy desired thirst:
in the which God shall performe the, thy Philosophicall Harmonie
in prayer. Thow knowest what I mean.

The Aeternall physitien minister his heuenly grace and continuall
blessings vppon you, to the Glorie of his name, execution
of your procedings, and holy and insatiable desires.

Δ Amen: O̅i̅potenti Deo, n̅r̅o̅,
Creatori Redēptori et
sanctificatori, o̅i̅s honor
laus et gratiarū actio.
Amen
[flourish]

Marginal notes:

line 2: All Officis

line 14: Δ: and E K, / and / A. Gilbert. [with line to 'other' (line 16)]

line 17: The erth — 1. E K
The Tree — 2. Δ
The planter — 3. A G

line 19: The Planter / may be separa / ted: from / Tree and Erth

line 23: Note Lerne / The Alfabet.

line 26: Δ* Philosophicall Harmonie / in prayer, is ment / by the prayer which / I dayly vse, & often. / Deus in. a.m. In. / D.a.a.m.f. G.p. / e. F.e.s. etc.

Jesus.

On good friday; After None

Δ There was a savor of fire felt by E K.

There semed one with a sword, suddenly to thrust out of the stone at E K his hed.

Whereat he started; and sayd he felt a thing (immediately) creeping within his hed,

and in that pang becam all in a [swete] sweat. And he remayned much misliking

the moving and creeping of the thing in his hed. At a quarter of an howre ende

it cam to one place: and so ceased somwhat: & then the Curten was drawn

away: and there appeared the Table, and the chayre covered.

Then cam three,* two went away and one remayned: as before was vsed.

E K held the paper of the letters in his hand: and Me bad him put it out of his hand.

Me The taste of this mercifull potion, yea the savour onely of the vessell worketh

most extremely agaynst the maymed drowsing of ignorance, yf the hand be heavy,

how weighty and ponderous shall the whole world be? What Will ye

△ this he sayd

[68b]

△ This he sayd vppon our silence after his former words. I answered, we desyred

to lerne the Mysteries of the boke.

The Boke now appeared (the cover of the chayre being taken away) the boke lying

lying vppon a rownd thing: which E K, was not able to discern what it is.

The first leaf ⌜side⌝ of the ⌜first leafce of the⌝ boke appeared full of the former letters, [consi] euery side

hauing 49 tymes 49 square places, with letters: some more then other.

M Euery side conteyneth 2400 and one [letter] od letter.

E K. All the letters semed to be of bluddy cullor, and wet: The lines

betwene the squares, semed to be like a shaddow.

In the first square were 7 letters.

Me Say after me: But pray first ere you begynne. △ We prayed

E.K. All became blak as pych in the boke

Then it becam light agayne.

Now he pointeth vp, with his rod of gold diuided into 3 equal partes, which

rod he toke from vnder the Table.

Me. Keph vam [he lifted his face to heven]

Don graph fam veh na.

E K. Now he kneleth down, and holdeth vp his hands

The letters of the first Square, ar 7.

Now he pointeth to the second

7	6	5	4	3	2	1

Med gal [E K. he turneth him self abowt.

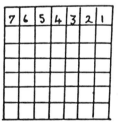

3. vn gal vn Mals na.

He Twise seven, Thre and All one: and his mercy endureth for euer.

4. Tal vn vrh.

5. Fam graph Fam.

6. Ged graph drux med.

7. vn van.

8. Tal vn don vr vn drux. sownded as 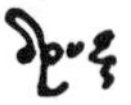

9. Med.

10. Tal van fam mals vn.

11. vn ged gon med gal.

12. Mals vn drux

13. Ged vn.

14. Fam graph fam.

15. ged vn tal mals graph gal vn keph

16. Veh vn mals veh drux graph na capcneh

17. ged med.

18. med gal.

19. Fam graph tal graph ur vn pa van ged graph drux

20. Gal med tal drux vn.

21. mals na gon vn tal

22. ged vn

23. van vn drux veh don vn drux.

24. Van don graph mals don graph fam

E K. Now he seemeth to wepe, and knock his brest. he pointeth with the rod, vp agayn, and sayd

25. vn gal graph mals gal

26 vn keph graph

27 Gal don van keph

28 Gisg vn don gal graph tal vn na.

Marginal notes:

line 6:
```
 49
 49
---
 441
196
----
2401
```

line 44: 100

[69a]

29. van vn

30. veh graph fam gisg fam

31. ged don vn mals vn gal. he stayed here a good while.

32. fam graph gal

33. van drux pa vn don

34 gal med tal gon med vrh

35 vn gal graph mals med vn gal

39.38.37.36. veh na graph van vn veh na. / Tal vn na / Med fam fam na graph / gal vn mals na /

40. med drux gon keph gal vn don. This is a word

41 mals vn drux ged graph mals na gon.

E K: Now he walked vp and down before the chayre: and cam agayn and pointed.

The letters now following seme to be written with Clay.

42. Med gal vn tal na

43. ged graph tal graph gal fam vn vr: eight letters

44. vn

45. gal gon drux med keph vn

46. na med pal mals med don. Now he walketh agayn, and loketh vpward.

Then he pointed agayn.

47. Vn gal mals van drux

48. Gal vn don

49. ged vn don tal graph fam: he walked betwene the shewing of tal and graph.

There are six letters in that word.

Me. Say after me (Shall I speak the Mysteries of thy glory, which thow hast secreted from the Inhabitants vppon the erth? yea lord, it is thy will, whose hed is high; and fete euery where, redy to revenge the blud of Innocents, and to call home the lost shepe.)

ch ses: the letters giue
Say after me Zuresk od adaph mal zez geno au marlan oh muzpa

ses pe z Kaphene
agiod pan ga zez gamphedax Kapene go le od

m phiam s
semelábugen donka fian ga vankran vreprez

d aze z keztz
ádeph avxe drux Tardemah va tzests grapad.

1.

vnbar
zed vnba domiól adepóad chieuak mah oshe daph

z
Onixdar pangepi adamh gemedsol a dinoxa hoxpor

gharmes
adpum dar garmes.

Me. I teache. let this lesson instruct the to read all that shalbe gathered out of this boke hereafter. It is not to be spoken, but in the time of his own time. It shalbe sufficient to instruct the: Fare well

E K. Now he couereth the boke with the veale.

Δ Prayses and Thankes be rendred to god, of vs his sely ones, now and euer. Amen.

Δ Note. All the former letters and words in the squares, were onely in the first or vpper row, [of the side] begynning at the right hand, and so going

orderly to the left. And secondly Note that this lesson he

red, pointing with his rod orderly vppon the same forsaid first row.

/flourish/

Marginal notes:

line 14: 100

line 27: Veresk and / Zuresk are / all one. / Δ perchance /

Zuresch, / with ch, for / K, and so / the word shalbe /

of [8] /7/ letters.

line 35: *Δ it is not to be / spoken or inter= / preted, but

whan / the time appointed, / is come

[69b]

Martij 31. Easter day after none abowt 4.

E K. hard first a sownd of Musicall harmonie

Δ The Veale was pluckt away

Three cam in, two went away, as before accustomed.

E K. Now he lyeth down. he riseth and pulleth the veale frō the chayre.

That veale was of cullor as a raynbow.

The boke appeared playne and evidently on the globe in the chayre.

E K felt the thing ronne in his hed as the other day it did.

He taketh out the rod from vnder the Table: he sayd

Aeternitas in Caelo

Δ vppon my staying from speche, he sayd, What wilt thow?

Δ The proceding instruction necessary for vnderstanding of the boke.

Me Mensuratur. Δ he putteth vp his rod to the boke

Me Sint oculi illorū clari, vt intelligant ⌊he held vp his hands and semed to pray.

He pointed now to the second row of the 49 rows of the first page of the boke; and sayd

Secundus a primo

1 Gon na graph na van fam veh na. Now he walketh vp and down.

2 Ged don med drux na vn gal med keph. he walketh agayn

3 [1.] Vn don gal graph drux ⌊he walked agayn.

4 [2.] med

5 [3.] drux vn ⌊he walked

6 [4.] ged graph tal mals ⌊he walketh⌋ vn vr med. ⌊7 letters.

7 [5.] med gon veh vn fam tal vn drux

8 [6.] van vn drux gal don graph fam

9 [7.] med don gal vn

10 [8.] van graph van graph gon vn na

11 [9.] drux med fam

12 [10.] mals vr gon ged drux vn mals na graph

13 [11:] Keph vn tal mals med drux med drux

14 [12.] vn drux graph mals na

15 [13.] med mals na graph [veh] gal : ⌊here, veh or gal is indifferēt

16 [14.] vn

17 [15.] Tal graph gal med [Keph] ⌊or rather⌋ pal ⌊so it shalbe better vnderstode

18 [16] Tal vn don van drux graph

19 [17] ged graph drux vn

20 [18] mals don graph fam ⌊Now he walketh

21 [19] drux med

22 [20] gal vn fam tal vn gisg

23 [21] van med don gisg fam

24 [22] tal vn drux ged graph gisg ⌊so it is

25 [23] {vn

[24] gal graph van drux graph}

26 [25] gal vn tal mals na

27 [26] drux vn pal gisg

28 [27] med fam

29 [28] van vn drux gal graph tal na drux vn pal vn gisg ⌊12 letters

med don

Marginal notes:

line 36:RH: △ Note this diuersitie / of sownd and / writing: as X for Z [with line to 'so' (line 35)]

[70a]

30 [29] med don med mals na vn fam

31 [30] van med don

32 [31] tal gon drux med gal vn vr

33 [32] vn tal van gal vn fam

34 [33] ged graph don

35 [34] mals vn

36 [35] med

37 [36] gal vn pal keph van tal

38 [37] pa vn drux veh graph fam

39 [38] med don gal vn drux. ⌊Now he maketh low obeysance to the chayreward.

40 [39] Mals vn Incomprehensibilis es in aeternitate tua.

41 [40] Mals don graph fam

42 van tal pa vr med fam gal vn

43 van med don pal

44 drux vn gal med drux

45 mals vn gisg don med mals na graph fam.

46 van drux gal graph fam.

47 vn gal med drux.

48 ged vn drux graph pa drux fam.

49 gom na graph na van gal keph

Me Shall I rede it? Δ we pray you

Gronhadoz oicasman
[2] [Iheh..ts] Ihehusch Gro[m]/n/adox arden, o na gempalo micasman

veueiah s
vandres orda beuegiah nox plignase zamponon aneph
[there is a stop]

e z e
Ophad a medox marune gena pras no dasmat. Vorts manget

vandemhnaxat
a deüne damph naxt os vandeminaxat. Orophas vor

c
minodal amudas ger pa o daxzum banzes ordan ma

pres vmblosda vorx nadon patrophes vndes adon ganebus

Ihehudz Δ Note: A deüne must be pronownced as one worde: like as Res publica, in latin.
els here wold seme to be .50. words. but,
A deüne, cam out of one square.

Δ Gehudz consisteth of 6 letters: but Gon na graph van gal keph consisteth of 7. I wold gladly be resolued of that dowt if it pleas you.

E K. he boweth down, and put the rod away, and than Kneled down.

Δ He rose and axed me what wilt thow?

Δ The former question to be soluted. Me Thow hast written [falh] fals:

for, it must be Ihehudz; and so it is of 7 letters.

Δ If euery side cõteyne 49 rows, and euery row will require so much tyme to be

receyued as this hath done it may seme that very long time will be requisite to this

doctrine receyuing: But if it be gods good liking, we wold fayne haue some abridgemẽt

[of] or compendious manner, wherby we might the soner be in the work of Gods seruyse

E K. The Chayre and the Table are snatched away, and seme to fly toward heven

And nothing appeared in the stone at all. But [the] was all transparent

clere.

Δ What this snatching away of Chayre and Table doth meane we know not: But

if the lord be offended with his yonglings, and Novices in this Mysteries, for propownding

or requiring a compendious Method etc Then we are very sorry, and ax forgivenes

for the rashnes at our lipps: and desyre his maiestie not to deale so rigorously

with

Marginal notes:

line 19 RH: Δ fortè van / Ax this dowte

line 42: Δ / Note / and take / hede from / hence forward

[70b]

with vs: as thowgh we had sufficient wisdom or warning, to beware of such motions or requests making

to his ministers. Let it not be so sayd of the holy one of Israel: but that his mercies abownd w/th/ vs to his

E K. Now commeth all down agayn as, before glorie. Amen

Me. What are the Sonnes of men, that they put time in her own bosom? or measure a Judgment that is vnsearchable

Δ

Me I help thy imperfections. What, man thinketh wisdome, is error in our

sight. But bicause my Nature is to cure, and set vp those that fall,

Thus much vnderstand

As I haue sayde: The 49 partes of this boke 49 voyces,

Wherevnto the so many powres, with theyr inferiors and

subiects, haue byn, are, and shalbe obedient

Euery Element in this mysterie is a world of vnderstanding

Euery one knoweth here what is his due obedience: and

this shall differ the in speche from a mortal Creature

Consider with thy self, How thow striuest against thyne own

light, and shaddowest the windows of thyne own vnderstanding

I haue sayde: Be it vnto the, as God will.

I am not a powre or whirlewynde that giueth occasion of offence.

Longe sumus a perversitate destructionis

This much I haue sayd, for thy reformation and vnderstanding

Δ

Me Lo, Vntill the secrets of this boke be written, I cōme no more.

neyther of me shall you haue any apparition. Yet, in powre,

my office shall be here

Say, what you here, for euery word shall be named vnto

you: it is somwhat a shorter way, and more according

to your desyre

Euery Element hath 49 manner of vnderstandings

Therin is comprehended so many languages

They are all spoken at ones, and seuerally, by them selues, by dis=

tinction may be spoken.

Vntill thow cōme to the Citie, thow canst not behold the beawty

thereof.

Nihil hic est, quod non est perfectum.

I go. I haue sayde, (and it is true,).

No vnclean thing shall enter:

Much less, then, here: For, it is the sight of whose Maiestie

We tremble and quake at

He shall teache, of him self; for we are /not7 [vn]worthy:

What then, of your selues? But such is his great and singular

fauor

Marginal notes:

line 10: Of the boke

line 11: 49 Powres with / theyr Inferiors / vide sup. 48 after / a sort: and .l. / vide Martij 24.

line 15: Angelicall / Language

line 24: Raphaël is / to be absent / for a certayn / time: but / his powre shall / be here

line 29: Of the boke

line 30: Languages

line 40: Δ / Note, that we / shalbe Theodi= / dacti, of god / him self and, / no Angel herein

---

[71a]

fauor, that, he is [of him] of him self, and with those, whome he choseth.

For, the ende of all things, is at hand,

and Powre must distinguish, or els nothing can prevayle

What you here, yea what thow feelest, by thy finger, Recorde,

and seale sure. This is all, and in this is conteyned all,

that comprehendeth all The almighty powre
and profunditie of his glory.

What els?

As thow seest, and till he see, whose sight, is the light of this his own
powre, His might is great. The dew of his stedfastnes
and glorious perfection hold vp and rectify the weaknes of your
fragilitie: Make you strong to the ende of his workmanship
to whome I commit you

E K. He plucketh the veale ouer all

A voyce afterward ———— Ne Ne Ne na Iabes

Δ Sanctus Sanctus Sanctus $\overline{\text{Dns}}$ Deus Zebaoth: Pleni sunt
caeli et terra gloria Maiestatis eius. Cui soli $\overline{\text{ois}}$
honor, laus et gloria:
Amen

[flourish]

Marginal notes:

line 1, supra: Potentia.

line 2: The ende / of all things / is at hand

line 9: The sight / of god.

1583. Aprilis 2. Tuesday Jesus. † . before none

Δ A voyce like a Thunder was first hard

The chayre and Table appered // therof

There appered fyre in the chayre, and burnt away the veal or covering [therf]

The cullor of the flame of the fire was [of] as of Aqua Vitae [bunt] burnt.

A voyce ———— Sum.

E K. There goeth a clowd or smoke from the chayre; and covereth the Table

That smoke filled all the place

A voyce ———— Impleta sunt oīa gloria et honore tuo

E K. All is becōme clere, saue the Table which remayned couered with the clowde still

A great thunder began agayn, and the chayre remayned all in fire.

Now the boke appeareth euidently, lying vppon the Globe in the chayre and the letters appered wet styll, as yf they were blud

There appered fire to be thrown oute of the stone, vppon E K.

The sownd of many voyces semed to pronownce this — Let all things prayse him and extoll his name for euer

E K. The fire is still in the chayre, but so transparēt, that the boke and letters therof may be well seen.

E K felt his hed as if it were one fire

A voyce —— Sic soleo errores hominum purificare.

A voyce —— Say what you see

E K. I see letters, as I saw before

A voyce —— Moue not from your places; for, this place is holy.

A Voyce —— Read. ———— E K, I cannot

Δ you shold

Marginal notes:

line 33: 

line 35: Note, fire

line 46: Moue not from / your places

[71b]

Δ you shold haue lerned the characters perfectly and theyr names, that you

mowght now haue redyly named them to me as you shold see them.

Then there flashed fire vppon E K agayne.

A Voyce —————— Say what thow thinkest. Δ he sayd so to E K.

E K. My hed is all on fire

A Voyce ———— What thow thinkest, euery word that speak.

E K. I can read all, now, most perfectly and in the Third row thus I see to be red.

Palc/s/e duxma ge na dem oh elóg da ved ge
ma fedes o ned a tha [h]lepah nes din.
Ihehudétha dan vangem onphe dabin oh [n] nax
palse ge dah maz gem fatesged oh mal dan
gemph naha Lax vu lutúdah ages magel osch.
macom adeph a dosch ma handa.

E K. Now it thundreth agayn

A voyce ——Ego sum qui in te Mihi ergo qui Sum

Δ Non nobis domine non nobis, sed nomini tuo damus gloriam.

Δ Then E K red the fowrth row, as followeth

Pah o mata nax lasco vana ar von zimah
la de de pah o gram mes ca pan amphan van:
zebog ahah danez öl ga. Van gedo oha ne
daph aged onédon pan le ges ma gas axa
nah alpod me alida phar or ad gemésad
argla mado oges.

Δ Blessed be the name of the Highest, who giveth light and vnderstanding.

E K. It thundreth agayn. All is covered.

A Voyce ———————————— Orate.

Δ We prayed and returning to the work agayn, the fire covered all still

and E K hard [voyces] voyces, singing (as a far of) very melodiously.

Then all became euident agayn vnto E K his perfect Judgment.

Δ E K then red thus

mises [pronownced]
Mabeth ar mices achaph pax mara geduth alídes

mansh
orcánor manch arseth. olontax ar geban vox portex

ah pamo agématon burise ganport. vdríos paseh

Machel

Marginal notes:

line 3: Fire agayn

line 9: Δ I dowt which of / these 3 must serve ⟨ z s c

line 10: The Third / row of the / first page.

line 18: The fowrth/row.

line 32: The fifth / row.

[72a]

Machel len arvin zembuges + Vox mara.

gons Ihehusch dah pársodan maHh alsplan

*adíper arkad
donglses adipr ágnot. archad dons a

dax van famlet a dex arge pa gens

Van danzan oripat es vami gest ageff

pasdas
ormaténodah zálpala doniton pasdaes gánpogan

Vndanpel adin achaph máradon oxámax

anólphe·dan ioh voxad mar vox iheduthar̄h

agga pal med lefe ₊ IAN lefa dox parnix

dros
O droes marsíbleh aho dan adeph uloh iads

akos
ascleh da verox ans dalph che damph lam achos

E K. There is a great Thundring agayn

Δ It is the hand of the highest, who will get him honor by his own works.

E K. The Voyce and sownd of pleasantnes and reioycing was hard: and all was

dark.

A small voyce ———————— Locus est hic sanctus.

An other voyce———————— Sacer est a te Domine

E K. All is now opened agayne.

Δ. Then E K, red thus

iah
Ámidan gah lesco van gedon amchih ax or

lesgomph
madol cramsa ne da vadgs lesgamph ar:

mara panosch aschedh or samhámphors <u>ascȯ</u>

pascadabaah <u>asto</u> a vdrios archads ors arni.

pamphíca lan gebed druxarh fres adma. nah

pamphes oÑ vanglor briafog, mahad ₊ no poho a

palgeh donla def arehas NA. Degel.

---

vnam
Vnaem palugh agan drosad ger max. fa lefe pandas

mars langed vndes mar. pachad odídos martíbah

Marginal notes:

line 3: *it is significatiue

line 6: The sixth / row.

line 17: Locus sanctus

line 21: The Seventh / row.

line 23: <u>Ascȯ</u>, with the prick / ouer the ȯ, is to be / pronownced as / Asto. :

line 29: The eight / row.

[72b]

v́dramah noges gar . lenges argrasphe drulthe
las aséraphos . gamled cam led caph Snicol
lumrad v ma. pa granse paphres a drimox a
demphe NA. geníle o danpha. Na ges a
me gaph a .

E K: The sownd of Melodie, begynneth agayne

Δ. The fire cam from E K his eyes, and went into the stone againe
And then; he could not perceyue, or read one worde
The Fyre flashed very thick and all was couered with a veale.

Δ Prayse we the lord, and extoll his name:
For, his hand hath wrought wundrous
Works, for his owne glorie.
[Whose name which]
Amen
[flourish]

Marginal note:

line 8: Note: this / Mysterie of / god his powre / drawn to him / self agayne.

Aprilis .3. Wensday, Forenone ☩

Δ First the Curten was drawn away: and then all appeared on fire. The whole place

all ouer. E k hard voyces, but could not discern any thing but the hummering

of them

Δ There cam fire agayn (out of the stone) vppon E K, all his body ouer

E K. The fire so diminisheth it self that the boke may be perceyued.

A Voyce ——————— Magnus Magnus Magnus

An other voyce ———— Locus sacer et acceptabilis Deo

E K felt the fire to gather vp into his hed

Shortly after he could read the boke, as he could do yesterday.

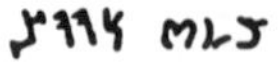

Vlla doh aco par semná gan var se gar on dun.

sebo dax se pal genso vax necra par sesqui nat.

axo nat sesqui ax (ex) olna dam var gen vox nap vax.

V̈ro varca cas nol vndat vom Sangef famsed oh.

sih ádra gad gesco vansax ora gal parsa.

Varo. nab vbrah NA pa uotol ged ade

pa

Marginal notes:

line 23: Locus Sacer

line 26: Δ / of the first character / Of Vlla, I dowt

line 27: The ninthe / Row

line 33: The Tenth.

som
pa cem na dax . van sebrá dah oghe aschin
o nap gem phe axo or . nee a ve da pongon
vdráh iohed
a moroh ah óha aspáh . nin ab vrdráh gohed
a carnat dan faxmal gamph . gamph nacro
vax asclad caf prac crúscanse .

Δ ———————————————————————————————

gan . ohe gemph ubráh ax . orpna
nex or napo, gemlo . a cheph can sedló
pam geman ange hanzu (ALLA .) Cáppo se
damo gan vas oro dax vá [ges /] ges palo
pal me pola .

E K. All these, (now red,) fall out and all the rows, before, likewise.

A Voyce ——————— Prayse God.

Δ We prayed. and after, was this shewed.

Gals ange no témpa ro sama dan genzé axe .
falod amruh ácurtoh saxx par mano gan vax
no . gramfa gem sadglá loh vrox sappóh
iad ah oha vara.

Δ ———————————————————————————————

Δ Now appeared an other row.

Se gors axol ma pa a oh la sabúlan . Caph
vns
ardox ampho nad v́rmah ud ago lan vams .
V́xa grad órmo dax palmes árisso dan vnra .
V́ansample galse not zablis óphide ALLA loh .
gaalah osson luze adaö max ʸanget or dámo ans .
leóz dasch lóöha dan se gláspa neh .

Δ ———————————————————————————————

———————————————————————————————

Marginal notes:

line 3: gohed, pronownced / as Iohed signifieth / One euerlasting / and all things de= / pending vppon One. / and gohed Ascha / is as much to say / as One god.

line 5 RH: canse, signifieth / mightie: and Crus= / canse, more / mightie.

line 7 RH supra: the a produced [refers to orpna]

line 7 LH: The eleuenth / Row.

line 8: All these which / haue lines vnder / them are eche / but one word / of diuerse sylla= / bles: being 9 / words of them.

line 8, over 'ceph...sedlo': the last h remissly sownded [refers to ceph]

line 11: Pola and Pala / signifie two: / Pola signifieth / two togither, and / Pala signifieth / Two separated:

line 15: Δ This was a / parcell of a / row, which onely / appered by him / self.

line 17: Δ / [At no, ende / 49, and so / here ar .10. over]

line 17, over 'madgla': á must be sownded long

line 21: This me is / the nine and fortyeth / word longing / to them before [with line to 'me' (line 21)]

line 22: The twelfth / row

[73b]

All becam dark, and it thundred

A Voyce ———————— Prayse God.

Δ We prayed

Δ Now appered three or four rows to gither

The boke seemed to fly, as if it wold fly a peces (the fyre remayning)

and to make a great sturring in the place where it lay.

Amprí apx ard ardo argá argés argáh ax .

osch nedo les icás . han andam von ga lax man .

sey

nosch . dóngo a yntar cey lude asch úrise alpé

.s

gem var dançet . [na]nap alped vrsbe temps a

vod mos gema o ulon mancepax oxné pricos

a gót . zalpa ne doxam órne .

A

Admag apa asco tar . gans oärz am seph

selqui quisben alman . gons sa ieh

mársibleh gron áscabb gamat . ney aden vdan

[phl]phand sempés nar narran al . cáno géme.

dansé álde nótes parcélah arb ner ga lum

s mysse . long

pançu príscas ábra músce an nox . napod

aske

a on dan sem ges asche

E K A sownd of many voyces, sayd —————— Orate

Mica surásche para te gámmes ádrios NA danos .

Vra lad pacad ur gesme crus a prásep ed .

a palse nax varno zum . zancú asdom baged

Vrmigar orch phaphes ustrá nox affod masco

gax cámles vnsanba a oh la gras par quas.

cónsaqual lat gemdax tantat ba vod .

talpah iam .

A

Marginal notes:

line 7: The 13

line 7: a long

line 9: [symbol] this with / a prick betow / keneth y.

line 14: pronownce / Asto

line 16: ẏ

line 19: E K vnderstode / the Langage: and wold / haue spoken somwhat but / he was willed to stay.

line 24, over 'crus': pronownced as we do Cruse a cup

[74a]

16

Gescó a taffom ges nat gam . pamphé ordáquaf

kid

costo chídmap mischná iaísg . iaiálphzudph a

s

dancét vnban caf ransembloh . dafma vp

gras

aschem graos chrámsa asco dah . vínna

gen álde os papéam och láuan vnad.

Oh dresad údrios nagel panzo ab sescú .

Vórge afcál valaffda mórsab gaf ham de

Peleh asca.

---

17 Δ This went away, when it was read

It waxed dark.

A voyce ——————— Orate Δ we prayed

E K. It beginneth to clere.

A Voyce to E K. ——————— Say

Ártosa geme oh gálsagen áxa loph gebed adóp:

zarcas vr vánta pas ámphe nóde alp^{4}an . nócas.
se ga ormácased lax naph talpt . pámphicas sandam
Voscméh iodh asclad ar . phan gas málse a
quaz nam vngem vansel gembúgel a gémbusez
áro tehl alta murt valtab bániffa faxed
ar [chyso]chlẏsod

A tam mat . glun asdeh ahlud gádre fam Shing
la dam . guinsé life arilsar zabulan cheuách se .
amph lesche andam var ges ar phex are .
NA tax páchel lapídox ar da vax malcos . vna
gra tassox varmára ud ga les vns ap se .
ne da ox lat ges ar .

Marginal notes:

line 1, over 'Gesco': o long

line 2: Sempiternall One / and indiuisible / God.

line 3: a very long

line 4: a reverent word / the a very long / and is, be it/ made with powre.

line 7, over 'gaf': a long

line 7: chal, iently, and / the a long

line 14 RH: The <div>ine powre creating / the <An>gel of the sonne [with line to 'galsagen' (line 15)]

line 16: 4 manner of cō= / structions in / that one word.

line 20: Aro is one / word diuided, / as respublica, / and here this / Word is diuided / into two squares / and so there / are 49.

line 24, over 'guinse': e long

line 24, over 'cheuach': a long

line 24: life lephe Lurfando / is a strong charge / to the wicked to tell / the truth

line 24, RH of above note: △ / This he sayd / to my/demand / of this phrase/ wherof I / had mention / many yeres / since.

line 25, over 'ar': pronownce ar

line 26: NA. The name of the / Trinitie, One / Separable / for a while

---

[74b]

19 Now it waxeth dark. △ We must pray: (sayd I) and so w< e did.> But E K prayed perfectly in this Angels language etc.

Asmo dahán pan casme co caph al oh .
san ged a bansaa vn adon a seb Ian .
aglaho dánfa zúna cap orcha (orka) dah os .
fámsah ON naäb ab nagah geha fastod .
hansey om hauan lagra gem gas mal .
parcóg dax nedo va geda leb árua ne cap sem carvan .

---

20 Onsem gelhóldim geb abníh ian .
oxpha bas cappó cars órdriph grip gars .
of víndres nah ges páhado vllónooh can vaz a .
fam gisril ag nóhol sep gérba dot vánca NA .
sem ah pa nex ar pah lad vamó iar séque .
Vad ro garb , ah sem dan van ged ah paleu

△ ---

Now the fire shot oute of E K his eyes, into the stone, agayne

And by and by he [sho] vnderstode nothing of all, neyther could reade any thing: nor remember what he had sayde. All becāme dark. Then was the curten drawne, and so we ended.

△ Gloria P̄ri et filio et spiritui sancto

nunc et semper

Amen

[flourish]

Marginal notes:

line 4, over 'bansaa': a long onely one a sownded

line 6: a sownded as au

line 8, over 'sem': in eius loco.

line 8: the g not ex= / pressly sownded. [refers to 'parzog]

line 14: it is but one / Word [refers to ar pah]

line 15, over 'paleu': sownded, palef

---

†

Aprilis .3. Wensday After none hor 5½

△ A prety while the veale remayned ouer all: then it was taken away

First fire was thrown vppon E K out of the stone

Many voyces concordantly sayd——Bonum est ô Deus, quia Bonitas īpa es.

An other voyce ———— Et magnum, quia tu magnitudo īpius Magnitudinis.

A voyce ———— Ádgmach ádgmach ádgmach

A great voyce ———— Sum, et sacer est hic locus.

A voyce ———— Ádgmach ádgmach ádgmach húcacha.

△ Then E K read the

row on this manner Padohó magebs (ghebs) galpz arps apá nal Si .

gámvagad al pódma gans NA . vr cas

nátmaz

Marginal notes:

line 31, over 'Adgmach': ⁙ much glory

line 32: Sacer locus

line 35, over 'arps': rede as arch

[75a]

nátmaz ándiglon ármvu . zántclumbar ar

naxócharmah . Sapoh lan gamnox vxála vors .

Sábse cap vax mar vinco . Labandáho nas gampbox

se
arce . dah gorhahálpstd gascámpho lan ge .

Béfes argédco nax arzulgh orh . semhaham

v́ncal laf garp oxox . loangah .

Δ Now apered Raphael or one like him, and sayde

Salus vobis in illo qui vobiscum

I am a medicine that must prevayle against your infirmities: and am

come to teache, and byd take hede

Yf you vse dubble repetition, in the things that follow, you shall both

write and work and all at ones: which mans nature can not performe.

The trubbles were so great that might ensue thereof, that your strength

were nothing to preuayle against them.

When it is written, reade it no more with voyce, till it be in practise

All wants shalbe opened vnto you

Where I fownd you, (with him, and there,) I leave you.

Cumfortable Instruction, is a necessarie Medicine

Farewell.

E K. The boke and the Chayre, and the rest were all out of sight while Raphael spake, and he lay down prostrate

E K. saw a great multitude in the farder side of the stone: They all cam in to the stone, and axed

What now?

[What now How now?.]

How now?

Vors mábberan ⁘ how now: what hast thow to do with vs?

Δ as I began thus to say (The God of powre, of wisdom,) they all interrupted my entended prayer to god for help etc and sayd We go We go.

Δ And so they went away.

Then the boke and the rest cam in agayne.

A Voyce —— One Note more, I haue to tell thee

Ax him not, What he sayeth, but write as thow hearest: for it is true

Δ Then, o lord, make my hearing sharp and strong, to perceyue sufficiently as the case requireth.

Rap. ———— Be it vnto the.

Δ Then E K red as followeth

Ors lah gemphe nahaoh ama natoph des garhul vanseph

iuma lat gedos lubah aha last gesto Vars macom des

curad Vals mors gaph gemsed pa campha zednu ábfada

máses lófgono Luruandah lesog iamle padel arphe

nades gulsad maf gescon lampharsad surem paphe arbasa

arzusen agade ghehol max vrdra paf gals macrom finistab
gelsaphan asten Vrnah

Marginal notes:

line 1: < ....> piller of Light / <stoo>de before the / <Bo>oke

line 3: [Vin in vinco must / be pronownced long / as if it were a / dubble i.]

line 4, over 'gascámpho': or gáscampho:

line 4, over above note: why didst thow so? as god said to Lucifer. The word / hath 64 significa= / tions

line 5: [Orh ∻ Deus sine fine / Gorh ∻ Deus a Deo]

line 5, over 'argedco': ∻ cum humilitate aduocamus te / cum adoratione Trinitatis.

line 5, over 'orh': This is the name of the spirit contrary to Befafes. [with a line to 'arzulgh' (line 5)]

line 5, RH beside 'semhaham': This word hath / 72 significations

line 5: Befes, the vocatiue / case of Befafes:/[Befes is as much to / say as cōme Be / fafes and see vs / [rule] / Befafes ô, is to / call vppon him as / on god / [rule] / Befafes oh, is as muche / to say, come Be= / fafes and be our / Witness.] / [rule] / Befafes his Etymologie / is as much to say / as, Lumen a, / Lumine. / Spiritus orh / secundus est in / grada imperfectiōis / tenebrarū. / Δ how can orh / signifie Deus sine / fine, if it be / the name of a / wicked spirit?

line 6, over 'loangah': of two syllables. [this wor]

line 8, over 'Raphael'. Me

line 43: Larvandah

line 45: △ Note these 55 / wordes stand in / 49 places: of which / 55, some two stand / in a [pla] square place/ some three, as I / haue noted.

[75b]

A Voyce ———————— Whatsoeuer thow settest down shalbe true

△ I thank god most hartilie: The case allso requireth it so to be.

23 Asch val íamles árcasa árcasan arcúsma íabso gliden
ieb af
paha parcadúra gebne óscarah gádne au arua las
genost cásme palsi uran vad gadeth axam pambo
cásmala sámnefa gárdomas árxad pámses gémulch
b
gápes lof lachef ástma vates garnsnas orue gad
garmah sárquel rúsan gages drusala phímacar aldech
oscom lat garset panoston.

---

4 gude laz miz lábac vsca losd pa Cópad dem sebas
gad váncro umas ges umas umas ges gabre umas umáscala
ghes
úmphazes umphagám maaga mosel iahal loges vapron
ghen
fémse dapax orgen láscod ia láscoda vága am lascafes
iarques préso tamisel vnsnapha ia dron goscam lápe voxa
chimlah aueaux losge auioxan lárgemah.

---

5 zureth axad lomah ied gura vancrásma ied sesch
lapod vonse avó avé lamsage zimah zemah zúmacah
Vormex artman voz vozcha tolcas zápne zarvex

ghi gafna
zorquem allahah giburod Ampátraton zimegauna

ask
zonze zámca aschma vlpa tapa van vorxvam

drusad Caph castárago grúmna cáncaphes absacáncaphes

zúmbala teuort granx zumcot lu graf saxma Cape.

---

26 Col age lam gem fam tepham vra ap du ca sampat

Vóxham Lúnzapha azquem Bobagélzod gaphémse lúnse

agni cam setquo teth gaphad oxámarah gímnephad

ie
vóxcanah vrn dage paphcod zámbuges zambe ach oha

zámbuges gásca lunpel zadphe zómephol zun zadchal

ureseh varún pachádah gusels vx amna pa gramia oh vz

Δ I think

Marginal notes:

line 3: There are no / points neyther / in the last / before . They / be parcells of / Invitations very / pleasant to good / Angels. / Before was, as / it were a pre= / face of the Crea= / tion and distinction / of Angels etc.

line 27: Bobagelzod

[76a]

Δ I think it will be dark by and by, and our Cumpany will expect our comming down

to supper. Therfore, if, without offense we might now leave of, it might seme good so to do

A voyce ———————— gemeganza × your will be done

Δ As I was discoursing with E K after we had done, and he seamed yet skylfull and hable to say much of the vnderstanding of the premises, and began to declare somwhat, How they did all apperteyne to Good Angels; Suddenly there cam the fyre from his eyes into tho stone agayne. And than he could say no more: nor remember any thing of that [w]he had seen or Vnderstode less than half a quarter of an howre before.

Δ Deo nro Viuo Vero et Oipoteti
sit ois laus et gra actio
nunc et semper Amen
[flourish]

Marginal notes:

line 12: [a few scribbled marks of the following nature:

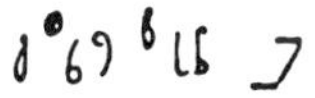

Aprilis 4. Thursday mane hor 5½

Δ I made a prayer

Δ A voyce ——— Quia ipo Deus Deus Deus nr cuius misericordia infinita.

Δ The fire immediately did shote out of the stone into E K, as before

His [tunc] therevppon did quake in his mowth

E K The Veale hangeth yet before.

Δ Then, all being vncouered, thus he red

Atra cas carmax pabámsed gero adol macom vaxt:

gestes ladúch carse ámages dascal panselcgen dursca zureóch (ie, ies)

pamcasáh vsca huldrongúnda malue ior . gáscama af

orthox VAN CORHG aspe zubra vaacáHh gandeuá
arinmaphel vax oh saoh abra iehudeh gamphe vndáxa
casmat lafet vncas laphet vanascor torx glust hahaha
ensède gumah galseds.

---

[28]

ie
Pacádpha palzé zuma carphah uzad capaden ýlsage
EXCOL PHAG MARTBH iasmadel vóscon sem abnérda
tohcoth iamphala páhath órcheth iesmog pasqué LabáHh
agas lada vng lasco ied ampha leda pageh gemze axax
ie ek
ózed caphzed campha voxal luthed gedan famech
iu
ártsnad gathad zuresch pascha lo guma hálphe
dax vancron patel zurad.

Marginal notes:

line 17: Note

line 31: This name cōpre= / hendeth the num= / ber of all the / fayries. who / are diuels / next to the/state and cō= / dition of man / etc.

[76b]

[29]

Canda lahad Bóbagen afna vorzed phadel
ies
NOBTDAMBTH gáscala axad vanges vodoth mured
ak
achna adcel damath zesvamcul pacadáah zimlos zoraston
geh galze mazad pathel cusma iaphes huráscah órphade
ies kel
loscad mages mat lumfamge detchel orze cámalah

pag
vndan padgze páthmataph zumad lepháda oháux

kan
[vs] vlschan zembloh agne phamgah iudad capex

Luzad vehech arse

---

ien
30 onda gams luzgaph vxan genzed pádex

filgh
CÓNGAMPHLGH ascath gadpham zurdah zamge

gloghcha sapax tastel v́nsada phatheth zúncapha

oxamáchad semteph ascle zuncas magzed dulm

pamfra húsage axad exóradad casmet ámphigel

iesk
adcath luza pathem nécotheth gesch labba doh

dóxa vascheth hoxan lamésde lampha iodoch gonzah

ies iel
hamges glutha óxmogel démapha vzed ascraph.

Kad ie
31 zudath chádgama ómsage hor gadsa gézes

na
ORPHÁMZAMNAHE gedod asphed voxa gémgah

lath gáphes zembloth chasca olphe dax marpha

sol ies
lothe sool separ marges bosqui laxa cosneth

gonse dadg voxma v́mage vnx gascheth lood

lo
adma loo ga zem_chá_na_phe ám_na_la ia

pacheth nox_da a_mah

---

32 Gedox al [sem_ga_na_da_bah o] SEM_GA_NA_DAH_BAH

ongagágeda phachel loódath haxna gu_na_pá_ge_pha

al se geda oh oŏda géhoph pachad enol adax loges

Marginal notes:

line 6: ⁙ iustitia a minime / diuino sine Labe

line 11: ⁙ fide that reviveth / ma<ns> brest mans / The holy ghoste:

[77a]

famgah laxqui hasche vadol vómsana gax ma deph na zad
gel panca vam sesquin oxal genoph voŏdal umadabah.

33 Asge lun zumia paxchádma enohol duran
ORCHLÓDMAPHAG mages oschan lod bunda cap
luzan lorpha leuandah orxzed famzad genósodath
phasélma gesda chom gas naph geth nag goth ládmano
Vmvar gezen vax gulzad margas luxt lapeh
iudath zomze van goth dah vorx guna ia ada
Vox hámana

34 Arze galsam vnza vcha pasel noxda
Nobróschom [GVNADÉPHOGAS] gunadéphogas dúnseph
man cax mal cás mah ied hah mel cár ha zemphe vncah
lethoph both ned ga phí cas mel ioth hath cha sad
ma ne ded ma gon zuna gothel pascheph nodax
vam phath mata

A voyce ——— Orate ——— Δ we prayed ∴

keth
35 Aphath zunca voxmor can zadcheth napha.

[Verd] VORDOMPHÁNCHES gauesgosadel gurah leth
agsnah orza max pace ieth cas lad fam pahógama
zon chás pha ma zum bles cha phax var gat ma gas ter
ne ho gat ma gan vn ga phax ma la gegath
laxqu goga lab naches

Δ

Therevppon the Vele was drawn, and the fire cam from E K his eyes again into the stone

Δ Deo opt. Max. o̅i̅s honor
laus et gloria Amen
[flourish]

Marginal notes:

line 6: 21, words hither

line 7, over 'goth': o long

line 13: in great letters [refers to Mobroschom']

line 17: Δ here are but / 48 words: I dowt / that there lacketh one.

line 23: Here seme to be to many by 3 or 4.

---

† [77b]

Aprilis .5. Friday a meridie hora 5½

Δ The Vele was taken away, without any speche vsed by me or E K
The boke and all the former furniture appeared very bright.

Δ I made a prayer to god, begynning Expectās expectaui Dominū etc

E K I here the sownd of men playing very melodiously on Instruments and singing

A Voyce ——— Serue God and take hede of Nettels. △ This was spoken to E K in respect of a great anger he was in yesternight, by reason that one had done him iniurie by speche at my table [Charles Sled.]

E K There appere a great many, a far of; as thowgh they appered beyond the
c
top /of7 a howse: and so semed far of behinde the stone: and they seme to haue no heds.

A Voyce ——— A peculier people, and shalbe restored

△ After this Voyce, the sayd hedles people disapered.

Then all appered fyre, and a clowd covered all: and in the top [of the] of the fyre in the chayre, appered three faces, and seemed to shute and close in one. The faces seemed, eche to turn rownd, and so ioyne in one afterward

A Voyce ——Prayse him in his glorie and wurship him, in his truth.

△ The fire entred into E K

A voyce ———Orate △ We prayed

△ Then thus appeared

gedóthar argo fa adóphanah gamsech olneh várasah

iusmach

A voyce ———Interpret not, till your vnderstanding be furnished.

Vschna phaól doa vah oho lazed la zu red ámma

donax valesto acaph lámphages ronox genma iudreth

loth adágma gonsaph godálga phareph iadsma zema

zunah
loa agnáphagon zunaha al me ionáphacas zeda ox arni.

---

agzelia ia
37 Adgzelga olms vánaph osma vages otholl dox an ga had

fáma
latqui dónaphe zu gar . phamah nordeph gasmat
gasque gasla gas NA gasmaphés gasmagél
gasnúnabe vamsech ábsechel gúlapha axnécho
demsa pámbochaph iehúsa gadaámah nosad
iurés chy almse orsa vax marde zun éffa
mochoéffa zuréheffa asga Lubeth bethlémcha máxiche
iehúscoth iaphan órnada vamne od ghim noh

Marginal notes:

line 6: Take hede of / Nettels.

line 12: Perhaps the / Jues shall / be restored

line 22, over 'iusmach': ℵ begotten

line 23: Interprete / not yet

line 29, over 'dox an ga had': one word

line 30, over 'fama': ℵ I will giue

[78a]

38 ned
Arphe lamse gaphnedg argaph zonze zumcoth
leg
Ómdopadáphaab nulech gaartha ancáphama soldémcah
casdra vges lapha ludasphándo galúbanoh apáchana
iedeph zembloh zamgýsel chéuacha laquet lozódma
ierinth onaph uzad máspela gýman orphámmagah
zoah
iumesbalégo archánphame . zamcheth zoach

---

39 Ámchana zeuoth luthámba ganeph iamda ox oho iephad

made noxa voscaph bámgephes noschol apeth iale
lod ga Na zuma datques vorzad numech
apheth nudach caseth iotha lax arseth
armi pli ca tar bám a co zamgeph gaseth vrnod
arispa iex han setha . oh lagnaph dothoth brazed
vamchach odoámaäh zembles gunza naspolge gáthme
orsoth zurath vámeth anseh .

40 Zalpe iédmacha ámphas nethoth alphax. durah
gethos ascheph nethoth iubad Laxmah ionsa max
dan do násdoga matastos lateth vnchas amse
gaf
Iacaph zembloágauh ad pha má gel lud cha dan sa
amphícatol arnópaa adapagémoh nodásma
machestépholon

41 Lumbor iemásch onzed gamphidárah go más cha pa
zeba zun amph naho zucath uomplinanohához machal
lozma dauangeth búches lauax orxod maches
donchaph luzath marpheth oz lanva don gáuah oschol
lúmasa phedeph omsa nax domágere angenophácha
phachadóna.

Marginal notes:

line 1, over 'Arphe': ⅹ I desire the O god

line 2: This was put in / and out a good / while before E K / could haue a / perfect vew to / rede it line 3, over 'apachana': ⁒ the slymie things / made of dust

line 6: Δ / here seme to / want 5 or 6 / names.

line 10: nu mech is / two wordes.

line 12: one word

line 15: These two words / are in one square.

line 19, over 'do nasdoga matastos': ⁒ the furious and perpetuall fire enclosed for the ponishment of them that / are banished from the glory.

line 19: one word of 7 / syllables: 4 in / the first part / and 3 in the / last.

[78b]

Óschala zamges onphá gemes phaches nolph
daxeth machésmachoh vastnálpoh gemas nach
loscheph daphmech noth chales zunech maschol
Lu gasnaph malces gethcaph madena (madna) oäh
gemsah pa luseth iorbástamax elcaph rusam
phanes domsath gel (iel) pachadóra amáxchano
Lumagéno armachaphámelon adro michó
natath iamesebáchola donádocha

Δ The fire went frō [E K.] his eyes to the stone agayn. Then his vnderstanding was gone allso.

E K

Δ Deo soli sit oīs laus honor
et gloria per infinita saeculo
saecula. Amen.

[flourish]

Marginal note:

line 4: [Lu] / ⁝X frō one

Aprilis 6. Saterday affore none hora 10½

Δ The fire shot into E K, as before was vsed: whereat he startled

All was vncovered, as the manner was. But E K had such a whirling

and beating inwardly in his hed, that he could not vse any Judgment to

discerne what appeared, for half a quarter of an howre almost.

A Voyce ———————— SVH

and agayn ——— a voyce ——— Gahoachma. [ ] ⁝X Sum quod sum, E K expownded <it.>

43 Asmar gehótha galseph achándas vnáscor sátquama

locat

látquataf hun gánses luximágelo ásquapa lochath

anses dosam váthne gálsador ansech gódamah

vonsepaléscoh ádmacah lu zámpha oh adma

zemblodárma varmíga zuna thotob amphichanósa

gemichanadabah Vademado Vaselapagédo

Δ ——————————————————— ▽

44 Amascabalonocha anódah aduradámah gonadephageno

vnachapesmacho geminadochapamica vuamsapálage

vocórthmoth achepasmácapha emcanidobah gedóah

Δ ——————————————————— ▽

[79a]

nostah

45 Nostoah geuámna da oscha lus palpal medna

gorumbalógeph acapnapádapha Volséma gonogédocha

ambusábaloh gemúsacha vamihópha zumnegadaphágepha

† iuréhoh

Δ ∇

[46] Zémnoda amni fa chebseth vsángrada bosadóma

zúmacoh aphinabácha buzádbazu amachapadomicha

zumanepassó NA vuamanábadoth

zumblegámpha zumblecaphamacha

Δ ∇

E K. All is couered with darknes. Terrible flashes of fire appered and they semed to wreath and wrap, one abowt an other. In the fire ouer the chayre appered, the three heds which appeared before.

A Voyce ———— Laua zuráah

Δ After our prayers was very hevenly noyce hard.

[47] Zudneph arni ioh pan zedco laniga nahad

lébale nochas arni cans lósmo iana olna dax

zémblocha zedman púsatha váma mah oxex párzu

drána ánza pasel lúmah cóxech ádamax gónboh

alze dah lúsache asneph gedma noxdrúma

Vamcáphnapham ástichel rátrugem abnath lonsas

masqueth tauínar tadna gehodód gaphrámsana

asclor drusáxpa

Δ ∇

[48] Amgédpha lazad ampha ladmaáchel galdamicháel

Vnza dédma Luz záceph pílathob ganó

vama zúnasch zemblagen ónman zuth catas

max ordru iadse lamad caphícha aschal

luz + ampna zodmínada excáphanog salgémphane

Marginal notes:

over line 1, centrally placed: .\: it was in the begynning. [with line to 'nostah' (line 1)]

line 4, to right of 'iurehoh': This last word was hid a prety while with a rym like a thin bladder / affore it: and when it was perfectly seen there appered a bluddy / cross over it. It is a Word signifying what <u>Christ did in hel</u>.

line 9: Δ here seme to / lack 5 words

line 14, to right of 'zuraah': .\: Vse humilitie in prayers to God, / that is fervently pray. it signifieth / <u>Pray into god</u>

line 20: Δ / pronownce as <u>che</u> / in chery

line 21: Δ / ratrugeem is one / of the 7 words on / the side of the Table / first prescribed

line 25: .\: I will begynne / anew

line 27: The 49th row followeth / after 2 leaves. / Arney vah nol etc

---

[79b]

Om vrza lat quartphe lasque deth Urad

<u>oxmaná</u> <u>gamges</u>

Δ Now the boke was couered with a <u>blew silk</u> sindall and vppon that blew covering appered letters of gold, conteyning these words

Amzes naghézes Hardeh

E K. it signifieth —— The vniversall name of him that created vniversally

be praysed and extolled for euer.

Δ Amen

A Clowde covered the boke.

A Voyce —————— Mighty is thy Name (ô lorde) for euer.

E K. it lightneth

A Voyce ———————— The place is Holy: stur not [sayd the three heds

△ Now appered to E K, some imperfection passed in the eleuenth row. And that

we wer towght how to amend it. and so we did.

△ Then the firy light went from E K into the stone agayn. and his

inspired perceyuerance and vnderstanding was gone: as often before

it vsed to be.

△ Gloriam laudemq nri Creatoris, oes Creaturae

indesinenter resc ent: Amen

Halleluiah Halleluiah Halleluiah

Amen

/flourish/

Marginal notes:

line 3: Blew

line 4: Note this / covering to / be made / for the boke

line 5 RH: ———— Note this to be pronownced / rowndly to gither.

line 16: Inspiration

Aprilis 6. Saterday after none

△ The Table, Chayre, boke and fyre appeared

And while I went into my oratorie to pray, fire cam thrise out of the stone

vppon E K, as he was at prayer, at my table in my study.

E K hard a voyce out of the fyre, saying } Why do the Children of men prolong the time of theyr perfect felicitie: or why are they dedicated to vanitie?

Many things ar yet to come: Notwithstanding, the

Time must be shortned,

I AM THAT I AM

A voyce —— Veniet (a) Vox eius, vt dicat filijs hoim quae ventura sunt.

E K There is a man, in white, come in, like Vriel, who cam first into the stone

Δ Benedictus qui venit in noie Domine —— Vr: Amen

Vr —— I teache: E K sayd that he turned toward me

Vr. What willt thow I shall answer the, as concerning this work?

E K He hath a ball of fire in his left hand and in his right hand

a Triangle of fyre

Δ What is most nedefull for vs to lerne herin, that is my chief desire.

Vriel —— Fowre monthes, are yet to come: The fifth is the

begynning of great miserie, <u>to the heauens</u>, to the earth

and to all liuing Creatures. Therfore must thow

nedes attend vppon the will of God: Things must

then

Marginal notes:

line 39: O Δ

line 43: A prophesie / Very dredfull / now at hand

[80a]

then be put in practise. A thing that knitteth vp all

must of force conteyn many celestiall Vertues

Therfore, in these doings, must things be furnished spedyly,
and with reuerence.
This, is the light, wherewith thow shalt be Kindled
This is it, that shall renew the: yea agayn and agayn,
and sevenly seuen tymes, agayn
Then shall thy eyes be clered from the dymnes
Thow shalt perceyue these things which haue [b] not byn seen,
No, not amongst the Sonnes of men.
This other haue I browght, whereof I will, now, bestow the seventith part
of the first part of seuenty seuen. The residue shall be fullfilled, in, and
with the; In, I say, and to gither, with the.
Behold (sayth the lord) I will breath vppon men, and they shall haue the
spirit of Vnderstanding
In 40 dayes must the boke of the Secrets, and key of this world be
Written: euen as it is manifest to the one of you in sight, and to the other
in faith. Therfore haue I browght it to the wyndow of thy senses,
and dores of thy Imagination: to the ende he may see and performe
the tyme of God his Abridgmēt. That shalt, thow, write down in
his propre and sanctified distinctions.
This other, (pointing to E K) shall haue it allwayes before him, and shall
daylie performe the office to him committed. Which if he do not,
the Lord shall raze his name from the number of his blessed, and those
that are annoynted with his blud
For, behold, what man, can speak, or talk with the spirit of God?

No flesh is hable to stand, whan the voyce of his Thunder shall
present the parte of the next Leaf vnto sight
You haue wauering myndes, and are drawn away with
the World: But brittle is the state therof:
small therfore are the Vanities of his Illusion
Be of sownd faith. Beleue. Great is the reward of those that
are faithfull
God Will not be dishonored, neyther will suffer them to receyue dishonor,
that honor him in holiness.
Behold, Behold, Mark ô and Behold: Eache line hath stretched
him self, euen to his ende: and the Middst is glorious to
the good, and dishonor to the wicked. Heuen and erth must
decay: so, shall not the words of this Testimonie.

△ Ecce seruus et misellus homuncio Dei $\overline{\text{nri}}$, fiat mihi iuxta beneplacitum voluntatis
suae. etc

△ Vriel toke a little of the fire in his left hand and flung it at E K: and
it went in at his mowth

Vr. My message is done.

△ May I Note Vr, (meaning Vriel,) for your name [that no] who now deale
with vs. ——— Vr ——— I am so

---

line 3: Spedily &
<&> reuerently

line 5: △. Vriel held / vp now the / Triangle of / fire [with hand]

line 9, over 'these': those

line 11: Δ / Vriel now / Holding vp / the Ball of / fire in his / left hand, / sayd as / here written ⌜with hand and joined by an integral to MN⌝

line 16: Liber / 

line 17, written vertically: Δ if frō the first day of / writing we accownt / than frō good friday the / reckoning doth begynne. / and so ende <this>

line 20: The Abridg= / m̄et of time

line 20: speaking to Δ

line 23: The danger / thretned, if / E K do not / his dutie

line 27: Note a / terrible / thing

line 37: The / ende of / all.

line 42: Note, by / the place / here before / what measure / in proportion / of powr and / vnderstanding / this was, in / respect of / the white ball / of fyre.

line joins 'seventith part' (line 11) to 'Vriel toke' (line 42).

[80b]

Δ I pray you to give vs advise what ⌜^{c}we⌝ are to doe in our affayres.

Vr. It is sayde

Δ he sayd to E K, Tell him, I haue told him, and seemed to smile.

Δ Of Mistres Haward (Jentlewoman of her Maties priuie chamber) I wold fayn know, wherfore we were ⌜^{c}not⌝ warned of her comming? [to make vs] she hath caused vs, now, for an howre or two, to intermit our exercise? Is it the Will of god, that for her great charitie vsed toward many, (as in procuring the Quenes Maties Almes to many [d] nedy persons) the lord entendeth to be mercifull to her? I meane at the pynche of these great miseries ensuing, now

(by you) told of. And that by her, I may do good seruice concerning

the Quenes Maiesties Cumfort?

Vr——— Who is he, that opened thy mowth, or hath told the of things to cōm< e?>

What thow hast sayd, is sayde. Mark the ende.

It is a sufficient answer.

Vr——— Loke vp. ———Δ he sayd so to E K. who loking vp, saw the boke

the chayre and the Globe a part, abroad, out of the stone, and then, none

remayning in the stone to be seene. and it cam nearer & nearer to

him, and it burned, as before.

Vr. So, set down, what thow seest.

What thow seest, deliuer vnto him.

As it is his will, so be it vnto the:

Do thy duty, wherevnto thow art moved,

and it shalbe sufficient.

[Vr] Farewell, for a time

Δ We put vp the stone: and the former boke and other furniture

appeared vppon the table hard by E K. and he was to write out as

he saw: Which he began to do, both in character and words: but

it was to cumbersome to him: and therfore he wrote onely the words

in latin lettres

Δ After he had written 28 lines there in that [boke th] paper boke, the

first word being Arney, and the last, being nah, suddenly all was taken away out of his sight: and so likewise his vnderstanding of that

he had written was quite gone. For, contynually as he wrote, he

Vnderstode the language and sense thereof, as if it had bvn english.

Δ After he had finished that second [✓] page of the first leafe, I then

Did copy it out as followeth

49 Arney vah nol gadeth adney ox vals nath gemseh ah

orza val gemáh, oh gedvá on zembáh nohhad vomfah

olden ampha nols admácha nonsah vamfas ornad,

alphol andax órzadah vos ansoh hanzah voh

adm< a>

Marginal notes:

line 7: Mistres Francis / Haward elected / to taste of god / his great mercy / for her charitable / hart. etc

line 19, RH: Δ The boke and writing was made / very playne to him.

line 35: [✓ forte Row]

line 38: Δ / forte, / Asney.

[81a]

In the tables expressed.	drux	1
drux	na	2
na	ger	3
ger	pa	4
pa	[na]	
van	van	5

or					or	6
pal					pal	7
med					med	8
gal	letters names,				[caph]	
ceph	vsed in sense				gal	9
vr					cheph	10
fam					vr	11
ged					[phm]	
vn					fam	12
mals					ged	13
					vn	14
					[mal	15.]
	veh				[nah]	
	graph	16	15		mals	15
	gisg[s]	17	16			
+	mals	18	17			
	don	19	18			
	gon	20	19			
	tal	21	20	L	△(d) { 1	
				b	a	

a [?]

Vad 7 [5] Vad 9

f [?]

[81b]

I finde diuerse dowts which I cannot order, to my contentment.

1. How many [of my ruled] leaves, shall I take for the writing of the first leafe

2. How shall I make the distinctions of the last [8] 9 lines of the first leafe answerable to all the ⌊former⌋ words: how to move them ⌊into⌋ this & ⌊place all⌋ of [th] these letters, & this 9 rows having but 49 letters.

.3. how shall I do for the true orthographie: Seing g and C and P etc haue so diuerse sownds: & not allways one as g sometymes as gh & sometymes as J: and C sometymes like K sometymes like S. p sometymes like ph, & sometymes p——— & sometyme f.

4 The number of the words in the first leafe,——— euery row, is not all one: nor 49 allwayes

5 of the ⌊wide⌋ Table, ⌊where⌋ is to be set downe all the tables following, all the Table ⌊over⌋, it will not agree to fill [vp] vp ⌊allso the⌋ all places, & to set down the ⌊rows⌋ pfectly.

Marginal note:

⌊written at top of page⌋: solgars

[82a]

adma iohá notma goth vamsed adges onseple ondemax orzan vnfa onmah vndabra gonsah gols' nahad NA.

---

2 Oxar varmol pan sampas os al pans orney andsu alsaph oucha cosdám onzagoles natmátatp max, olnah von ganse pacath olnoh vor nasquah loth adnay

nonsah oxansah vals nodax vonqueth lan sandquat ox ardánh [ozabel] onzâbel ormach douquin astmax [al|] arpagels ontipodah omvah nosch als mantquts, [ar] armad notgals . Vantantquah †

---

2 [3] Ondroh als vrh + panchah orn sandvah loh andah nol pan, sedmah zugeh als abmicadampâget ordomph, axah gethol vav axel anthath gorsan vax parsah vort lanq ándamsah getheol, vrchan navádah óxembles armax lothar, vos antath, orsé vax alnoth, other mals olnah gethom várdamach, alls +, Orgeth

---

3 [4] Or pasquah omzádah vorts, angénodah varsáua onch aldúmph, ánget ónsaual galta oth aneth ax pa gesné ouád ax orneh aldumbáges voscómph alze ax, orzad andah gost astoh nadah vortes, astmah notesma goth nathad omza, geth altéth ox, degáth onda voxa gemnaché adna dansa als alst

---

4 [5] arsah + Orthath ols gast ardoh max vármah doth novámq lath, adnab gothan, ardrínoh astómagel arpáget asteth arde obzá, ols (NA) gemnapálabamida orsat nahah

---

Marginal notes:

line 4: <I> dowt / <w>hich is n / <a>nd which is / u.

line 10: a dowte whether / ar mad be / two words or / one.

line 17: Δ / Ω

Odmázen ándulphel, ox ambrássah oxah géth nor vamfah genoh daqueth als astna, oh tatóh, alsah goth necor andeoh neo alda nah

---

5 [6] Vanlah oha demagens on sunfah, paphah olemneh, ózadcha lax ornah vor adme ox vastmah gu labazna, gamnách<o> asthmah ochádo landrídah vons sah, lúgho iahat nabscham nohads vandispa rossámod androch alphoh, zúmbloh ásnah gonfageph aldeh lo dah vax orh asmo, gad au dansequa deo, dath vax nograh vor segbat Mon.

---

6 [7] Arni olbah galpa lohánaha gáupumagénsah osso var se darsah goho álbumiclámácapáloth ieho nad veslah vors ardno inmony asquam rath als vásmah génda loggahah astmu

---

7 [8] Arnah notah lax vart luhoh désmaph, ol capraminacah oxandanvah gemneloriplitonpha accamplahnostapha ormaxadahahar orzemblizadmah panchefelogedoh áschah ólmah ledóh vaxma

---

8 [9] Gans na cap lan seda ax nor vorza vo laspral onsa gem gemah noph gázo na von santfa nostradg ansel vnsa pah vort velsa or alda viax nor adroh semneh ols vandésqual olzah nolpax pahah lothor ax ru vansar glímnaph gath ardot ardri axa noh gaga leth arde maxa.

---

9 [10] Corsal mabah noplich alps arsod vord vanfax oriox nabat gemnepoh laphet Ióda nat vombal nams ar

geth alloah néphirt. lauda noxa voxtaf ardno
ándroch labmageh ossu állmáglo ardot nalbar vanse
dar to vorts parsan vr vnrah vor gádeth leth orze
nax vomreh agelpha, legar or nembla ar va Su

Marginal notes:

line 3: here seme to / be 50 names and / so, one to many

line 14: here are but 38

line 32: 48

[83a]

<10> ~~11~~ Zanchumáchaseph olzaminóah Valseburáah nodaligánax
orsápnago darságnapha nobsiblith armipyth
arsepólonitantons
Iembúlsamar lebóge axpar ornáza oldaxardacoah

11 ~~12~~ Semno ah al chi do á cha da Selpaginodah adahubámicanoh
dam pha gli ás cha nor oxompaminapho lemp, na, gón sa pha
ne co ál pha [aspa] as pa gé mo cal na tú ra ge

12 ~~13~~ Sen gál se quar rus fa glan súx taft ormaca
ox i no dál ge brah nop tar ná gel vom na ches pál ma cax,
arsep as dón sadg asc lan fán che dah nor vi car máx coh
zum bla zánpha ad geh do ca ba ah

13 ~~14~~ Ar gém na ca pál fax, or[r] nido hab cas pigan alpuh
gágah loth ral sá bra dan go sá pax vólsan qués tan

ondapha opicab or zy lá pa achrapa máles

[adm m] ad má car pah oxalps on dá pa, gém na de vór guse

---

[15] lat gans sa par sat lasteáh lor ádah nóxax ardéphis

nónson andoh gvmzi vor sab líboh ad ni sa pa loth gaho lar

va noxa oho lan sempah noxa Vriah sephah lúsaz

odgálsax nottaph ax vrnoc árpos arta zem zubah

lothor gas lubah vom zá da phi cár no

---

5 [16] Alsótaphe [no] ondah vor ban sanphar pa loth agno iam

nésroh am algórs vrrábah geuseh alde ox nah vors

d

púrblox ámphicab nóstrohh admág or napsú asmo lon

gamphi arbel nof ámphi on Saubloth aschi nur laffax

beth

las doxa pra gem a Sestrox amphi nax var sembbh

Marginal notes:

line 3: <h>ere are / <.....4.>

line 7: .50. words

[83b]

6 [17] Angésel oxapácad onz adq ochádah ólzah vor náh

orpogógraphel al sa gem ua ca pí coh vl da pa pór sah

naxor vonsa [n] rons vrbanf lab dún zaph algadef

fe

loh gem vortáoh amph ahoha za vaxorza leph oxor

neoh ah va dunaca pi ca lodox ard nah.

---

7 [18] Iahod vox ar pi cah lot tár pi ges nol zim na plah

ge ó gra plih ne gó ah va lu gán zed am phí la doh

Zan veh al nex oh al pha ze goth gedóth axor van zebá
al cá pa

Luma ges ard de oh ah

---

18 ~~19~~

Onchas lagod van Sebageh oxangam pah gos dah manzeh ocondah
vardol Sebagh ol madan NA obal Sepaget, otoxen narvah
lubatan ansem nofet au naba notoh ax arsah mans Vstgam
pahod pah mal sednah gestons amphes al manso gapalebâton
arra nax vamfes amah dot agen nalphat ar zamne oh Sages

---

19 ~~20~~

nax lerua nath Zembloh axpadabamah Sanzápas
gunzanquah ona var demneh gah lod vmnah doxa val tarquat
mans ol gem nageph au zanbat vx [na] anzach al pambóha
naxtath ol nada vam nonsal aua nal gedot vorx alge lah
despa[g] gu prominabâmîgah olpaz ord gamnat lem paz
cath normadah on demq

---

20 ~~21~~

Laffah ie ogg dalseph abrimanadg oldomph ledothnar
ymnachar onze vam sepno voxauaret ol zantqur amph
nas Sages om nartal vor miscam bemcax lappad gesso
drux capgol ass letnar vom
sausah or gamprida ornat vol asmd onza duh get hansa
gorh hubra galsaropah nequax dap gemno ab pnidah
noxd lumbam

---

21 ~~22~~

al gethroz ax arvan oh zempal guh arvax no demnat ar
pambals nop nonsal geh axor pam vartop ab vbrah cardax
lon songes au dumax ar nephar lu gemne om Asda

Vorts

Marginal notes:

line 10: here seme to / be 50.

line 19: of the n and / u of this word / I dowt. [refers to 'gunzanquah']

line 28: At vom was / a † to note / the ende of a / line: But both / these mak but / 49 names.

[84a]

vorts vmrod val manqh noh Sam, naga vrbrast Lurvandax
vpplod dam zurtax loa an avarn nar gemplicabnadah oxa

Δ ∇

2> 23 nooa Babna ampha dum nonsap vrs daluah marsasqual orma
nabath Sabaothal netma vol sempra isch laue ondeh noh
semblax or mansa macapal vngenel vorsepax vrsabada noxanquah
vndalph asmoh vxa na Gaspar vmpaxal Lapproh Iadd nomval
vp setquam nol astma vors: vrdem gnasplat bef affafefafed noxtah
Volls laydam ovs nac

Δ ∇

3 24 cedah or manveh geh axax nolsp damva dor demgoh apoxan
subliganaxnarod orchal vamnad vez gemlehox ar drulalpa
ax vr samfah oladmax vr sappoh Luah vr pabmax luro
lam faxno dem vombres adusx or sembal on vamne
oh lemne val se quap vn nap nastosm dah voz mazaz
lumato games on neda.

Δ ∇

4 25 voh gemse[1] ax pah losquan nof afma dol vamna vn samses
oh set, quamsa ol danfa dot santa on anma ol subracah
Babalad vansag olso pas gonred vorn chechust axaroh

rugho am nadom val sequot ne texpa vors vrs al pam vans na tomvamal ansipamals notems anq$_k$, arxe al

25 [26] pangef offd ne pamfah aliboh a nostâfâges almesed vrmast geus vrmax au semblox satq quayntah luzez arne noh pamna sams bantes orn volsax vors vnisapa monsel dah nox ah pah vomreb doth danséquox anzazed onz anfal nom vamreh volts vrnacapácapah noshan yalt gelfay nor sentqbt onbanzar luntaf val sentepax

26 [27] ornisa nor Pampals anz alpah nox noxa gendah von gamne dah vors ad na lepnazu acheldaph var honza gune alsaph nal vomsan vns alpd a domph ar zemnip ans vrnach vancef ban yanzem oh aha vons nabrah vh asmo drat vormez al pasquar no gems nah zem lasquith apsantah.

Marginal notes:

line 16: 51 words

[84b]

27 [28] Vol zans alphi ne gansad ol pam ro dah vor vngef a deoh nad vnsemel apodmacah vnsap val vndar ban cefna dux hansel yax nolpah volts quayntah gam vemneg oh asq al panst ans vntah hunsansa Apnad ratq a sanst nel odogamanázar + olzah guh oh nah varsa vpangah neoh aho

28 [29] Notgah ox vr auonsad vl dath nox lat ges orn val

sedcoh leth arney vas ars galep odámpha nol axar vox apracas nolph admi adpálsah noh vrh gednach vax varsablox vrdam pagel admax lor vamtage oxandah lamfó not vorsah axpáa, ols nugaphar ádras vxár nostrílgan ampacoh vortes lesqual exoh.

29 [30] Ses vah nómre gal sables orzah, get les part, ox ar se de cólmachu ardéh lox gempha lar vamra goh naxa vors admah gebah, semfúgel admá geod alzeh orzam vánchet [ket], oxam prah geh orzad Val nexo, vam seleph oxa, noha par gúmsah askeph nox adroh lestof ad moxa nonsúrrach

30 [31] Vomchál as pu gán san var, sem quáh lah set gedoh argli oranza vor zina sedcátah zuréhoh admich, ors arsah varsab, oliba vortes lúnsanfah, adnah vor semquáx, vorsan lap varsah gebdah voxlar geoh, gemfel ad gvns. aldah gor vanlah, gehudan vor sableth, gedvel ax ors, manch var sembloh.

1 [32] Ar dam fa gé do hah Luxh arcan Mans lubrah vor semblas adna gor partat, nor vílso ádchu apri sed amphle nox arua getol. Vor sambla geth, arse pax vor sah gelh aho gethmah or gemfa nah prax chilad ascham na prah oxáh var setqua lexoh vor sámbleh zubrah.

2 [33] Lax or setquáh vah lox rémah Nol sadma vort, famfa le gem nah or sepah vartef a geh Oha lon gaza Onsa ges

adrux: vombalzah ah vaxtal. noh sedo lam, vom

tántas

Marginal note:

line 26: 48

[85a]

tántas oxárzah Mechól va zebn geth adna vax, ormacha lorni adrah, Gens arnah vor, Arsad odícoh alida nepho.

⟨33⟩ ~~34~~ Hastan bah ges loh ru mal; vrabo den varsah, Mah vox idah ru gebna demphe, ors amvi ar, Genbá, óxad va ges leth vriop: nal pas vi me ró to ádnavah ged anse lah verbrod vn gelpa, lux árd do ah: vast vor Gemafánoh

⟨34⟩ ~~35~~ Amles ondanfaha noxt vradah gel núbrod Arb á cha lo pe go há pa ra zem che pár ma la Na burá doh gem la pa orzin fax nol ad micápar vó si pi cá la ton andrah vox ardno, get na ca ploh gálzun

⟨3⟩5 ~~36~~ Ór ge mah luza cá poh nox tráh víoxah nebo hu ge o mí lah cox chá dah or na hú da vol sa pah: No bro ch, ál pa chídomph náb la grux la vx ar gá fam gel ne do gá lah vo sa pah

36 ~~37~~ Gu la gé dop áx ix óx a max lun sá gem pah orsa devímah Gé pa cha vor sí ma coh alduth gempfa: Nox gal max ar hú gaf gli nó rob va gen lá car du zum ox ám pli zam

zu latmah ge gé ma ohahah.

---

[38] Ga lá pa drux váx ma geb lá geb or ché plon gan zéd ah Vox ár vox gelet ar gahad, gan pá gan doruminaplah vor zinach cu pa chef ardrah óx ox pol sa gal máx nah guth ardéth on zupra cró cro gah var sa má nal

---

[39] Ar sa bá cho as noh al geh oh, ax ár pa gal olza deh or za zú max exoh eh, or [cha] cah pal donzahá onza zethas: nor sáp se pah onzap a palmah aldoh voh náblebah gemnápam os malsa or naoh zar bu lagém pah neó ha brah

---

[40] Tal gep ar sep nah doh, vors alsa doh necoh am ar geth na ges alpran odox malsápnah, gohor ahoh gadmah

---

[85b]

ol dáneph aludar dónzagab ólsagah nebthuh or sapnar balgonph nep gemloh, ax amna duth achár laspá, voha, náxvolh gas vergol ah pratnom

i
geá nostuámph

---

[41] Ván sa pal sah gón so gon ge la bu rá doh tato lang, ge mé fe ran ón da pans ge lá brah: or pa gé mal on sán fan gen ólc ma cha lan Von sé gor a prí cas nor vá gel om brá cau cohadal.

---

a	d	r	o	s,	a,	c	l	o	d́	f	a	ç	d	o	g	é	p	n	a	h,	l	a	p	c	a	n,	m	o	c	d	á	c	o	d	o,	f	a	m	ó	n,	t	u	a	l	c,	d	o	m,
v́	r	a	s	n	a	g	e	p	h,	a	m	p	h	i	d	o	n,	g	á	n	s	e	l,	v	a	x,	ó	r	e	h	a	m	a	h,	v	ó	r	s	a	f	a	n	s	a,	u	c	a	s
d	a	m	í	f	a	g	a,	n	a	b	u	l	a	x,	Q	r	s	a	g	e	h,	n	a	ḿ	v	a	h,	o	c	a	r,	l	u	n	s	a	n	g	e	l,	c	a	r	p	a	c	o	a
l	u	n	s	e	m	n	e	p	h,	o	d	á	r	n	a	c	n	o	h,	z	e	m	b	l	o	h,	o	b	l	í	c	a	n	d	o	n,	g	a	l	s	o	r	x	v	l	á	g	a
f	ó	m	n	a	p	h,	a	p	á	n	s	a	g	e	h,	l	o	n	s	ú	g	a	l	a	n,	g	r	a	s	t,	v	b	l	á	n	s	o,	a	r	n	o	x,	v	o	n	s	á	o
t	a	l	t	é	m	a	p	h	e	c	h,	ó	r	m	a	c	h	a	d	á	g	e	n	o	x,	v	r	s	t	á	m	v	a	h,	n	a	d	v	a	r	e	h,	o	n	s,	a	r	[illegible]
z	u	c	á	n	z	u,	n	a	p	l	i	o	r	a	h,	n	o	r	g	e,	n	a	h	a	n	a	h	a,	v	s	p	l	a	h,	r	r	a	d	ú	n	v	a	h,	n	a	v	í	o
a	r	s	a	h,	v	ó	n	r	o	g	e	n,	d	a	h	v	a	l	a	h,	o	r	z	a	p,	c	v	l,	c	a	r	s	e	d,	a,	p	o	r	s	a	l,	q	á	s	t	a	v	a,
g	a	n	f	ú	m	a	r	a	b	ó	m	o	n	a	h,	g	á	s	t	a	g	e	s,	ó	r	d	o	l	p	h,	n	a	q	a	s,	o	r	g	e	m	v	a	h,	n	o	x	a	d

Δ And this is the later ende of the second page of the first leafe of this excellent boke.

Booke. The other leaves are written, apart, in ⌈a^{c}n⌉ other boke[s] as may appere

But with these 9 rowes and the former 41, doth arise the some of 50: which is one

more then 49: Therfore I am not onely of this but of diuerse other imperfections yet

remayning in this page, to ax the solution and reformation.

Δ Whan I had told this my dowte to E K. he answered me that the first row of these

last .50. before set down, was the last of the first page of this first leafe: and

true it is that in the first page were first sett down 48 rows, of which eight and

& fortith row begynneth with this word Amgédpha etc And therfore the next

next row following, (begynning with Arney vah nol gadeth etc) is the nyne and

& fortyth row of the first page and so the last row of that page: And therby,

=by allso the second page of the first leaf hath these 49 rowes here noted: And

And so is one dowte taken away: The other is of the [imperfect] numbers of words

/words/ (with a "c" written above) in some of the 49 rows of this second page:

Aprilis 10. hor .9. △ As we wer talking of the Macedonian (the greciā), who yesterday cam w/th/ M/r/

Sanford his letters, there appeared in the corner of my study a blak shaddow: and I did

did charge that shaddow to declare who he was: There cam a voyce and sayd that it

it was the Macedonian: and abowt his hat was written in great letters

this word Κατάστικτος which E K wrote out: and it signifieth

maculosus, or condemnatus etc and the Voyce sayd, that word was sufficiēt

adding Est, △ God be thanked and praysed.

Marginal notes:

line 2: the copy had / ouyna / I <could> not <conjecture>

line 39: [firmus]— -

[86a]

To me <deli>uered by M^{r}

Edward Kelly

1583. Martij 22

friday

Mr Husy cam wth

him from blockley

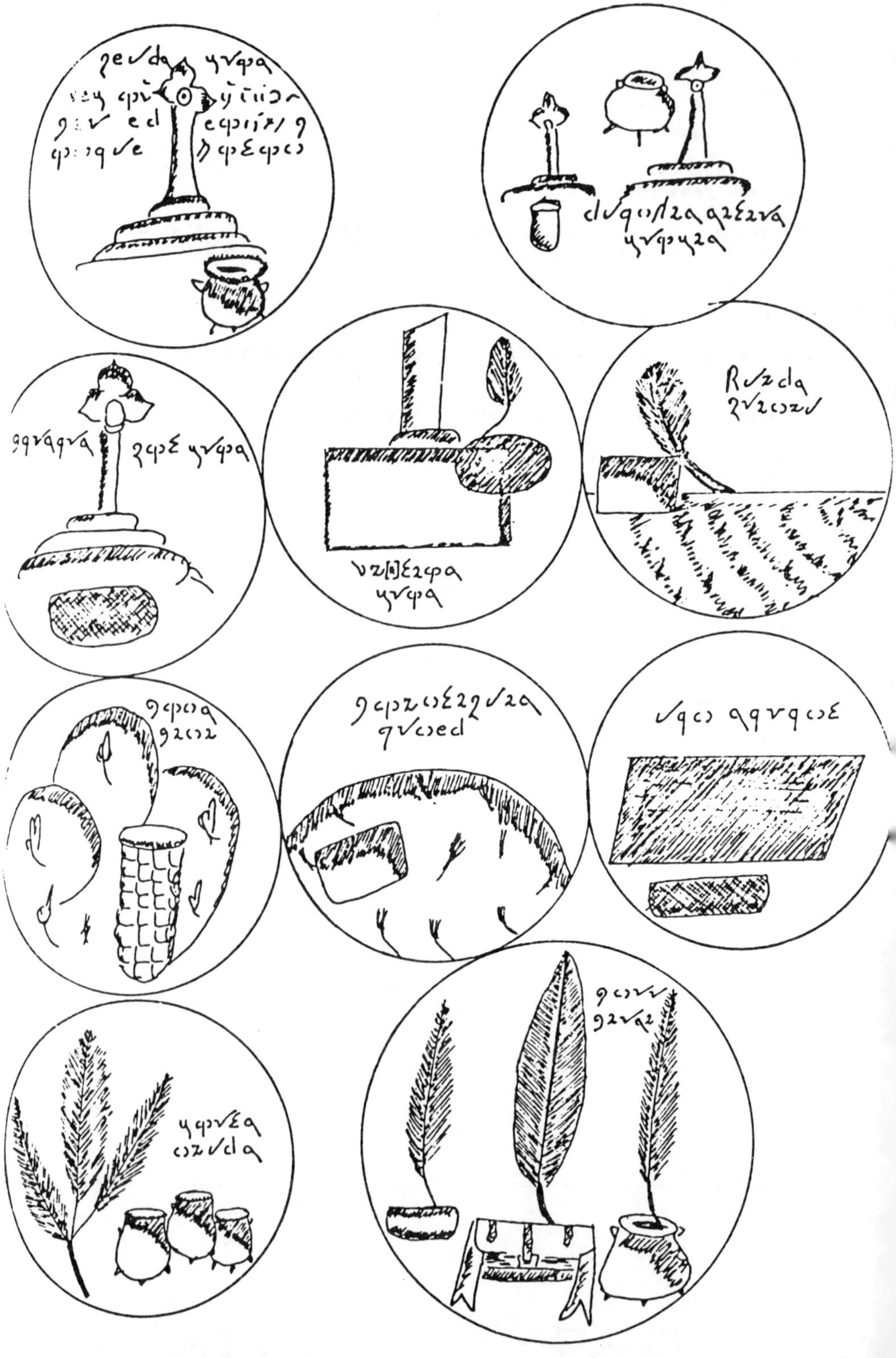

[87a]

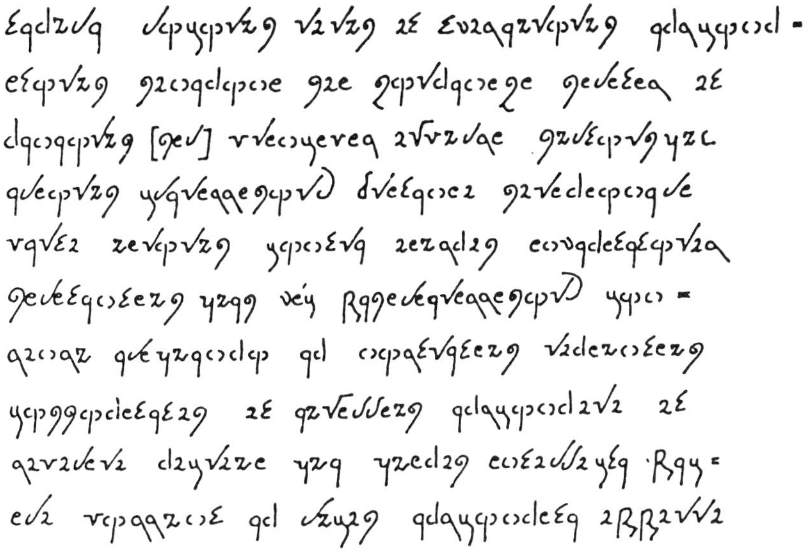

[flourish]

[87b]

[blank]

[88a]

Aprilis. 11. Thursday

Δ After my comming home from the court, abowt 4 of the clok after none, and after my being in my study a while, it cam into my hed to assay to deciphre the cifre which before is spoken of, and was browght me by E K, as he was willed to do. And at the first I was half out of hope: but yet making many assayes, and gessing [at] (with c written above) it (at the length) to be latine, I fownd this

to be the true Alfabet. God giving me the perceyverance.

A b c d e f g h i k l m n o p q r

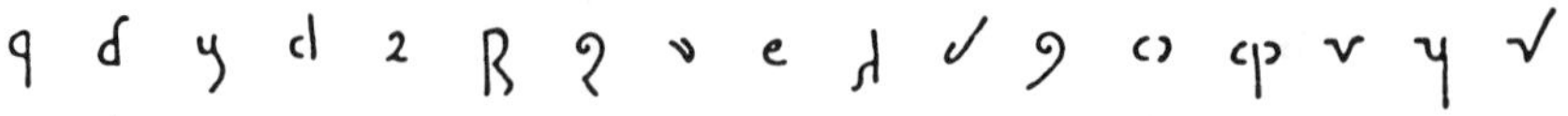

s t v x y z w.

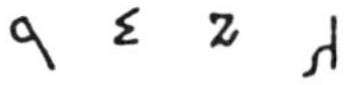

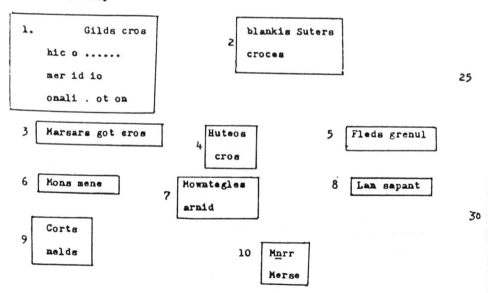

And, the first longer writing, was thus,

Tabula locorum rerum et Thesaurorum absconditorū Menahani, mei Gordanili, militis et Danaorū Principis, expulsi, multorumq aliorum clarissimorū (Britanie meridionali parte) virorū, contra eiusdem inhabitatores militantium: quam, hîc, familiarissimorum consensu, aliquando ad nostratium rediuntium commoditatem et auxilium abscondere et sepelire decreui: Qua quidem intellecta, facile possunt ad lucem abscondita efferre.

And the Notes of the ten places, here by, [notified] affixed are thus to be red orderly

1. Gilds cros
hic o ......
mer id io
onali . ot on

2 blankis Suters
croces

3 Marsars got cros

4 Huteos
cros

5 Fleds grenul

6 Mons mene

7 Mowntegles
arnid

8 Lan sapant

9 Corts
nelds

10 Mnrr
Merse

Marginal notes:

line 5: They were / fownd at / Huets Cross / as the spirituall / creature affirmed / when he lèd them / to the finding / of this Monimēt/ & < a> boke of / Magik & / Alchimie. / Perhaps that is / <the> Cros called / Huteos Cros / being the / fowrth of / them below

line 15: Note / J Dee the / last being of / the Danes / here, was / abowt the / year 1040

line 23: 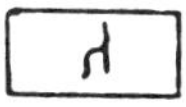 / of this K / I dowt yet

line 32: △ fortè Marr

[88b]

Aprilis 15 Monday

△ As E K was writing the eighteenth leafe which was of the spirites of the earth, (in the after none abowt 4½ of the clok) he red a parcell therof, playnely ⌈& alo^c^wde⌉ to him self, and herevppon suddenly at his side appeared three or fowre spirituall creatures like laboring men, hauing spades in theyr hands & theyr heares hanginging abowt theyr eares, and hastely asked E K what [they] ⌈he⌉ wold haue & wherfore he called them. He answered that he called them not. & they replyed, & sayed that he called them: Then I began to say, they lyed: for his intent was not ⌈to⌉ call them, but onely to read and repeat that which he had written: and that euery man who readeth a prayer to perceyue the sense thereof, prayeth not. No more, did he call them and I bad them be packing out of the place. and therevppon remoued from my desk (where I was ruling of paper for his writing) to the grene chayre which was by my chymney: and presently he cryed out and sayd they had nipped him and broken his left arme by the wrest: and he shewed the bare arme and there appered both on the vpperayde and lower side imprinted depe in, two circles as brode as grotes thus  very red: And I seeing that, sowght for a stik and in the meane while, they assalted him, and he rose, and cryed to me (saying) they cōme flying on me, they cōme; and he put the stole, which he sat on, betwene him and them. but still they cam gaping or gyrning at him. Then I axed him where they were: and he poynted to the place and then I toke the stik and cam to the place, and in the name of Jesus commaunded those Baggagis to avoyde /and smitt a cross stroke at them7 and presently they avoyded.

All thanks be to the onely /one7 Almighty, and everlasting God

Whose name be praysed now & euer. Amen

Aprilis 18. Thursday morning. hor. 8. circiter

△ As E K cam to write out the Tables according as he was wont: and to haue the letters appearing in the ayre hard by him, he saw nothing but a blak clowde seuen cornered. and after I had put the stone agayn into the frame, and therevppon did make long and oft request, for answer hauing, There appered nothing, neyther was any thing seen in the stone. Then I fell to prayer agayn, and at length, there appeared written vpon, or [out of] yssuing out of the clowde, this sentence

He promised, be not carful:

E K. The letters semed to stand at fingers endes, (being 21): and so euery finger had a letter on it: and the fingers semed to be placed at the Corners of the Heptagonall clowde: and assone as the sentence was red the fingers which seemed to issue out of the Heptagonū did shrink in agayn and disapere

Δ All laude honor and thanksgiving, be to the highest, our most louing mercifull and almighty God, now and euer amen.

The stone out of the frame

Marginal notes:

line 29: Note. Now / 30 Tables, / being writtē / since good / friday: and / dayes onely / 21 passed / since good / friday.

line 37: Δ as who shold / say αυτος /εψα , ipe / dixit dēʒ / Deus.

line 37, RH: Δ Note, here are iust 21. letters

line joins 'stone' (line 32) to 'stone' (line 44)

[89a]

Thursday. Aprilis 18. after dynner.

We being desirous to know the cause of this stay making, in the Tables shewing as before was accustomed; and now (24 leaves being written, a dark clowde to hang in the place of a glorious boke, did greatly disquiet our myndes, and browght vs in feare of some offence lately committed, by any ore, or both of vs,

whereby the Indignation of the lord might be kindled against vs.

Herevppon we prayed severally: and at length, (no alteration, or better

Cumfort hapening to vs, [w] I prayed in the hearing of E K, [at my]

(by my desk, on my knees) in great agony of mynde; and Behold there

appeared one standing vppon, or rather somwhat behynde the Heptagonall clowde

who sayd I am sent, to vnderstand the cause of your greif, and

to answer your dowtes.

Δ I, then, declared my mynde breifly, according to the effect of my prayer.

wherevnto he answered at large, reproving my appointing of god a tyme

or to abridge the tyme spoken of. and among his manifold grave speaches

he had these words

Prepare all things, For tyme is at hand

His Justice is great, and his arme stronge

How darest thow dowt or dreame, saying: Lo, God, this may be done

in shorter time etc. But such is flesh.

Be rocks in faith

▲ It is not the manner of vs, good Angels, to be trubbled so oft.

At the time appointed, thow shalt practise: While sorrow shall be

measured, thow shalt bynde vp thy fardell.

Great is the light of Gods sinceritie.

Appoint God no tyme. Fullfill that which is commaunded

God maketh clere when it pleaseth him. Be you constant and avoyde

Temptations: For True it is, that is sayde: And lastly I say,

It shall be performed

What is it now thow woldest desyre to be made playner?

Δ still he proceded vppon my answers: and at length he sayd

Neyther is the time of mans Justification known vntyll he hath byn tryed.

You are chosen by God his mercy to an ende and purpose: Which ende shall be made manifest by the first begynning in knowledg in these Mysteries.

God shall make clere whan it pleaseth him: & open all the secrets of wisdome whan he vnlocketh. Therfore seke not to know the mysteries of this boke, tyll the very howre that he shall call the. For then shall his powre be so full amongst you, that the flesh shall not be perceyued, in respect of his great glory

But was there euer any, that tasted of gods mercies so asuredly, that wanted due reuerence? Can you bow to Nature, and will not honor the workman? Is it not sayd, that this place is holy?

What are the works of holines? I do aduertise you: for, God will be honored. Neyther will he be wrasted, in any thing he speaketh,

Think not, that you could speak or talk with me, vnleast I did greatly abase my self, in taking vppon me so vnlikely a thing in forme, as to my self. etc

But he doth [it] /this7 not for your causes, not for your deserts, but for the Glorie of his own name.

One

Marginal notes:

line 16: Prepare / all things

line 22: Good Angels

line 23: [hand]

line 32: Tyme of Justi= / fication known / Whan / The ende / of our elec= / tion

line 39: Tyll the very / howre

line 42: want of due / reuerence Vsing / <in> our actions / <is> reproved.

line 47: Angels abase / them selues, to / pleasure man by / theyr instructions / when they tak / vppon them, or / vse any sensi / ble evidence of / them selves / <or> voyces. etc

---

[89b]

One is not to be lightened, but all. And which all? The two fethered fow<l> to gither with the Captayn

Ask What thow wilt: for, vntyll the 40 dayes be ended, shalt thow haue no one more shew of vs.

Δ Whether shall we give Cownsayle, or consent to the Captayne to go down into the Cuntry, as, presently he entendeth

Vr——— As he listeth

Δ E K. sayd that this was Vriel who now had appered and answered all this.

Vr.——I will ask the one question. Haue we any voyce or no?

Δ I do think you haue no organs or instruments apt for voyce: but are mere spirituall and nothing corporall: but that you haue the powre and property frō god to insi= nuate your message or meaning to eare or eye, in such sort as mans Ima= gination shall be, that both they here and see you sensibly.

Vr.——we haue no voyce, but a full noyce that filleth euery place: which

whan you ones taste of, Distance shall make no separation.

Let there one cōme that may better answer: not in respect of thy self

but one, more nerer to thy estate.——Do thy Duty.

Δ He sayd this, to one who cam in, and he departed him self.

Δ This new come Creature sayd, Wold you haue any thing with me, Il?

Δ Who art thow: Art thow one that loveth and honoreth our Creator?

Il——will you see my hart——E K. he openeth his body and sheweth his hart

and theron appered written EL.

Δ he semed to be a very mery Creature, and skypped here and there, his apparell was

like as ^{c}/of/ a vyce in a play: and so was his gesture and his skoffing, as the

outward shew therof was to be vulgarly demed. but I did carefully ponder the

der the pith of the words which he spake: and so forbare to write very much which he

spake at the begynning, by reason E K did so much mistake him, and in <a>

in a manner toke him to be an Illuder.

Δ As you are appointed to answer vs by the Messager of God, so answer vs, (who desyre the

pure and playne verity,) as may be correspondent to his credit that assigned you, and

to the honor of God who created vs.

Il——My answer is Threefold——I answer by gesture by my apparayle and

will answer the by my wordes.

Δ Do you know where the Arabik boke is that I had: which was written in tables and

numbers?

Il——It is in Scotland——A minister hath it: it is nothing worth. The boke conteyneth fals and illuding Witchcrafts. All lawde honor and p^r^ayse be to

the One and euerlasting God: for euer and euer.

△ The Lord Threasorer, hath he, any bokes belonging to Soyga? Il——— he hath

none: but certain Introductions to all artes.

△ But it was reported to me by this skryer that he had: certayn peculier bokes pertayning

to Soyga. otherwise named ysoga, and Agyos, literis transpositis.

Il——— Soyga signifieth not Agyos. Soyga alca miketh.

△ What signifieth those wordes? The true measure of the Will of God in iudgment

which is by wisdome.

△ What language is that, I pray you? Il——— a language towght in Paradise

△ To whome? Il——— by infusion, to Adam. △ To whome did Adam

vse it? Il——— vnto Chevah △ Did his posteritie vse the same?

Il——— yea, vntyll the Ayrie Towre was destroyed. △ Be there any

any letters of that Language yet extant among vs mortall men?

Il <....> that there be △ Where are they? Il——— ô, syr, I shall

make

Marginal notes:

line 1: Three are / to be lighte= / ned.

line 3: 40 dayes.

line 5: A.G.

line 14: Vox ange= / lorū

line 16: Vriel putteth / one in his / place.

line 19: △ / Il or El

line 22: El.

line 23: IL

line 32: Note / Threfold / answer

line 34: Liber Ara= / bicus

line 38: E K: he / Kneleth down.

line 41: Note

line 46: The lan= / guage towght / in Paradise

[there is an illegible note at the bottom left hand corner of the folio]

[90a]

make you in loue with your Masterships boke.

△ Did Adam write any thing in that Language. Il——That is no questio< n.>

△ Belike than, they were deliuered from one to an other by tradition. or els

[△] Enoch his boke, or prophesie, doth, or may seme, to be written in the same language: bycause mention is made of it in the new Testament in Jude his epistle where he hath, Prophetauit autem de his Septimus ab Adam, Enoch, dicens, Ecce venit Dominus in sanctis millibus suis facere iudicium contra ōes, et arguere ōes impios, de omnibus op̄ibus impietatis eorū, quibus impiè egerunt; et de omnibus duris quae locuti sunt contra Deum peccatores impij. etc

Il.——— I must distinguish with you. Before the flud, the spirit of God was not vtterly obscured in man. Theyr memories were greater, theyr vnderstanding more clere, and theyr traditions, most, vnsearchable. Nothing remayned of [Enoch] Enoch but (and if it pleas your mastership) mowght haue byn carryed in a cart.

I can not bring you the brass, but I can shew you the bokes.

Slepe* 28 dayes, and you shall fynde them, vnder your pillow whan you do rise.

Δ As concerning Esdras bokes, which are missing, what say you?

Il——— The prophets of the Jues haue them. Δ But we can hardely, trust any thing in the Jues hands, concerning the pure Veritie: They are a stiffnecked people and dispersed all the world ouer.

Il——— I will shew you a trik. Δ he lifted vp his fote, and shewed the sole of his shoo: and there appeared the picture of a man, who seemed to haue a a skorf or fowle skynne on his face: which one toke of: and then there appered on his forhed these two figures 88

I will shew you more then that, to. and will speak to a man shortly, that shall bring Water to wash euery mans face.

Δ What mean you, by euery man? shall all men, be made cleane?

Il——— There is a difference in washing of faces.

EK. This creature seemeth to be a Woman by his face: his apparell semeth to be like a Vice in a play.

E K. Are you not a Kinsman to syngolla?

Il I syr, and so are you a kinsman to synfulla.

Δ A man may finde corn in chaf.

Il——— So may you (perchaunce) finde me an honest man in my ragged clothes.

Δ This other day, whan I was in dowt of the Grecian (the Macedonian) whether he had any good and profownd lerning or no, he was represented spiritually, and abowt his hat in great letters was written this greke word Κατάστικτος I pray you what doth it signifie? I axed the grecian and he sayd βεβαιος

Il. Loke in your boke. Δ I toke the common lexicon: and he sayd, No

Not that: Then I axed if I shold take φαuorinus his lexicon: and he

answered. Nor that. and I axed which then: and he sayd your boke covered

with a white parchmēt. and I axed, that of Misteries of Latine greke

and hebrue? and he sayd, yea: and there you shall finde that Maculo=

sus hath onely that one word Καταςικτe longing to it. I loked &

so I fownd it which satisfyed me very well.

Δ I pray you what say you of Gariladrah; do you know him? who long

sins did deale with me?

Il——Yf he were lesser then I, /Iͨ/ durst speak [of] /tͨo/ him: But bycause he is greater

then /Iͨ/, I am not to speak to him. All vnder, and nothing above me, I deale.

Loke on your Tables, and there you shall <u>finde an other name of his.</u>

Δ I remēber no such thing: Il——Consider who hath set me here

Yf the Truth thow hast allready, be of a greater then my self, then is

it sufficiēt. Δ what day was that name given me?

Il ——Immediately, sir, after your Worships last cōming

Δ That was Raphaël: And I remēber that Gariladrah sayd that he must leave me and

his better (Raphael) shold be my instructor, and that then the same Raphael was in

my hed then. etc.

Marginal notes:

line 4: Enoch

line 11: Note / excellent / Memories, / for Traditions / contynuing and / preseruing.

line 15: Δ forte 18. / Note 28 dayes / more do make / iust the 40 / dayes, before / notified.

line 17: Esdras / bokes

line 18: The Jues

line 24: Δ this might / seme to signi- / fie the calling / home of the / Jews, A° 1588. / to come

line 29: Note, El / semed to / be woman.

line 46: Gariladrah

line 51: That was / Vriel / pag. precedete.

line 54: *he pointed / to E K.

[90b]

Δ Sing a song to his prayse, who created vs.

Il I will sing a short song.
Your doings are of GOD: your calling great:
Go down and seke the Threasor, and you shall obteyn it.
Take no care: for, this Boke shall be done in 40 dayes
Begyn to practise in August. Serue god before.
You shall know all thing, ictu oculi.
And so, prayse, glory, and eternall singing
with incessant humilitie be vnto the Creator [t] that
hath framed, made and created all things, for
euer and euer, Now say you (yf you will)
Amen Δ Amen Amen Amen

After the ende of 40 dayes, go down for the Threasor

Whan those 40 dayes are done, than this boke shall be finished. The rest of the time Vntyll August, is for rest, labor, and prayer.

Δ What labor? Il——In digging vp of those Threasors.

Δ Must we nedes dig for them? Il——otherwise, yf thow willt.

Δ How, I pray you? For to dig without lycence of the Prince, is dangerous by reason of the lawes: and to ax licence is half an odious sute.

Il——yf thow haue a parcell or part out of euery place of the erth, in any small quantitie, thow mayst work by the Creatures, whose powre it is to work in such causes: which will bring it (neuer trust me) before you can tell twenty.

Δ he meaneth. Neuer trust him, if it be not so, as he hath sayd.

Il——No, neuer trust me, if it be not so.

Δ you mean those ten places, marked in the Table, which last day, I deciphred.

Il——I mary, now you hit it. yea sir, and your chest allso, it wold do no hurt. Give me one: and I will make 40: and give you twenty an<d> take twenty to my self: and when you haue it, I pray you let me hau<e> some little portion for my wife /and/ children.

Δ As concerning that Chest, I pray you how cam the Macedonian, or M/r/ Sanford to know of it, so particularly as he did?

Il——Husey told of it, openly, at the bord at braynford in the hearing of diuers

The Grecian will seke him oute.

The Greke in grecia perhaps can finde out Threasor, but not in Anglia.

The Greke hath a Threasor in his hed, that will enriche him to be a fole line 20: wthout dig= / ging.

line 26: Ten places

line 27: The chest / 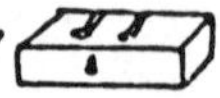

line 39: △ True it is, / I had hidden / there in a / capcase the / recordes of / any doings wth / Saule & other / etc.

line 44: The boke / The powder / the rest of / the roll.

[91a]

Quinti libri Mysteriorum

Appendix

Aprilis 20 ——— Saterday

△ This Saterday had byn great and eger pangs betwene E K and me: while

he wold vtterly discredit the whole process of our actions: as, to be done by evill

and illuding spirites: seking his destruction. saying that he hath often heretofore

byn told things true, but of illuding diuells: and Now, how can this be other, than

a mockery, to haue a cornerd dark clowd to be shewed him in steade of the playn

writing which hitherto he had written out of? and that whan they shold do good in dede

that then they shrank from vs. and that he was not thus to leese his time: But that

he is to study, to lerne some knowledge, whereby he may liue: and that he was a c<umber>

to my howse, and that he dwelled here as in a prison: that it [was] wer better for him

to be nere Cotsall playne where he might walk abroade, without danger

[and or] to be cumbred /or vexed/ with such sklaunderous fellows as yesterday he was, with one

I was yesterday at Londom, I met with a blak dyer. He had a cupple of rings, that wold giue better instructions

Your Chymney here will speak agaynst you anon: yet I am no bricklayer I must be gone.

Δ God, for his infinite mercyes be allwayes praysed, glorified, and extolled of all his Creatures: Amen.

He advised E K to communicate to me the boke, and the powder, and so al<l> the rest of the roll, which was there fownd: saying, true friendes <vse> not to hide any thing eche from other.

Δ An old proverb it is Amicorum oia coia

Vnde, Deo soli ois exhibeatur

laus honor et gloria

Amen.

[flourish]

Note: There followeth Quinti Li<bri>

Mysteriorum Appendix

Marginal notes:

line 4: Thesaurus absconditus

line 5: 40. dayes. —

line 6: August —

line 7: Knowledge to be / infused Ietu / Oculi.

line 13: Thesaurus / abs.

line 14: 40

line 15: Note: / till Au= / gust

little Ned dwelling at the black raven in Westminster: who rayeld at him for bearing

witnes of a bargayn made [by] betwene the same Ned (or Edward) and one Lush

A Surgoen, who was now fallen in poverty, a very honest man etc. With a

great deale of more matter, melancholik, and cross overthwartly to the

good and patient vsing of our selues to the accomplyshing of this action.

I replyed, and sayd, that we might finde our selfe answered [yest] on

thursday, as, That God wold clere when it pleased him: and that

we were not to appoint God a time to performe his mysteries and mercies

in; [shot] shorter then he hath spoken of: And that vndowtedly, the

occasion of this blak clowd, was some imperfection of oures, to be amended

and that then, all, wold be to our furder cumfort. And as concerning his dowting

the goodnes of the creatures, (dealing with vs) he was to blame, to say [the] or dowt

the tree to be yll that bringeth furth good frute. for of these creatures, from

the begynning of theyr dealing with vs vnto the last howre, we never hard other than

the prayse of god, instructions and exhortations to humilitie, patience, constancy,

fayth etc. The things they promise be such as god can performe, and

is for his servyce and glory to performe: and such as haue byn imparted to man

before: and therfore neyther impossible for man to enioye agayn, nor

vnmete for vs to hope for. and thowgh his trubbled mynde did dowt, yet

my quiet mynde, which god hath made [straight] ioyfull throwgh his mercyes, and which accuseth me not in this action of any ambition, hypocrisie, or disorderly longing, but onely is bent and settled in awayting the Lord his helping hand to make me wise for his servyce, (according as long tyme my daylie prayer to him hath byn.) and seing I haue and do ax wisdome at the lord his hands, and put my trust in him, he will not suffer me to be so confownded: nether will he offer a stone to his seely children, when in tyme of nede they ax bred at his hands: besides that Voluntatē timentium se faciet deus: and (by his graces) I feare him so, and am so carefull, to do that shold pleas him, that I make no accownt of all this world possessing, vnleast I might enioy his fauor, his mercies and graces And whereas he complayned of want, I sayd, my want is greater than his: for I was in det all of 300 pownds, had a greater charge than he, and yet for all my 40 yeres course of study, many hunderd pownds spending, many hunderd myles travayling, many an incredible byte and forcing of my witt in study vaing to lerne or to bowlt out some good lifing, [ye] etc. yet for all this I wold be very well pleased to be deferred yet longer, (a yere or more) and to go vp and down Ēgland clothed in a blanket, to beg my bred, so that I might, at the ende be assure<d> to atteyn to godly wisdome, whereby to ⌈$\overset{c}{\text{do}}$⌉ God some service for his glory. And to be playne, that I was resolued, eyther willingly to leave this world presently that, so, I might in spirit enioye the bottomles fowntayne of all wisdome, or

Marginal notes:

line 28: /hand/

line 38: Sapientia

line 46: 1s / 300 det.

[91b]

els to pass furth my dayes on earth wth gods favor and assurance of enioying

here his mercifull mighty blessings, to vnderstand his mysteries, mete for the

performing of [of] true actions, such as might sett furth his glory, so, as it mig< ht>

be evident and confessed, that such things wer done Dextera Domini.

And many other dyscourses and answers made vnto his obiections and dowtes:

After ward I began to speak of the trubbles and misery foreshewed to be nere at hand, and

by that tyme I had entred a little into the Consideration and talk of the matter, he appered

that sayd he was called El or Il, and sayed

——— Now to the matter.

Δ what matter?

Il.——— I must haue a Wallet to carry your witt and myne own in.

Δ Benedictus qui venit in noie Dni

Il——— Then I perceyue that I shall haue a blessing

Blessed is the physitien that hath care of his patient, before the pangs of death

doth viset him.

Δ——— What think you of that clowdy Heptagonu?

Il.——— Dost thow consider, I go abowt it?

I told the, euery thing I did, was an Instruction. As I can not

stand stedfastly vppon this, (it self one and one perfect:)

so can not my mowth declare, much lesse speak, that you may

comprehend it, what this is wherevppon I go.

E K. He went on the Heptagonon, as one might go on the top of a turning

whele: (as sōme horses vse to turn wheles as may appere in Georgius

Agricola de re metallica)

Il.—— I know, what all your talk hath byn: But such myndes, such Infection,

such Infection, such corruption: and must nedes haue a potion appliable for the

cure. But how will you do? I haue forgotten all my drvggs behinde me.

But since I know that sōme of you are well stored with sufficient oyntments,

I do entend to viset you onely with theyr help. you see, all my boxes

ar empty?——— E K he sheweth, a great bundell of empty poticharie boxes,

and they seme[d] to my hearing to rattle

Δ How commeth it, that you pretend to cōme frō a favorable diuine powre to pleasure vs

us and your boxes ar empty.

Il——— you sayd euen now in your talk: Jovis oīa plena: yf my empty

boxes be Vertuous, how much more shall any thing be, which I bring not empty?

Δ Then I pray you, to say somwhat of the vertue of your empty boxes, bycause

we may haue the better confidence of your fullnes

Il.—— Will you haue my bill? Δ shall we go to the Apothecaries,

with your Bill?

Il.—— I will shew it: serve it, where you list.

Iudra galgol astel.

△ you know we, vnderstand it not: how can it bè serued?

Il.—— you must nedes haue an expositor

What boke of physik is that, that lyeth by you?

[△ There lay by me on my desk, Marcus Heremita de Lege spirituali in greke and latine

but the latin translation lay open before, on the left side of which, the sentence began

Non raro per negligentiā, quae circa alicuius rei operationē comittitur, etiā Cognitio obscuratur

And on the right side, began Corpus sine mente nihil p̄t perficere etc]

Il.———— Mary here is good physik in dede

you fownd my name the other day. go to my name. [△ so I turned

to the second boke and browght sigillū AEmeth. and there chose the

word Ilemese. he than axed me, which letter of this name I liked best

and I sayd, L: bycause it conteyned the name representing God. El. etc

then he sayd somwhat furder of the letters, which I wrote not.

Il———— Go to great M, the second: for this is it shall serue his turne

yf

Marginal notes:

line 6: A meridie ——

line 11: El

[92a]

yf this can not serue him, he shall haue a medicine, that a horse can not

abyde. Vse this, and I warrant you, your blindenes will be gone.

Δ It is here, greatly, to be Noted: that I turned in this boke of Marcus, 27 leaues furder: tyll I cam to the Quaternie of M, the second and there I fownd this sentence notified (by my lines drawn, and a Note in the margent, Cor contritum) Sine corde contritio impossibile est omnino liberari a malitia et vitijs. Conterit autem cor tripartita temperantia somni dico et cibi et corporalis licentiae. Caeterum horum excessus et abundantia voluptatem generat. Voluptas autem prauas cogitationes ingerit repugnat verò praecationi et convenienti Cogitationi

Δ This being considered by vs, we ceased and this instant and thanked God of his mercies, that it wold pleas him to make vs vnderstand some iust cause whie clowdes now appeared in stede of brightnes etc.

Soli Deo ōis honor laus et gloria Amen.

[flourish]

Marginal notes:

line 1: <A> remedy for / <the> blyndenes / <of> E K at / <t>his instant

line 3: Δ / and so many / dayes yet / wanted of / the 40, yf we / accownt frō / the 6 day of / Aprill: but / if frō the tyme / of the begynning / to write them, / then there wan= / teth not so / much by 9 / or 10 dayes

---

Aprilis 23. Tuesday. mane. hor 8.

Δ After our prayer iointly, and my long prayer, at my desk requesting God to deale with vs, so, as might be most for his glory, in his mercies: not according to our deserts, and

frowardnes: etc. At length appeared in the stone a white clowde, seven cornered.

And behinde the Clowd a Thunder seemed to yssue

A Voyce ———— Whan I gathered you, you were chosen of the myddest of Iniquitie:

Whome I haue clothed with garments made and fashioned with my owne

hand ———— I, AM, Therfore Beleue:

Δ I prayed, and thanked the highest, that so mercifully regarded our miserie

A Voyce ———————— I, AM.

E K. Now standeth Vriel vppon the clowde, and semeth to loke downward

and kneled, saying

AEternitie, Maiestie, Dominion and all powre, in heuen

the earth and in the secret partes below, is thyne, thyne

yea thyne; and to none els is due, but vnto the: whose

mercies are infinite; which respectest the glorie of thy owne

name above the frowardnes, and perversnes of mans nature:

which swarmeth with synnes, and is couered with Iniquitie: and

in the which, there is fownde no place free from filthynes and

abhomination. Glorie be to the; ô, all powre: and

magnified be thow, in the workmanship of thy own hands, from

time to time, and with out ende of time, from generation

to generation: and euen amidst and in the number of those, for

whome thow hast prepared the flowres of thy aeternall Garland.

Beare with them (ô lord) for thy mercyes sake. for, woldest thow

seeke Δ in the myddst of miserie? Whom yf thow sholdest

iudge according to [ius] thy iustice, How shold thy Name be glorified so in thy
self, to thy own determination, and writing, sealed before the Creation
of the Worldes? The fire of thy Justice consumeth thyne own seat.
and in the, is no powre wanting, whan it pleaseth the, to cast down,
and gather them to gither, as the wynde doth the snow, and in hemme

them

Marginal notes:

line 21: Nos

line 26: Vr.

line 41: △ here I mist / the hering of / a word or / more.

[92b]

them with the mowntaynes, that they may not arrise, [..] /to/ synne

But what thow art, thow art: and what thow willt, thow canst.

Amen

△ Amen.

Vr.——I haue measured time (sayth the lord) and it is so: I haue appointed
to the heauens theyr course, and they shall not pass it.
The synnes of man shall decay, in despite of the enemy: But the fire
of aeternitie shall neuer be quenched, nor neuer fayle
More, then is, can not, nor may not be sayde
We can not be Witnesses to him, which witnesseth of him self
But (this sayeth the Lord). Behold yf you trubble me
ones more, or towche the wings of my excellency, before I shall

move my self, I will raze you from the earth, as children of perdition and will endue [that] those that are of quiet myndes, with the strength of my powre. You are not faithfull, sayeth the lorde whome you beleue not. Notwithstanding I haue hardened the hart of One of you, yea, I haue hardened him as /the/[c] flynt, and burnt him to gither with the ashes of a Cedar: to the entent he may be proued iust in my work, and great in the Strength of my Glory. Neyther shall his mynde consent to /the/[c] wyckednes of Iniquitie For, from Iniquitie I haue chosen him, to be a first erthely witnes of my Dignitie.

Your words are, yet, not offensive vnto God: Therfore, will not we, be offended at any thing that is spoken: For it must be done /caret/ and shall stand; yea and in the number /which/[c] I haue allready chosen.

But this sayeth the lorde: Yf you vse me like worldlings I will surely stretch out my arme vppon you, and that heuily Lastly, I say

Be Faithfull,
Honor God truely
Beleue him hartily.

E K. he kneleth down, and semeth to pray.——Now he standeth vp

Vr. Lo, As a number increasing is allwayes bigger: so in this world decreasing, the Lord must be mightily glorified Striue not with God. But receyue, as he imparteth. The Mercy of my message, quencheth the obscuritie and dullnes of your sowles. I mean of the Infection, wherewithall they are poysoned.

Lo, how the Earth cryeth vengeance. Come, for thy Glory sake, it is tyme Amen

Δ Seing it is sayd that in 40 dayes [and before 40 dayes] the boke shalbe finished: and seing it is sayed that our former Instructers shall not come nor appeare to vs tyll the boke be finished. And seing heretofore the boke vsed to appere to E K, that he might write, whan so euer he bent him self therto: and seing the same

---

Marginal notes:

line 11: 

line 12: NOTA et / Caue.

line 17: One of vs is / by the Lord / confirmed in / constant purpose

line 21: Election / confirmed

line 25: △ I think / sayeth the Lord / [caret] is forgotten / here

line 27: Note / 

line 33: 

line 35: Note

line 39: Vengeance / cryed for

[93a]

same boke appeareth not so now: and seing we are desyrous to be fownd diligent in this work, and to omitt no Opportunitie wherein the writing therof might be furdred: We wold gladly know, What token or warning shall be giuen vs, henceforward, whan due tyme serueth for the same purpose.

Vr——Dy in the folly: I haue sayde

E K. It thundreth and lightneth abowt the clowde: and now all
is vanished away

△ E K sayd, that at the very begynning of this days action, when he
expressed the first Voyce (this day), hard by him, his belly did
seame to him, to be full of fyre: and that he thowght veryly,
that his bowells did burne: And that he loked downward
toward his leggs, to see if any thing appeared on fire: calling
to his mynde the late chance that befell to the Adulterous man
and woman by Sainct Brydes church in London. etc
Allso that whan he had made an ende, he thowght his belly
to be wyder, and enlarged, much more then it was before.

△ I sayde certayn prayers to the Almightie our God and most
mercifull father, on my knees; and E K on his knees
likewise, answered diuers times, Amen.

After this, we made A G. to vnderstand these the mercies of the
Highest: and he reioyced greatly, and praysed the Lorde:
And, So E K, was fully satisfied of his Dowtes:
And A G, and he, were reconciled of the great discorde
which, yesterday, had byn betwene them etc.

Non nobis, Domine, Non nobis,
sed nomini tuo [da] Gloriam omnem
Laudem et honorē damus et
dabimus in perpetuum
Amen
[flourish]

Marginal note:

line 21: A.G,

[93b]

[blank]

[94a]

Aprilis 26. fryday

Δ Note

By the prouidence of god, and Mr Gilbert his meanes, and pacifying of E K his vehement passions and pangs, he cam agayn to my howse: and my wife very willing, and quietted in mynde, and very frendely to E K in Word, [and][c] cowntenance: and a new pacification [on][c] all partes] confirmed: and all vppon the Confidence of God his servyce, [to][c] be] faythfully and cherfly intended, and followed in and by our actions, throwgh the grace and mercy of the highest.

[flourish]

1583 Aprilis 28. Sonday: after Dynner. abowt 4 of the clok.

Δ As I and E K had diuerse talks and dyscourses of Transposition of letters: and I had declared him my rule for to know certaynly how many wayes, any number of letters (propownded,) might be transposed or altered in place or order: Behold, suddenly appered, the spirituall creature, IL, and sayd

Il—Here is a goodly disputation of transposition of letters Chuse, whether you will dispute with me, of Transposition, or I shall lerne you

Δ I had rather lerne then dispute. And first I think, that those letters of our Adamicall Alphabet haue a due peculier vnchangeable proportion of theyr formes, —— and likewise that theyr order is allso Mystical

Il—These letters represent the Creation of man: and therfore they must be in

proportion. They represent the Workmanship wherewithall the sowle

of man was made like vnto his Creator.

But I vnderstand you shall haue a paynter shortly.

Δ—I pray you, what paynter may best [serue] serve for the purpose? Can master

Lyne serue the turn well?

Il.—Dost thow think that God can be glorified in hell, or can diuells dishonor him?

Can Wickednes of a paynter, deface the mysteries of God?

The truth is, I am cōme to aduertise you, least with a small error

you be led, far, a syde.

Let me see the forme of your Table

Δ—I shewed him the Characters and words which were to be paynted

rownd abowt in the border of the Table.

Il—How do you like [it?] those letters? Δ I know not well what I

may say. For, perhaps, that which I shuld like, wer not so to be lyked:

and contrarywise what I shold think well of, might be nothing worth.

Il—Thow sayest well.

Behold, great is the fauor and mercy of God toward those whome he

fauoreth. All things are perfect but onely that: Neyther

was that shewed or deliuered by any good and perfect messager

from God. A wicked powre did intrude him self, not

onely into your societie, but allso into the Workmanship of Gods mysteries

Sathan dare presume to speak of the Almighty. Those Charac=

ters are diuilish: and a secret band of the Diuell. But, this sayeth the lord, I will rayse them vp, whom he hath ouer thrown: and blott

oute his fote steps where they resist my glorie. Neyther will

I

Marginal notes:

line 22: The mysticall / Alphabet.

line 32: The Table / of Practise

line 42: Illuding / spirits thrus= / ting in them / selues.

[94b]

I suffer the faithfull to be led vtterly awry: nor finally permi< t darkness>

to enhemme them for euer. He sayeth, I AM, and they ar<e most untrue.>

But behold I haue browght the the truth: that the Prince of reas< on,> Go< d>

of Vnderstanding may be apparent in euery part of his Caelestiall de=

monstration. Therfore, as thow saydst vnto me ones,

So say I now to the: Serue god.

Make a square, of 6 ynches euery way

The border therof let it be (here) but half a inche: but on the Table it

self, let it be an inche broad.

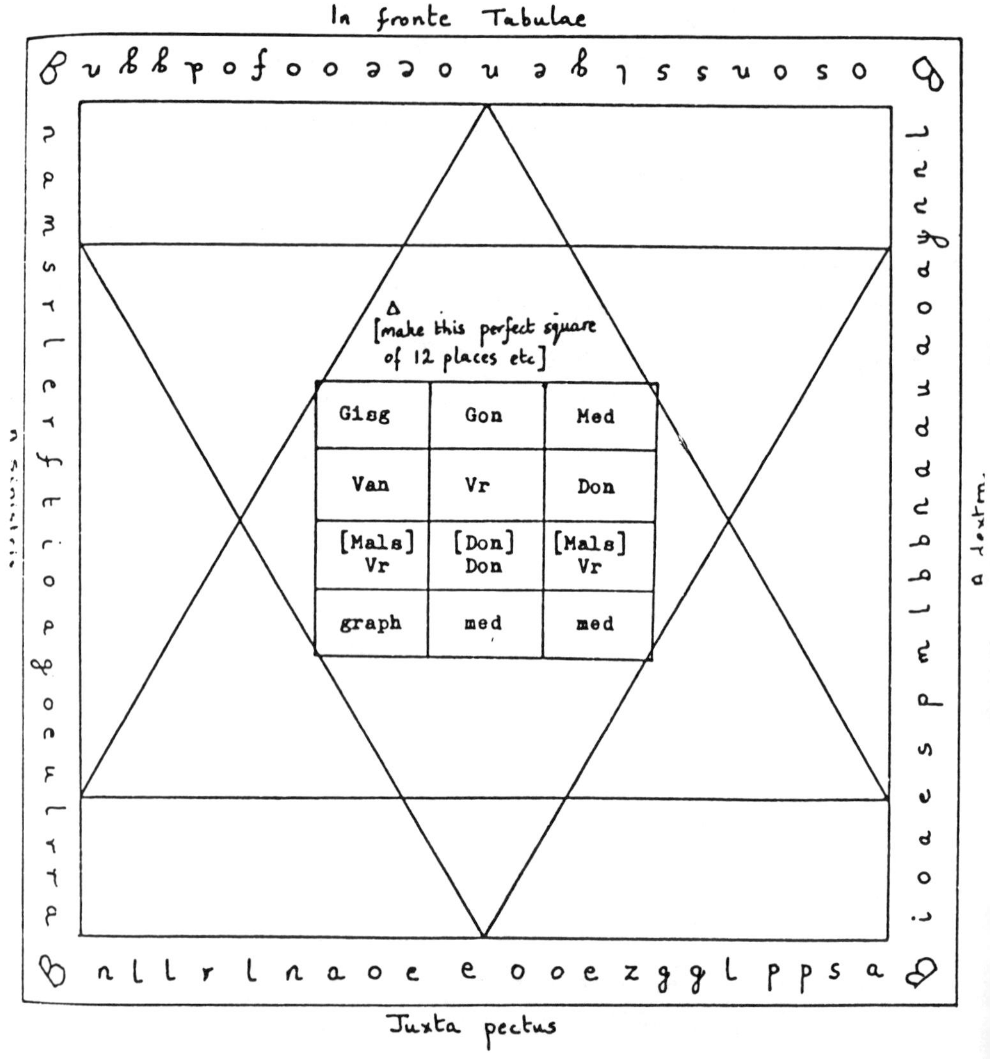
In fronte Tabulae
Δ [make this perfect square of 12 places etc]
Gisg
Gon
Med
Van
Vr
Don
[Mals] Vr
[Don] Don
[Mals] Vr
graph
med
med
Juxta pectus

Euery one of those [sy] sides must haue 21 Characters

But, first, at euery corner make a great B

Prayer is the key of all good things:

Δ After

Marginal notes:

line 2: *I vnderstand / that the Charac / ters are most Vntrue

line 7: Δ* / The inner / square, of / 6 ynches;

line 10, RH upside down: Δ vide post. [2] foliā[e], et etiā in / Tabula cordis, carnis et / Cutis, nam in lineis def= / endentibus, ibidem habes / hanc tabula hic incipiendo / sed in primo omittendo l et accipiendo o [with hand pointing to first 'o' of top border of the table ('in fronte Tabulae')]

[95a]

Δ After our prayers made, E K had sight (in the stone) of innumerable letters

and after a little while, they wer browght into a lesser square and fewer letters.

first appered in the [opposite] border opposite to our standing place (which I haue

vsed to call, in fronte Tabulae) these letters following: beginning at the right

hand, and proceding toward the left.

.1.	2	3	4
Med	drux	drux	gon
fam	vn	vr	med
med	tal	vr	vn
drux	fam	don	graph
fam	don	vr	fam
fam	vr	drux	mals
Vr	graph	vn	tal
ged	don	med	vr
graph	or	graph	pa
drux	gisg	graph	pa
In fronte Tabulae	A sinistris	Juxta pectus	A dextris

med	gon	med	drux	
graph	med	med	vn	
graph	vn	graph	vn	
tal	ged	ceph	van	
med	med	ged	vn	
or	graph	ged	med	
med	van	vr	vn	
gal	vr	mals	gon	w th a prik
ged	don	mals	drux	
ged	don	fam	drux	
drux	vn	vn	vr	

Il——What haue you in the myddle of the Table? △ Nothing
IL. sigillum Emeth,

is to be sett there

Il——The rest, after supper.

△ Soli Deo Omnipotenti sit laus perennis.

Amen

/flourish/

Marginal notes:

line 20: forte med

line 29: Sigillū / Emeth.

After supper, returning to our businesse, I first dowted of the heds of the letters in the bordes, to be written, which way they ought to be turned, to /the/ center ward of the Table or from the center ward.

I1.———The heds of the letters must be next or toward the center of the square Table or Figure

Diuide that written by 12 and 7

△ I diuided it

I1.——— Grace, mercy and peace be vnto the liuely branches of his florishing

kingdom: and strong art thow in thy glory, which dost vnknytt the

secret partes of thy liuely workmanship: and that, before the weak

vnderstanding of man

Herein is thy powre and Magnificence opened vnto man: and why?

bycause thy diuinitie and secret powre is here shut vp in Numero

Ternario et Quaternario: à $\overset{o}{q}$ principium et fundamentum

omna huius est tui sanctissimi operis

For, yf thow (o God) be wunderfull and incomprehensible in thyne

owne substance, it must nedes follow, that thy works are likewise

incomprehensible. But, Lo, they shall now beleue, bycause they

see, which heretofore could skarsly beleue. strong is the

Influence of thy supercelestiall powre, and mighty is the force of

that arme, which overcommeth all things: let all powre

therfore rest in the. Amen.

Marginal notes:

line 39: Note of / the Square / within

line 47: Ternarius et / Quaternarius

[95b]

△ The spirituall creature seamed to eate fyre, like balls of fyre: hauing his face toward me, and his bak toward E K.

Il——Leave oute the Bees of the 7 names of the [Kings] seven Kings, and 7 Princis: and place them in a table diuided by 12 and 7: the 7 spaces being vppermost: and therein write, in the vpper line, the letters of the king, with the letters of his Prince following next after his name: and so of the six other, and theyr Princis: And read them on the right hand from the vpper part to the lowest, and thow shalt finde, then, the Composition of this Table.

Therein they are all comprehended, sauing certayn letters, which are not to be put in here: By reason that the Kings and Princis do spring from God; and not God from the Kings and Princis. Which excellency is comprehended, and is allso manifest, in that Third and Fowrth member.

Rownd abowt the sides [of this square] is euery letter of the 14 names, of the 7 kings and Princis

Hereafter shall you perceyue that the Glorie of this Table surmownteth the glorie of the sonne

All things els appertayning [to it] vnto it, are allready prescribed by your former instruction.

I haue no more to say, but God transpose your myndes, according to his own will and pleasure. You talked of Transposition.

Tomorrow I will be with you agayn. But Call not for me, least you incurre the danger of the former Curse.

l	o	m	e	g	a	n	o	g	i	l	a
o	g	o	n	r	o	l	e	g	o	b	o
s	e	f	a	f	e	l	e	l	a	b	a
o	n	o	m	t	u	r	o	p	e	n	y
n	o	d	s	i	l	l	o	p	s	a	n
s	e	g	r	o	r	n	e	[p] s	[s] p	a	n
s	e	g	l	a	r	a	z	a	m	u	l

[flourish]

Marginal notes:

line 4: 12 }
7

line 10: Note of / these kings / and Princis

line 15: The dignitie / of the Table / of Practise.

line 20: He alludeth / to our talk / [of Talk] had / of Transposi= / tion of letters

line 22: Note danger / of violating / precepts of / doctrine

line 28, RH: fortè / s p

[96a]

Aprilis 29. Monday, a meridie

Δ As E K and I wer talking of my [boke] boke Soyga, or Aldaraia: and I at length sayd that, (as far, as I did remember) Zadzaczadlin, was Adam by the Alphabet thereof, suddenly appeared the spirituall creature, which sayd yesterday that he wold cōme agayn, this day, vncalled: and at his first comming he sayd Then, à primo

Δ Qui primus est et nouissimus, Alpha et omega, misereatur n̄ri.

Il——Amen. Glorie be to the, which art one, and comprehending all.

Mervaylous is thy wisdome, in those, of whome, thow willt be comprehended.

A short prayer, but appliable to my purpose

Euery prayse, with vs, is a prayer.

Δ he taketh of, his pyed coat, threw it vp on the corner of my desk.

and then he seemed clothed in an ancient doctorly apparayle: and on his

hed he had a wrethe of white sylk of three braydes.

Il.——Well I will give you my lesson, and so byd you farewell

First I am to perswade you to put away wavering myndes.

Secondly, for your Instruction, in these necessarie occasions, thus it is:

The owtsides or skyn must be the centre. There is one fowndation.

The Flesh must be the owtside.

The Centre it self must be disseuered into 4 aequall partes.

There is your lesson

Δ We vnderstand not, this dark lesson

Il——The hart must be the fowrth part of the body; and yet the body

perfect and sownd. The skynne must occupy the place of the hart

and yet without deformitie

God is the begynning of all things: The fardest parte of all things is in

the hands of God.

The like shalbe fownd amongst the number of his One and most holy name:

The Erth is a fowndation to euery thing: and differeth but onely in forme

In the forme of his own application wherevnto it is applied.

God is the begynning of all things, but not after one sorte, nor to

euery one alike

But it is three manner of works, with his name:

The One, in respect of Dignification:

The Second, in respect of Conciliation:

The Third, in respect of an ende and determined Operation.

Now syr, to what ende, wold you were your Character?

△ at our two first dealings to gither, it was answered by a spirituall

creature (whome we toke to be Vriel,) sigillum hoc in auro

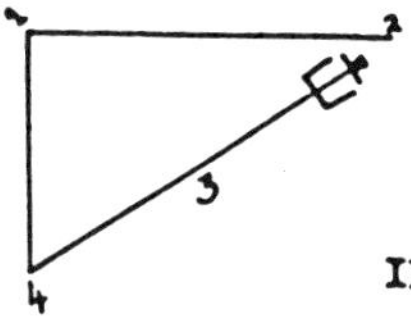

sculpendum, ad defensionem Corporis omni loco, tempore

et occasione, et in pectus gestandum.

IL—— But how do I teache?

The Character is an Instrumēt appliable onely

to Dignification

But there is no Dignification (syr) but that which

doth procede, and hath his perfect Composition,

Centrally, in the square number of 3 and 4

The Centre whereof shall be equall to the

greatest.

△ We Vnderstand not. IL—— Hereby you may gather

Marginal notes:

line 3: Adam

line 12: Apparayle / changed.

line 18: an aenigmat= /ticall lesson

line 28: Note

line 34: Three manner / of works with / God his Name

line 40: Vide inscriptionē / suo loco, / a° 1582 / Martij die / 10 / f. 6

[96b]

Note here of the 7 Tables of Creation how they apperteyn to the 7 kings and Princis.

not onely, to what ende, the blessed Character, (wherewith thow shalt be
dignified) is prepared, but allso the nature of all other Characters.

To the second——————Δ Conciliation you meane.

Il——The Table is an Instrument of Conciliation.
And so are the other 7 Characters: which you call by the
name of Tables, squared out into the forme of Armes: which
are propre to euery king and Prince according to theyr
order.

Now to the last: Δ As concerning the ende and determined Operation

Il——It onely consisteth in the mercy of God, and the Characters of these
bokes. For, Behold, As there is nothing that commeth or
springeth from God, but it is as God, and hath a secret Maiesticall and inexplicable Operation in it: So euery
letter here bringeth furth the Names of God: But, (in dede),
they are but one Name; But according to the locall and
former being, to comprehend the vniversall generation corruptible
and incorruptible of euery thing. It followeth, then, it must
nedes comprehend the ende of all things

This much, hitherto

The Character is fals and diuilish

He that dwelleth in the, hath told the, so, long ago

The former Diuel, did not onely insinuat him self, but these things

Δ I do mervayle, that we had no warning hereof ere now, and that I was

often tymes called on, to prepare those /thing^c^s/ (character and Table): and yet they

were fals

Il——— Yf it shold haue byn gon abowt to be made, it shuld not haue byn suffred

to [pass r] pass vnder the forme of wyckednes.

The Truth is to be gathered vppon the first Demonstration (my de=

monstration and yours are not all one: you will not be offended w/th/

me, syr).

I gaue the a certayn principle, which in it self is a sufficient demons

stration: I told the, the placing of the Centre, the forme of

it, with a lineamentall placing and ordring of that which

thow lookest for Δ But truely I vnderstand not.

Il——— I teache. Take cleane paper

It must be made 4 inches square

Pray. Δ We prayed.

Il—— These letters, which I shall speak now thow shalt, afterward,

put them in theyr propre characters:

Write: Neuer since the begynning of the world was this

secret deliuered, nor this holy mysterie set open, before

the Weaklings of this world

Write in the vppermost prik O,

and h on the right hand, and g on the left etc

The two extreme priks, one on the right hand, a and the other

---

Marginal notes:

line 4: The Nature / of all Charac= / ters.

line 7: Instruments / of Concilia= / tion

line 9: NOTE

line 10: Order

line 14: This boke / of 48 Tables

line 17: Note of the / Names of / God.

line 19: Generatiō — corrup

line 20: — incor.

line 23: The Charac= / ter allso / was a falls / tradition

line 29: Note

line 32: * / lepidè, mathe- / maticas meas / demonstrationes / denotat

line 37: *he meaneth / my propre / Character / truely made

line 41: Note. These / to be put in / propre Charac= / ters

[97a]

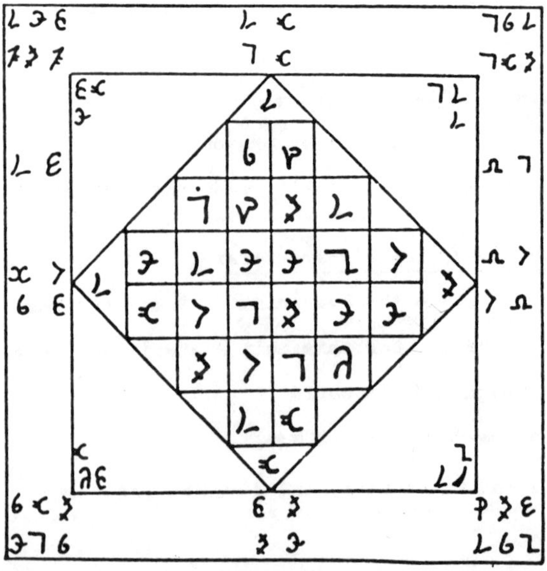

[97b]

/blank/

[98a]

other, on the left o etc

There is the Whole

Δ We prayed (vnbidden) in respect of the mysterie revealed.

E K, was skarse able to abide or endure the voyce of the spirituall Creature, when he spake of these things now: [it] the sownd was so forcible to his hed that it made it ake vehemently.

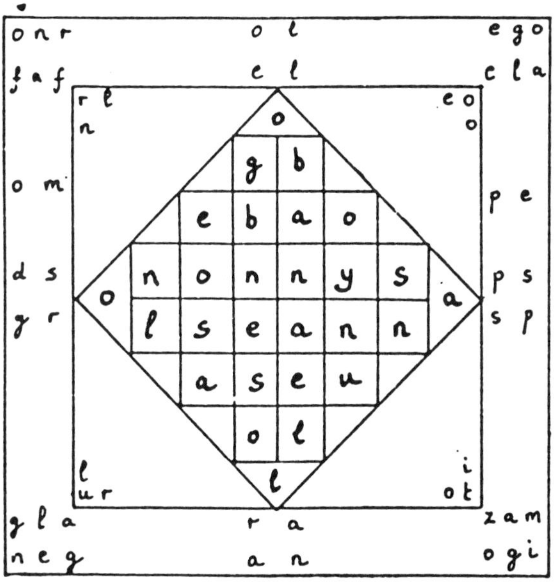

I1——Set down the kings, and theyr Princis in a Table (as thow knowest them:

with theyr letters backward: excepting theyr Bees, from the right hand, to the left.

Let Bobogel be first, and Bornogo, is his prince.

o	g	o	n	r	o	l	e	g	o	b	o
s	e	f	a	f	e	l	e	l	a	b	a
o	n	o	m	t	u	r	o	p	e	n	y
n	o	d	s	i	l	l	o	p	s	a	n
s	e	g	r	o	r	n	e	s	p	a	n
s	e	g	l	a	r	a	z	a	m	u	l
l	o	n	e	g	a	n	o	g	i	l	a

IL.——Here is the skynn turned into the Centre: and the Centre turned into 4 partes

of the body

Δ I see now allso, how, the flesh, is become the owtside: o g e l o r n o etc.

Il. I haue done tyll sone.

Δ Deo nro Oipotenti perennis laus sit et immensa gloria Amen

[flourish]

Marginal note:

line 11: Δ/ Note here the / three diuerse man= / ners how the letters / ar encumpassed. / The midder is called / .1. the Hart or centre / those abowt enclo= / sing the hart, ar / .2. called the flesh, / and the two owtside / pillers (of two letters / in a row) is cowne / .3. and the skyn.

NOTE

Δ After that these things were finished, [and] E K rose vp from y^e table and went to ^{c}/the/ west window, to reade a letter which was, euen than, browght him from his wife: which being done, he toke a little prayer*boke (in english meter made by one William Hunnis which m^r Adrian Gilbert had [left] here and it lay on the Table by vs all the while of this last action) and with this boke, he went into his bed chamber, intending to pray on it, a certayn prayer, which he liked: and as he opened the boke, his ey espied strange writing in the spare white paper at the bokes ende and beholding it, iudged it verily to be his own letters, and the thing of his own doing: but being assured that he never saw the like of this Character [for Conciliation], and that other, (notified by the hart or Center, skyn and flesh before this present howre, he ^{c}/be/ cam astonied, ^{c}/and/ in great wrath; and behold, suddenly, One appered to him and sayd, Lo, this is as good as that other. meaning that, which we had receyued, and is here before sett down on the former page.

With this newes cam E K to me, as I was writing down fayre this last Action, and sayd, I haue strange matter to impart vnto you: The<n> sayd I what is that? and at the fyrst (being yet tossed in his mynde with this great iniurie of the suttle supplanter of man, [and] ambitiously intruding him self, to rob god of his glory) he sayd, you shall know, and at length shewed me this little paper, here, by, being the one of the white leafes in the ende of the /forsayd/[c] little prayer boke. And I vewing it to be ment to be the counterfeat of ours; but, with all, imperfect diuerse wayes, after the order of our method: yea thowgh[t] the words, out of which it had sprong had bin good, and sufficient: and thereat laughed at, and derided the Wicked enemy, for his envy, his ass hedded folish ambition, and in dede mere blyndenes to do any thing well. To conclude, we fownd, that with an incredible spede this Diuilish figure was written down by some Wicked spirit, to bring our perfect doings in dowt with vs: thereby eyther to provoke vs to /vtter/[c] vndue speaches of gods good creatures, or to wavering myndes of the Worthynes and goodnes of the same /things receyued/[c], and so eyther to leaue of, or with fayntharted wavering to procede. But I /by gods grace/[c] (contrary to such inconveniency) [being] /was/ armed with constancie, and confident good hope, that God wold not suffer me, (putting my trust in his goodnes and mercy, to receyue wisdome from him) to be so vniustly dealt withall or vnkindely or vnfatherly vsed at his hands etc. and entended after supper to make my ernest complaint to the diuine Maiestie [of] /against/ this wicked intrusion and temptation of the Illuding diuell: and so we went to supper.

Marginal notes:

line 4: * / The Title of the / boke was Seuen / sobs of a sorrowfull / sowle for synne.

1583. Aprilis 29. Monday. after supper. hora 8.

△ I went into my oratorie, and made a fervent prayer agaynst the spirituall enemy: specially meaning the wicked one who had so suddenly so suttily and so liuely cownterfeted the hand and letters of E K: as is here before declared, and by the thing it self may appere here: Likewise E K on his knees (at the greene chayre standing before my chymney) did pray: after which prayers ended, I yea, rather, before they were ended, on my behalf, E K espyed a spirituall creature cōme to my Table: whome he toke to be IL. and so, a lowd, sayd He is here. and therevppon I cam to my desk, to write as occasion shold serue: [or receyue] And before I began to do any thing I rehersed part of my intent, vttred to god by prayer and half turned my specha to god him self, as the cause did seme to require Therevppon that spirituall /creature/ [c] who, as yet had sayd nothing, suddenly vsed these words ——————— I give place to my better.

E K. There semeth to me Vriel to come, and IL to be gone away. △ Then began that new come Creature to say thus

---

Marginal notes:

line 39: △ —— prayed

line 43: E K prayed

o	r	i	a	m	s	e	a	e	h a
o	r	i	a	n	b	s	e	a	h a
o	r	i	a	n	h	s	e	a	h a
a	r	h	i	a	n	h	s	e	a h
a	r	n	a	x	o		d	a	x o
p	a	l	g	a	n		h	a	h o
n	a	x	a	p	h		a	r	o

a l n	g a	d a x
n o p	e x	a l g
	o e a u a o r h a	
a r	b r a h	t a
	a m o f t[h] m o v n t e r h	
n o	a r v a[h]	q r
	i e[h]	
a l	a a l l x a p	a r
a h r	n o	t o x
a h a	x a	a l g

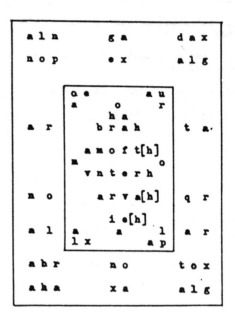

Marginal notes:

line 1, RH: o h a h r a h a m o x [E K's hand]

line 11, RH: △ / Belmagel / his cownter= / feating of ♉ / instruction re= / ceyued frō god, / and to E K / his hand, as / likely as could be [Dee's hand]

[99b]

[blank]

to say thus

Most abundant and plentifull are the great mercies of God vnto them which truely and vnfaynedly feare, honor and beleue him The Lord hath hard thy prayers, and I am VRIEL, and I haue browght the peace of God, which shall from henceforth viset you.

If I had not made this action perfect (sayeth the lord) and wrowght some perfection in you, to the ende you might performe: yea, if I had not had mercies (sayeth the lord) over the infinite number and multitude of sowles, which are yet to put on the vilenes and corruption of the flesh, Or if it wer not time to loke down, and behold the sorrow of my Temple, Yet wold I, for my promiss sake, and the establishing of my kingdom, verifie my mercies vppon the sonns of men: Wherevnto I haue Chosen three of you, as the mowthes and Instruments of my determined purpose. Therfore (sayeth the Lorde) Be of stowte and courragious mynde in me, for me, and for my truth sake: And Fear not the assales of temptation, For I haue sayd, I am with you. But as mercy is necessary for those that repent, and faithfully forget theyr offenses, so is Temptation requisite and must ordinarilie follow those, whome it pleaseth to illuminate with the beames of triumphant sanctification

Yf Temptation wer not, how shold the sonnes of men (sayeth the lord) know me to be mercifull? But I am honored in hell, and wurshipped with the blasphemers: *Pugna erit, vobis autem victoria*: yet, albeit, (thus sayeth my message) I will defend you from [the] crueltie of these dayes to come and will make you perfect: that perfectly you may begynne in the works

of my perfection: But, what? and doost thow (sathan) think to
triumph? Behold (sayeth the God of Justice) I will banish thy servants
from this place and region; and will set stumbling bloks before the feete
of thy ministers: Therfore, be it vnto the, as thow hast deserued: And
be it to this people, and holie place, (as it is, the will of god; which I
do pronownce) light without darkness, Truth without falshode,
righteousnes without the works of wickednes. I haue pronownced it,
and it is done
But thow, o yongling (but, old synner,) why dost thow suffer thy
blyndenes thus to encrease: or why dost thow not yeld thy lymmes to
the service and fullfilling of an aeternall veritie?
Pluck vp thy hart. Let it not be hardened. Follow the waye
that leadeth to the knowledge of the ende; the open sight of god his word
verified for his kingdoms sake.
you began in Tables, and that of small accownt: But be faithfull: for
you shalbe written within Tables of perfect and euerlasting remembrance. Considering the truth, which is the message of him which is
the fowntayne and life of the true, perfect and most glorious life to come,
Follow, loue, and diligently Contemplate the mysteries therein.
He that hath done this euill, hath not onely synned against the, but against
God, and against his truth. Judgment is not of me, and therefore
I cannot

Marginal notes:

line 41: Vriel

line 9: Note, sowles / created before / the bodies are / begotten

line 13: Three elected

line 15: Fortitudo in deo / et propter Deum.

line 19: Temptation / necessarie

line 25: A perfect be= / gynning

line 27: Sentencia cōtra / istū Malignum / spūm qui nobis / imponere voluit.

line 34: * / He spake to E K.

[100b]

I can not pronownce it: But what his Judgment is, he knoweth in him self. His name is BELMAGEL and he is the fyrebrand which hath followed thy sowle from the begynning; yea seking his destruction. Who can better cownterfeat, than he, that in thy wyckednes is chief lord and Master of thy spirites: or who hath byn acquaynted with the secrets of mans fingers so much as /⌐[c that] 7 hath byn directer? My sayings are no accusation: neyther is it my propertie to be defyled with such profession. But I cownsayle you generally; and aduertise you [throwgh] throwgh the grace and by the spirit of vnspeakable mercy. This night, yf your prayers had not byn, yea, if they had not perced into the seat of him which sitteth aboue: Thow, yea (I say) thow hadst byn carryed, and taken awaye, this night, into a willdernesse, so far distant hence Northward, that thy destruction had followed. Therfore lay away thy works of youth; and fly from fleshly Vanities yf not vppon Joye and pleasure of this presence, yet for the glorie of him that hath chosen you.

I say be strong: Be humble, with Obedience: For,
All the things, that haue byn spoken of, shall co͞me to pass: And there shall not be a letter of the boke of this prophesie perish.
Finally, God hath blessed you, and will kepe you from temptation and will be mercifull vnto you: and perfect you, for the dignitie of your profession sake: Which, world without ende, for euer and euer, with vs and all creatures, and in the light of his own cowntenance, be honored.

Amen Amen Amen

Δ Herevppon I made most humble prayer wth harty thanks to our God, for his help, cumfort, and Judgment against our enemie, in this case, (so greatly concerning his glorie). And at my standing vp I vnderstode that Vriel was out of sight to E K. yet I held on my purpose to thank him, and to prayse god for Vriel that his so faithfull [and frutefull] ministerie vnto his diuine Maiestie, executed to our nedefull comfort in so vehement a temptation.

Deo n͞ro Omnipotenti, sit o͞is laus, honor, et gratiarum actio, nunc et in perpetuu͞

Amen

[flourish]

Marginal notes:

line 2: Angelus malus / proprius ip͞ius / E K.

line 7: Δ / Diuels are / accusers pro= / prely.

line 11: E K had byn car= / ryed away in the / wrath of God / if fervent prayer / had not byn, as / may appere in the / begynning of this / mightie Action.

line 19: The boke of / this Prophesie / shall contynue

line 20: Δ ∻ a malo Temp / tationis

line 22: Δ / Professio mea / est Philosophia / vera. / vide Libro / primo.

[101a]

/5./ Maij [4] Sonday. a meridie hor. 4 vel circiter.

Δ Forasmuch as, on fryday last, while my frende E K was abowt writing

of the Tables he was told that the same shuld be finished on monday next:

and that on sonday before, (it is to wete, this present sonday) at after none,

all dowtes shold be [and] answered; after, the after /^{c}none/ had so passed, as tyll

somewhat past 4 of the clok: Then, we fell to prayer, and after a

quarter of an howres invocation to god, and prayers made, E K sayd, here

is one. whome ([in dede]) we toke to be Vriel: as he was, in dede

I had layd 28 questions or articles of dowtes in writing vppon my desk,

open, ready for me to rede (vppon occasion) to our spirituall instructor: who,

thus began his speche, after I had vsed a few wordes begynning

with this sentence. Beati pedes, evangclizantiā pacem etc

Vriel—The very light and true wisdome (which is the somme of my message,

and will of him that sent me) make you perfect and establish those things, which he hath sayd, and /hath/[c] decreed: and likewise your myndes, that you may be apt vesselis to receyve so abundant mercies. Amen. △ Amen, per te Jesu Christe: Amen.

Vr —— This boke, and holy key, which vnlocketh the secrets of god his determination, as concerning the begynning, present being, and ende of this world, is so reuerent and holy: that I wonder (I speak in your sense) whie it is deliuered to those, that shall decay: so excellent and great are the Mysteries therein conteyned, aboue the capacitie of man: This boke (I say) shall, to morrow be finished: One thing excepted: which is the vse thereof. Vnto the which the lord hath appointed a day. But (bycause I will speak to you after the manner of men) See that all things be in redynes agaynst the first day of August next. Humble your selues nine dayes before: yea, vnrip (I say) the cankers of your infected sowles that you may be apt and meet to vnderstand the secrets, that shalbe deliuered. For why? The Lord hath sent his angels allready to viset the earth, and to gather the synnes thereof to gither, that they may be wayed before him in the balance of Justice: and Then is the tyme that the promise of God, shalbe fullfilled. Dowt not for, we are good Angells.

The second of the greatest prophesie is this (o ye mortall men). For the first was of him self, that He shold come: And this, is from him. [self]: in respect /of/[c] that he will come. Neyther are you to speak the wordes of this Testimonie, in one place, or in one people,

but, that the Nations of the whole world may knowe

that there is a GOD which forgetteth not the truth of his

promise, nor the sauegarde of his chosen, for the

greatnes of his glory.

Marginal notes:

line 18: This Holy / boke

line 23: The boke to be / finished to morrow / /rule/

line 24: The day appoin= / ted for the Vse / of this boke / Augusti .1. / /rule/

line 27: Our nine / dayes contrition / preparatiue / /rule/

line 31: Angels sent / to viset the / heaps of sinnes / in the world / abownding etc.

line 35: Good Angels.

line 36: The second / of the greatest / prophesie, is / this.

line 40: Our Testi= / mony of this / Prophesie, / all the World / ouer, to be (by / Vs) published.

[101b]

Therfore (I say) prepare your bodies, that they may be strong enowgh,

for armors of great profe. Of your selfs, you cannot: But desire

c
/ssire/ and it shall be giuen vnto you. For Now, is euen that wicked childe·

c
grown vp [vnto] /vnto/ perfection: and the fier tungs red to open his Jaws

Wo therfore shalbe to the Nations of the Earth: and Wo Wo

innumerable to those that say, We Yelde:

Wickednes (o lorde) is crept vp, and /hath/ [c] filled the dores of thy holy sanctuarie: defyled the dwelling places of thy holy Angels: and poysenned the earth, as her own seat.

Im 40 dayes more must this boke be perfyted in his own marks to the intent that you allso may be perfyted in the workman=ship of him, which hath sealed it.

=ner

Oute of this, shall be restored the holy bokes, which haue perished euen from the begynning, and from the first that liued

And herein shalbe deciphred perfect truth from imperfect falshode, True religion from fals and damnable errors,

With all Artes: which are propre to the vse of man, the first and sanctified perfection: Which when it hath spred spread ⟨a⟩ a While, THEN COMMETH THE ENDE.

Thy Character must haue the names of the fiue Angels (written in the myddst of Sigillum Emeth) graven vppon the other side in a circle. In the myddst whereof, must the stone be,

Which was allso browght: Wherein, thow shallt, at all times behold, (priuately to thy self,) the state of gods people throwgh the Whole [world] earth.

The fowre fete of the Table must haue hollow things of swete wood, wherevppon, they may stand: within the hollownes wherof, thy seales may be kept vnperished.

One month is all, for the Vse thereof.

Thus sayeth the Lord, when I browght you vp in likenes of birds, encreasing you, and suffring you to touche the skyes, [and call the sterrs to testimonie thereof] I opened vnto you the ende of your reioycing: For, this Doctrine shall towche the skyes, and call the sterrs to testimonie therof: And your fotesteps shall viset (allmost) [all] the partes of the [world] whole world.

The sylk, must be of diuerse cullors, the most changeable that can be gotten. For, who, is hable to behold the glory of the seat of God?

All

Marginal notes:

line 1: Our bodyes to / be made / strong

line 4: Antichriste / is allmost / ready for / his practise

line 10: 40 dayes more / for the tables / writing in their / own Characters.

line 13: The frute / of this boke

line 21: The backside / of my Cha= / racter.

line 22: The Vse of / the stone / which a good / Angel browght / to me the / last yere. / Remember it is / half an inche thik

line 26: The 4 hollow / fete of the / Table

line 29: The Vse of the / Table of prac= / tise is onely / for one Month.

line 31: * / Vide sup^{a} / A^{o} 1582 Maij 4.

line 35: Great long / iornayes to / be gon of vs two

line 37: The Cullor / of the silk / for the Table

[102a]

All these things must be vsed, as that day.

All errors and dowtes ells may be amended by the rules of reason: But Notwithstanding, Ask, and thow shalt be answered.

Δ. As concerning Mals don mals, what is the veritie to be placed in the middle of my practise Table?

Vr. — Write

o	o	e	rather thus	t	i	o
l	r	l		u	l	r
r	l	u		l	r	l
o	i	t		e	o	o

Δ from whense, are these taken?

Vr. They owght to be gathered of those names, which are first ga= thered by the, [by] by ordre: (In the myddst of them:) [the] the Kings and Princis being placed, as thow (of thy invention) [dost] diddst gather them: Not putting theyr own princis, next to the kings: but as they follow in Tabula, collecta by the: as thus

a	l	i	g	o	n	o	r	n	o	g	o
o	b	o	g	e	l	e	f	a	f	e	s
a	b	a	l	e	l	u	t	m	o	n	o
y	n	e	p	o	r	l	i	s	d	o	n
n	a	s	p	o	l	r	o	r	g	e	s
n	a	p	s	e	n	r	a	l	g	e	s
l	u	m	a	z	a	a	g	e	n	o	l

Δ Wherfore is the Table of Kings and Princis set down in so diuerse manners?

.1: as, one, to haue Bobogel and Bornogo in the first row: an other to haue

.2: Baligon and Bagenol (his prince) in the first row: and here thirdly

.3. Baligon and Bornogo: and in the Heptagonon Blumaza semeth to be first, discoursed of, and his prince and Ministers: but very secretly:

4. Vr. Blumaza is the first, in respect (And so all the rest, are the first in

respect) of theyr own being. That secret is not to be deliuered but by the distinction of the boke. Notwithstanding, thow hast truely considered of it all ready.

Δ I required the perfect forme of the 21 letters, that I might imitate the same in the Table of practise, and in the holy boke writing etc.

[Vr They shall be deliuered to morrow.

Whether is the King his Name Bnaspen, or Bnapsen?

[Vr. Bnapsen.

Δ The Character or Lamine for me was noted (Noueb 17. A° 1582 /1p.85/) that it shold cōteyne sōme token of my name: and now, in this, (accownted the true Character of Dignification) I perceyue no peculier mark, or letters of my name

[Vr. The forme in euery corner, considereth thy name. Δ you meane there to be a certayn shaddow of Δelta. Vr. Well.

Δ Bycause many things do seeme to be taken from vnder the Table, as out of a stoare howse, shall there be any shelf framed vnder our square Table of Practise or handsome stole set in apt place to lay things on?

Vr. These things that were deliuered by show, vnder an Imagined Table, were

the

Marginal notes:

line 1: <.....> the / <fir>st of / August / next.

line 6, RH: Δ So they seeme / to haue byn / ment in the figure / of the Table / of practise / before described.

line 15: The Princis / here not / put next / to their / kings.

line 25: Note. / .4. diuerse / Wayes.

line 30: A Secret of / preeminence / due to the Kings / etc: as in Astro / logy. I vse to mak / every planet a / base / or a / grownd / in his / propre / signification etc / & so every / howse of / the 12 / &c. in respect of / his proper and / essentiall signifi= / cation.

line 42: The Sym / bolum of / my name / in my character / how and where

---

[102b]

The mēbres of God his secret Prouidence,

the members of God his [prouidence] secret Prouidence, distributed vnto his Ang< ells>

as the Principals of theyr Officis. But vnder thy Table is nothing to be set.

Δ What more vses are there of the great Circle or globe, wherein there are Capitall letters vnder the Kings names and Characters: and allso there are other letters with numbers: of which we haue receyued no instruction: and more ou͡t of these letters, sōme are aversed and some euersed, etc?

Vr —The letters turned bak to bak, (⌈bei^c^ng⌉ [the] Capitall letters,) ar aequally to be diuided, according to their numbers, with a circle cumpassing the name and Cha= racter of the king vnder which they are placed

The other letters, whose greatest number doth not excede 7, are certayn By notes of wicked and euill powres: which cannot, any way, but by the towchestone of truth be deciphred from the good. Wherof Notice shall be given at large by the boke.

He that standeth in the myddst of the globe, signifieth Nature

wherevppon, in the first point, is the Vse and practise of this work

that is to say, as concerning the first part. for it is sayde before

The Boke conteyneth three kinde of Knowledges

.3. 1 The knowledge of GOD, truely

.2. 2 The number, and doing of Angels, perfectly

.1. 3 The begynning and ending of Nature, substantially.

And this hath answered a great dowte.

Δ What is the vse of the 7 lamines, (like armes,) and from what grownde

are they framed or deriued?

Vriel—— They are the ensignes of the Creation; wherewithall they were created by God:

known onely by theyr acquayntance, and the manner of theyr doings.

Δ Are they to be made in any mettall?

Vr ——— They are to be made in [pure tynne] purified tynne: And to be vsed at the time

of theyr Call

Δ Ar the letters there to be altered into the holy [Ch] Alphabet letters or characters?

Vr Into theyr propre Characters. Δ May I not vse them as they ar, vnaltered? Vr —— < .... >

Δ How to be vsed; hanged or layd?

Vr To be layd before the vppon the Table. Or thow mayst place them, (yf thow

wilt,) contynually at the 7 angles of the Holy seale: laying them

besides, and against the points or Angles of the Holy Seale: 7 ynches

from the Vtter border of the holy Seale, all at ones: Or els they may be paynted, On the Table.

Δ What is the [vse] fowndation of the first 40 letters, in the principall, or

holy seale Emeth: and what other vses haue they, then yet hath byn

spoken of: And what is the reason of suche theyr consequence, or

following eache other, seing in our practise we cull them out by a pa

culier order?

Vr ——— Thow hast nothing there, but what hath byn sufficiently spoken of.

Δ yf 42 letters be 42 names, and 42 persons, how shall distinction be made

betwene any two or three, of one name and in one row?

Vr ——— How canst thow distinguish any thing with god?

Δ Lord I know not

Vr ——— Yet, by the boke it shall be perfectly known: but by skyll aboue

nature.

Δ Hau<e>

Marginal notes

line 3, over 'pals' of 'Principals': ples

line 9:

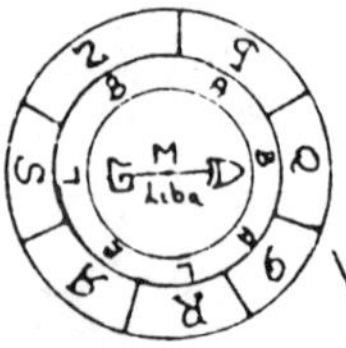

Δ perhaps somewhat like this

line 15: The man in the / myddst of the / globe or circle

line 18: Three kinde of / Knowledges in / this boke.

line 23, over 'lamines': Tables
line 25: The 7 ensignes / of creation
line 28: At the time / of theyr call.
line 31: Letters / to be / altred
line 37: The 7 ensignes / to be paynted on / the Table.
line 43: sup

a line joins 'Nature' (line 15) to 'Nature' (line 21), then to 'first part' (line 17) and then to '.1.' (line 21).

[103a]

Δ Haue I rightly applyed the dayes to the Kings?

Vr—The dayes are rightly applyed to the Kings

Δ How is the phrase The fifth of the seventh vnderstode, which Befafes speaketh of him self?

Vr—He speaketh so of him self, in respect that he shall be the fifth that shall be Vsed. In consideration of Nature he is the fifth, allthowgh not consequently in the Order of Operation

Δ It was promised that we shold be instructed, whan the Day (in this practise) is to be accownted to begynne.

Vr—It is not to be enquired, which is sufficiētly towght, it is a thing most easy, and perfectly deliuered.

Δ Adrian Gilbert how far, or in what points is he to be made priuie of our practise? seing it was sayd, That none shall enter into the Knowledge of these mysteries with me, but onely this worker. Truely the man is very cumfortable to our societie.

Vr—He may be made priuie of some things: such as shall be necessarie for the necessitie of the Necessities wherevnto he shall be driuen.

Δ The phrase of the last Ternarie, which, Baligom (otherwise named Carmara, or Marmara) vsed, I vnderstand not.

Vr—He is the ende of the Three last corruptible times: wherof, this is the last.

Δ The one, at Noes flud ended, the second at Christ his first comming and this is the third.

Vr—It is so.

Δ The Characters and words ānexed to the Kings names in the vtter circumference of the great circle or Globe: How are they to be vsed?

Vr—They are to be paynted vppom swete wood: and so to be held in thy hand, as thow shallt haue cause to vse them.

Δ For the bringing of the erthes hither from the places of hidden Threasor, what is your order and direction?

Vr—After you haue eaten, it shall be told you.

Δ We prayed, and so went to supper

/flourish/

Marginal notes:

line 1: <......> Dayes and there / <....>ngs

line 4: Befafes

line 12: A G.

line 13: sup§

line 18: The last / Ternarie.

line 21: Three / times

line 24: Vide supra pa= / gina praecedente.

line 27: Δ / The 7 / characters / of the 7 kings / as on the / former page / is Babalel / Liba etc.

1583

The same sonday. [M] Maij .5. [after supper hora 8½

Δ After diuerse our eiaculations and pangs of prayer and thanks vnto god, this was sayed

Vr—Be it thus vnto you [He prayeth in his own language]

After this holy boke is finished, then is it necessarie with expedition that the foresayd commaundemēt, as concerning the fatching of the earth, be fullfilled and performed. And be it vnto you as HE will. And HE sayeth thus.

My angel shall be amongst you, and shall direct his iornay: and will bring his feete, euen into the place and places, where that erthly filth and Corruption lieth. Behold I will deale mercifully with him. For, Error shall not deceyue him. Notwithstanding what I will haue done with it

---

Marginal note :

line 39: Expedition

[103b]

or how it shall be bestowed, is yet to be enquired of.

Secret are the determinations, and vnsearchable purposes, wherewithall the most mightiest dealeth with worldlings, and loketh vnto the v< se> and necessarie application of worldly things. Many temptations shall assayle him in following this commaundement. But it is sayd, I Will be with him. God will deale mercifully with you This is sufficient.

Yet ones more. Yf thow haue any dowte herein it shall be satisfied.

Δ What if he go first to Nubery, and with the erth being taken thence, to procede to the other places noted in the skroll and then with the erth of those ten places, the rest of the skroll, the boke therewith fovnd, and the red congeled thing in the hollow stone, to cōme directly hither: and then the rest of the peculier practise for enioying the premisses, to be lerned. or how els will you haue him order his iornay

Vr— As thow wilt herein, so shall it be browght to pas.

Δ As concerning the Victorious Captayn [The Lord Albert Laski] [Alasko] the Polake who so much desyreth my acquayntance, and Conference, how sha<11> I vse my self, to God his best liking, my Cuntries honor, and my own good Credit?

Vr—Remember, it is sayde, that the Princis of the earth shall not discredit, much lesse work thy Confusion. He that dwelleth in the, above worldes: and shall give the sufficient discretion worldly, in worldly occasions. For, Where the blessings of God are, euery thing is perfyted.

Δ As concerning the Chamber for Practise, appointed by me, and the half pace whereon the Table standeth, how is allowed <of?>

Vr—The place can not sanctifie the Action, but the Action the place But I answer the, after the manner of men, It is sufficient

Δ The 4 hollow feete for comprehending the 4 letter seales, how great owght they to be?

Vr. According to the fete, of the nearest proportion And so, as the heith of the Table, be, as it, now, is.

E K. He semeth now to sit in the ayre: but I perceyue no chayre behinde him.

△ Are all these things of this dayes Action to be Noted with your name: as Vriel?

I am Vriel, which allwayes will answer vntill this Action be finished

I teache. Be Mercifull, Thankfull, and mery in him, and for him for whose name you shall susteyne much bodyly sadnes

More then my mesage, I may not: And it is done

△ As

Marginal notes:

line 1: How the / Threasor is to / be vsed

line 13: The Skroll / The Boke / The red powder

line 18: Albertus / Laski, / Palatinus / Siradiensis / venit ex / Polonia Londiniū / 1583. Maij initio

line 24: My good Angel.

line 30: ∴ Hereby may many / other answers / be cōsidered

line 40: VRIEL

line 43: Multa nobis / perpetienda / propter Deū / nostrum / Ōipotētem

---

[104a]

△ As concerning the Vision which yester night was presented (vnloked for) to the sight of E K as he sat at supper with me, in my hall, I meane: the appering of the very sea, and many ships thereon, and the Cutting of the hed of a woman, by a tall blak man, What are we to imagin therof?

Vr — The One, did signifie the prouision of forrayn powres against the Welfare of this land: which they shall shortly put in practise:

The other, the death of the Quene of Scotts It is not long vnto it.

The Maiestie of his invisible powre, which overcommeth all things be among you, vppon you, and rest with you for euer

Δ Amen

E K. At his last words he flung fyre with his hands from him toward vs, and it spred it self in the manner of a Crosse.

Δ Gloria sit sempiterna Deo nr̄o

Omnipotenti et AEterno

Amen

[flourish]

Marginal notes:

line 4:

line 8: Note The Quene / of Scotts / to be behedded. / [rule] / So she was / A^{o} 1587 at / Fodringham Castell / And allso the / same yere a / great preparation / of ships against / Ēgland by the / King of Spayn / the Pope and / other Princis / called Catholik / etc

---

Maij: 6. Monday, I went to london,: and E K remayned [writing the Tables] attending the accomplishing of the promise, for the Tables ending and for the perfect forme of the holy letters receyuing: Which two points (when I cam home that after none), I fownd done. But it is to be Noted, that, When E K could not aptly imitate the forme of the Characters, or letters, as they were shewed: that then they appered drawn on his paper with a light yelow cullor, which he drew the blak vppon, and so the yellow cullor disapearing there remayned onely the shape of the letter in blak: after this mann͡ and iust of this quantitie and proportion

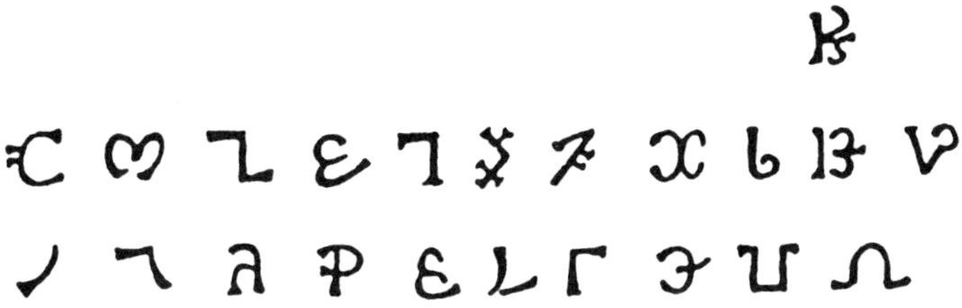

[flourish]

Marginal note:

line 27: Note.

[104b]

<Ma>ij 8. Wensday. After dynner hora circiter 4

△ Being desyrous to furder all things on my part to be performed, and < n.. > to lack the Cumpany of E K going for the Erthes (before spoken of) and to be away 10 or 12 dayes: and for as much as the boke was to be written in 40 dayes before August next: and vncertayn of those dayes whan they shold begynne: and allso for that I wold do all things (gladly) by warranty of cownsayle of our Instructor, I was desyrous to know whether the boke were to be written in paper or parchem̄et: in what cullor the lynes were to be ruled, grene or blew etc. and of diuerse other dowtes, necessary to be dissolued, I was carefull

to haue had some aduertisement. After long prayers of vs both,

Nothing was eyther seen in the ayre, or hard. Then it cam in my hed

to set furth the stone.

E K. sayd that assone as he loked into the stone, he saw there the Table, Chayr,

and three, com into the stone. Vriel sat down in the chayre: the

other two, inclined theyr body to him reverently: and then, stode by; one on the

one side of the chayre, the other, on the other side.

The sides of the Table cloth were turned vp, and a thing like an yong

shepe, bigger then a lamb, appered vnder the Table. Then they two did

knele before Vriel and sayd

Verus et sanctus et sempiternus.

Δ Then they rose agayn. and they semed to haue talk, a conference togither

and therevppon Vriel sayd

Vr Be it so, bycause powre is giuen vnto him.

E K. The Table, Chayre and all the [rest] three do disapere: and

therevppon immediately appered in the stone a fayre Pallace: and out

of the pallace cam a tall wellfauored man, very richely apparayled

with a braue hat and a fether on his hed: and after him followed a

great number, all like curteours. and this braue man sayd

Man—How pitifull a thing is it, when the wise, are deluded?

Δ—I smell the smoke; procede Syr, in your purpose.

Man I come hither, for the desyre I haue to do the good.

Δ —— Come you, or are you sent. Tell the Veritie I charge the, in the name and by the powre of the aeternall Veritie.

Δ Note: After I perceyued euidently that it was a wicked tempter, who had powr permitted him at this instant, I began with some Zeale and egreness to rebuke, and to charge him. But he stiffly and stowtely did contemne me a good while, mock me, and at length thretten to destroy me, my wife, and children. etc

Δ I therevppon made my ernest prayers to god agaynst this spirituall enemy: but he in the myddle of my prayers, sayed thus.

Man —— As truely as the Lord liueth, all that is done, is lies

Δ That, thy sentence, will I record agaynst the; to be layde to thy charge at the dredful day:

Δ After this great turmoyle past, was this voyce (following), hard of E K.

A voyce ——— Pereant tenebrae, cum Principe Tenebrarum

Δ All went suddenly out of sight, Prince and pallace and all

And the Chayre and Table and Vriel appeared againe

[Vr —— Arme] Vr ——

Marginal notes:

line 3: The Erthes

line 8: The boke

line 13: Note the / stone

line 19: The shepe / Vnder the / Table

line 26: A Temptation / permitted by God.

a line joins 'powre' (line 24) to 'powr' (line 35).

[Vr:—]—Arme your selues; for, great shall be the temptation followin<g>

You shall be hindred, in all, that may be.

Nothing can hinder god his determined purposes.

Δ— Man may hinder his owne saluation

Vr:—Fullfill those things that are commaunded.

Forme, and write the boke after thyne own Judgment.

God his determination is iust; Therfore putto your hands

More then hath byn sayd, and more plainely, cannot be Vttred.

His works are true, for, and to the ende.

Δ Forasmuch as expedition is to be made for the erthes fatching and diuers other things: and we haue made assay to get an horse: But we could get none as we wold: and without somme better prouision of mony then we haue, we cannot redress the case. Therfore, if it might pleas god, that of the ten places Noted, we might haue but the possession of the smallest of them, deliuered here, vnto vs, at this pynche, it might greatly pleasure vs.

Vr.———— Will these worldlings hold on in theyr iniquitie?

E K They pulle the leggs of the Table away, and seme to carry all away in a bundell like a clowde. and so disapered vtterly.

Δ Herevppon I was exceding sorrowful: and betoke my self to a lamentable pang of prayer.

Δ After long prayer, appered in the stone a thing like a Tunge

all on fyre thus hanging downward 

and from it cam this voyce

Tung ——Thow hast deliuered thy self vnto the desires of thy hart, and

hast done that which is not Convenient.

Thow hast spoken iniquitie, and therfore dothe the Veritie

of Gods Doings by Vs, decay, in your Wickedness.

△ I dowt of the Veritie of that tung.

Tung —— Man (o God) beleueth him self in his own Imagination

Therfore Wipe our holines from the face of the erth

And Justifie our doings, where we lawde and prayse the.

△ I becam now abashed of my former speche, and perceyued my error:

axed forgivenes bitterly at the Lord his hand. and at length

it was sayde

Tung ——Do that, which is commaunded, the Lord is Just.

△ O lord, forgiue me my trespaces, and deale not with me according

to Justice: for, then I, and all mankinde shall vtterly perish;

Vnleast thy mercy be our savegard, destruction is our desert.

Tung ——It is forgiuen: but it shall be punished.

E K. The tung mownted vp toward heven, and he saw it in the

ayre out and above the stone aboue a hand bredth, mownting vpward

△ Thy Name be praysed, in AEternitie, Ô God

Amen

△ Herevppon

Marginal notes:

line 1: Temptations & / hinderances

line 6: The forme / of the boke / committed to / my discretion

---

Herevppon I was in an exceding great hevines, and sorrow of mynde: A<nd>
sundry tymes, bewayled my case to God: and promissed a greater care
henceforeward, of Governing my Tung: and consenting to any
vnlawfull or vnconvenient desire of my hert: yea, [or] /to forbeare/[c] to accum<pany>
with my own wife, carnally,: otherwise then by hevenly leave
and permission, or /if vppon/[c] my protestation making in the hardines of the conflict
that vnleast the lord order /and redress/[c] my cause, I shall be overcome: That if
I shall, so deliberately call for help, and not withstanding be entrapped,
That then, such trespace, shall not be imputed vnto /me/[c], as gladly, gredyly,
or willingly committed [etc] of me etc.

/flourish/

Maij 9. Holly Thursday in the morning.

△ Being desyrous (before E K. his going down into the Cuntrie) to haue som<e>
Cumfort and token of free forgiuenes at Gods hands I browght furth
the stone. Then I went into my Oratorie first requesting the
Almighty God to respect the harty sorrowfull paines [I] I had endured for
my offences; /to regarde/[c] the Vows and intent of /my/[c] better hede taking henceforth
etc. and prayed the 22 Psalm in the conclusion of the pang.

E K——One, all in white appeareth in the stone, who sayde
————It is written: It is written: yea, it is written:
Euen as the father his compassion is great over his yonglings
and Children: So, is the abundance of thy mercy (o lord)
great and vnspeakable to the long offences and sinnes

of thy servant. For, it is written, the light of
thy eyes haue beheld those that feare the: and those that trust
in thy mercy, shall not be confownded
Be it, what it was: And be you, what you were:
For, the Lord, is euen the same, that he was, before:
But be you Warned
Behold, my armes ar longer then my body, and I haue eyes
rownd abowt me: I am that, which [g] GOD pronownceth
vppon you: Be it as I haue sayde [flourish]
Δ Therevppon he disapered; and immediately, appered Vriel,
who sayd
Vri.——— Actum est. Δ Then the other two, and the Table and
Chayre, and the ancient furniture appeared, agayn restored,
and more bewtifull, then in foretyme.
Vri——Thus, sayeth the Lord: Euen as the Tabernacle which I
restore, is ten times brighter then it was, So may your
Worthynes deserue brightnes ten tymes cl<er>er then this
The rising of synners doth greatly reioyce vs [and]
That, he hath sayde, Do good vnto those that feare me: and
defend them, bycause they know my name. For in Justice
they

Marginal notes:

line 20: Δ fortè / Annaël

line 29: [hand]

line 30: Misericordia / Dei.

line 36: NOTE

they shall finde me theyr God: & in mercy their great Comforter. Therfore we say, In thy name (o thou most highest) fiat.

fiat.

Justifie not your self:

Be humble and diligent:

Continue to the ende. For great is the reward of them that feare the Lorde stedfastly.

Δ Whereas the /ordring of[c] the7 boke is referred to my Judgment: in my mynde it semeth requisite /that[c]7 as all the writing and reding of that holy language is from the right hand to the left, so the begynning of the bok<e> must be, (as it were, in respect of our most vsuall manner of bokes, in all languages of latin, greke, english etc) at th<e> ende of the boke: and the ende, at the begynning, as in the hebr<ew> bible. secondly the first leafe cannot be written in such little and aequall squares, as [the] all the rest of the 47 leaves are: bycause, the first leafe, except 9 lines (of the [last] second page) therof: is all of words: some conteyning many letters, and sōme few, very diuersly: wherfore, I entend to make many leaves, serve to distinguish the 49 rowes of the firs<t> leafe: and at the ende of euery word to draw a line of partition, vp and down, betwene the two next parallell lines. etc. or as shall cōme in my mynde then.

Vr——He, that sayeth, DO this, directeth thy Judgment.

E K. Now is there a veale drawn before all: and all things appere far bewtifuller then euer they did.

Δ I rendred thanks to the highest, and became in mynde
Very Joyfull, that the Lord had pardoned my
offences: whose name be praysed, extolled and
magnifyed world with out ende. Amen.
I prayed after this the short psalme Jubilate Deo
quotquot in terra versamini etc.

[flourish]

E K, immediately was to take bote and so to go to London: ther< e>
to buy a saddell, brydle, and bote hose: for he had (here) yesterday, bowght a
prety dun Mare, of goodman Pentecost: for iij^{ls}, redy mony, in angels [god]
God be his guyde, help, and defense
Amen.

[flourish]

Marginal notes:

line 1: Justice

line 10: The boke.

line 14: Note

[106b]

Thursday. Maij 23. Circa 10½ mane.

Δ E K being cōme [home] yesterday [frō his ior] againe & hauing.......
the erthes of the eleuen places before specifyed: Wee being desirous to....
the furder pleasure of the highest therein, and in other matters p̱teyn[g]: to our Actions
in hand: I made prayer to such intent, both in my oratory & at my desk, rendring

thanks for E K his safe retorne, and for the benefit receyued of late of the Governor and assistants for the Mines Royall: (which I perceyued, was the extraordinary working of god ⌈for⌉[c] theyr ⌈inward⌉[c] perswasion; ⌈they⌉[c] being ⌈els⌉[c] very vnwilling so to let the lease, as I obteyned it.) and moving somwhat towching Albert Lasky

At length, E K hard a Melody ⌈a far of⌉[c], and the voyce of many, singing, these words

Pinzu[a] Lephe ganiúrax Kelpadman pacaph

Δ At the length the curten was taken away, and there appered a clere whitis<h> fume, but not fyre

After that, cam the three, which were wont to cōme in.

Michael——— Grauida est terra, laborat iniquitatibus inimicorum lucis.

Maledicta [est] igitur est, quia quod in vtero perditio<nis> et tenebrarum est.

Vriel——— Sordida est, et odiosa nobis.

Raphael——— Proprijs sese flagellat tremulis.

E K. They loke abowt them, as thowgh they loked for somwhat or at somwhat

Rap. ——— Veh dicat, sed non est qui audiat

Gementem vidimus, sed non est, qui misereat.

Sancticemur igitur Sanctum eius, quia <n>os sanctificamur in illo

Mich. ——— Fiat.

E K. He plucketh all the vsuall hangings down abowt the place and now they take the Table away, and the Chayre: And where the Chayre was semeth a Canapy or cloth of state to hang

Michael———— Transeunt vetera, Incipiunt nova.

E K. Now seeme like clowdes to cōme abowt the Canapy being very beawtifull: and the bottom or flowr of the place, all couered with pretious stone, bigger then ones fist.

Mi ———— This
Vriel ———— That
Rap ———— We
} [they sayd, pointing abowt the howse.

E K. They bring in a Throne like a Judges seat or Throne and set it vp with the back of it to the Wall.

Mich ———— Be it couered for a season: For euer and euer and

Marginal notes:

line 3: <T>he Erthes.

line 7: <T>he stone / 

line 11: <T>his [a] was / <s>ownded to the / <e>nde of pinzu / <a>s we vse in / <e>nglish balads / <a>s with this / <w>ord down / <a> is sownded / <h>ey downa / <d>own a down a / etc.

line 32: Nova

[107a]

c
/and7 [ever] ever is thy Justice, O GOD [all three sayd] E K. And there cam light fire flashing from the Throne]

There commeth a beame from the Throne, and throwgh Raphael his head, and semeth to cōme out at his mowth. The other two seeme to knele downe: Michael on his right hand, and Vriel on his left.

Raphael.—— I will speak (o lord) bycause it is iust that thow hast commaunded.

Your rashnes (o worldlings is trodden vnderfote: He sayeth, (I say not) your synns are forgiven

△ O blessed God; ô prayse we his mercyes for euer: ô Cumfortable newes.

Raph.———— For, whome I will viset, those do I clense (sayeth the Lord)

Whan other things decay by reason of theyr age and filthynes quae nunc sunt in summo gradu, and I will not suffer them to move one fote farder [(], sayeth the lord,) Then shall your branches begyn to appere: And I will make you florish, for my gloryes sake, And my testimonies are true, and the wordes of my covenant iust: My pathes are thorny, but my dwelling place, is cumfortab<le>

[And lift vp your harts, as from the strength of an other] [But be you vnto me]. My hand is heuy, but my help is great. Be ye cumforted in me: for from me, in my self, I am your Cumforter: and lift vp your harts as from the strength of an other. But be you vnto me a new people: bycause I am to you no new god. Dwell with me to the ende bycause I haue byn with you from the begynning: For Who soeuer shall arrise agaynst you (Behold) I am With you.

Your fathers liued in darknes, and yet were revived yea your fathers were in light, and yet they saw not Truth. But I will be known: yea the Nations vppon earth, shall say

}Lo this is he, whome we haue risen agaynst I AM. therfore
}reioyce

All three sayd] We perish (o lord) for our vnrighteousnes
sake [and therew/th/

they fell down] But in the we were created and in the

We rise agayn: Huseh Huseh Huseh garmal, Peleh Peleh Peleh
pacád=

uasam

Gyrd your gyrdles togither and pluck vp your myndes: I say,
ope< n>

your eyes: and yf you haue eares, heare: for we tremble and

quake. This mercy was never: no not in Israël

Decedant mali, et pereant.

Depart o ye blasphemers, and workers of Iniquitie: For,

Here is Glory, Justification, with Sanctification

I answere the. / △ Note: he meaneth, now to such matters as

I propownded first of my self, and this
Poland< er>

prince etc to give answer. The Prince had

left with me these questions:

.1. De Vita Stephani Regis Poloniae quid [st...]
dici po< ssit?>

2. An successor eius erit Albertus Lasky an ex
domo Austria< ca?>

3. An Albertus Lasky Palatinus Siradiensis habebit
regnū Molda< uiae?>

Marginal notes:

line 6: Just:

line 9: Peccatorū rem / missio

line 17: The Thorny path / sup^a: Mar: / 24.

line 31: Angeli iniusti respectu / Justitiae Divinae

line 37: Mercy,

Behold you thanked God, and it is accepted.

I say, Althowgh we require speede of the and of you: yet ....

.... speede of vs, you haue a Master, we are his mowth ...

are Schollars, without vs, you could * not heare him: Ney ....

we heare him of our selves.

Consider the first, respect the second: Measure your selues,

as the third.

For what you were & shalbe is allready appointed

And What He Was, is and shalbe, it is not of our determination

His purposes are without ende: yet, to an ende; in you, to an ende

Therfore When you shall be called vppon, DO that which

is commaunded: But appoint no forme vnto god his buil=

ding. Many wyndes are to cōme: but theyr furey is in

Vayne: It is sayd: The Conquest shall be yours.

To the purpose. Who puft vp this princis father with desire to

Viset these cuntries: or who hath prevented him? euen he that hath

prouided him a sonne, as an arme vnto his chosen

Truely the hills shalbe couered with blud: The Valleys shall take vp

the Cedar trees vnframed: He seeth these places, but knoweth not

to what ende. He is dead, in respect of his absence: But honor

them, whome God hath sanctified. For, Behold, the Lord

hath sayd: Thow shalt gouern a people: a time there is, which

is prefixed: and it is the course of the sonne: Then sh< all> it be

sayd vnto him, O King.

When you semed to be carryed vnto mowntaynes, you towched his [his] ...

Behold (sayeth He). Fornication shall not prevayle:

the very stones shall be taken away: and the Tables shalbe couered with blud: and theyr dayly bankett shall be Wo Wo.

Whatsoeuer thow takest in hand, First loke vp: see if it be Just: yf it be, put furth thy hand: for it is [redacted] graunted.

It is sayed, I haue giuen the powre; and thy perswasion shall <be> like fire: and for my names sake, thow shalt triumphe agaynst the mightiest. But beware of Pride.

Many Witches and enchanters, yea many diuels haue rosen vp against this stranger, and they haue sayd, We will preuayle against him: for why? There is one that aspireth and he it is, that seeketh his confusion. But I will graunt him his desire. He shall do good with many: your names are in one boke. Feare not, therfore; Love togither

There

Marginal notes:

line 1: .... / .... / require none at / Gods hands in / this Case.

line 11: Note / we shalbe / called vpon.

line 17: Albertus / Lasky

line 20: The dead / man [hand]

line 22: Prophetia de / regno Alberti a / Lasky. sed ipē / noluit constanter / se convertere ad / Deum: et ad= / herere Deo / &c.

line 26: Fornication

line 29: Justa / facienda.

line 32: Perswasion / △

line 35: Alb. Lasky ℭ

line 39: Alb. Lasky his / name in one boke / with our names.

[108a]

There shall arise, saying, let ....
talked with strangers: But I ....
I will driue them from they< r> own ....
the bones which are buryed a far of ....
They do spit vengeance agaynst ....
them in theyr own filthynes ....
All men loke vppon the ....ause it is glorified .....
Happy are they, whose faces are marked, and in w.....
is a percing fyre of workmanship.
I will move the Prince (sayeth the Lord) Be .....
shall shortly say, Ô give me Cownsayle: for th.....
cownsayled me, conspire agaynst me
Behold, such as shewed the, little frendeship, are rather such ..
dede (as thow iustly hast confessed,) as were forced to doe ...
good: I say they, begyn to repine at that, they haue ...
Let those which are of tyme, yelde to time
One euerlasting cumfort of grace, and perfect loue,
be amongst you: to the honor and glory of him that
loueth you.
Beleue, for the teacher his sake.
All thow demaundest, is answered.
Of our selues, (we say,) We desire to be with you:
And what is of vs, the same be it vnto you
E K. They pluck the curten, affore the stone, all ouer.
The curten is like beaten gold:

Δ Semper sit benedictus Trinus et vnus.

AEternus et omnipotens Deus n̄r̄.

Amen

/flourish/

Liber sexti [et sancti] Mysterioru̅ (et sancti)

[Noualissim] parallelus, [sequitur] Noualisq

sequitur

Marginal notes:

line 4: < ....rie bones / .... be / .... to>

line 8: Fa= / <Fa>ces marked

line 11, over 'for th': ⁄ forte they that

line 13: * / The Cumpany / for the mines / royall which / had made A.G. / and me a lease / for Deuonshire / mynes etc

line 14, below 'doe': forte done

line 16, RH: ⌐ Δ we were called to / dynner often / so he ended.

line 25, RH: ⌐The other curtens did not /not/ cover all so wholy / as this did.

Appendix

Bibliography

Manuscripts

a) British Museum Library:

Additional MS 36674. Material by Forman, Dr. Caius and others; scrying experiments of H.G. and Jo. Davis (fols 58-62); invocations for consecrating a glass or crystal.

Cotton MS Appendix XLVI, parts 1 & 2. Dee's Actions with spirits later published by Meric Casaubon as a True and Faithful Relation.

Cotton Charter XIII, art. 39. A chart drawn by Dee in 1570 outlining how to 'Make this Kingdome Flourishing, Triumphant, Famous, and Blessed'.

Cotton Charter XIV, art. 1. Traces the ancestry of Queen Elizabeth and John Dee back to the earliest Welsh kings.

Cotton MS Vitellius C.VII, arts 1-6. A Compendious Rehearsal; 'Perspectiva, sive de arte mensurandi'; 'Of Famous and Rich Discoveries'; 'De trigono circinoque analogico'; 'De speculis comburentibus'; Supplication to Queen Mary. All are in Dee's hand.

Harleian MS 249, art. 13. Tract on British sea limits and a letter from Dee to Dyer dated 8 September 1597 concerning Manchester College (fols 104-105).

Harleian MS 1879, arts 1, 5 & 6. Catalogue by Dee of some 230 manuscripts in his possession; catalogue by Dee of printed books in his library; catalogue by Dee of manuscripts in his library. The last two items are dated 6 September 1583.

Harleian MS 6986, art. 26. Letter from Dee to Queen Elizabeth concerning his return from the Continent, dated 10 November 1588.

Lansdowne MS 19, art. 38. Letter from Dee to Burghley dated 3 October 1574.

Lansdowne MS 61, art. 58. Letter from Dee to Burghley dated 22 August 1589.

Sloane MS 3188. Dee's Actions with spirits between 22 December 1581 and 23 May 1583.

Sloane MS 3189. The Book of Enoch, in Kelly's hand.

Sloane MS 3191. '48 Claues angelicae'; 'Liber scientiae auxilii et victoriae terrestris'; 'De heptarchia mystica'; 'Tabula bonorum angelorum invocationes'. All are in Dee's hand.

Sloane MS 3677. Ashmole's copy of the contents of Sloane MS 3188.

Sloane MS 3678. Ashmole's copy of the contents of Sloane MS 3191.

Sloane MS 3824. A number of instructions for summoning angels and experiments in the art of scrying. 17th century.

Sloane MS 3848, fols 148-161. Invocations for use with mirrors and crystals in the art of scrying. 17th century.

Sloane MS 3851, fol. 50 ff. Instructions for summoning angels into a crystal. 17th century.

b) Bodleian Library:

Ashmole MS 423, art. 122. Ashmole's transcript of Dee's personal memoranda found in the margins of Stoffler's Ephemerides, covering the period from 1543 to 1566.

Ashmole MS 487. The Ephemerides of Stadius for 1554-1600 (Cologne 1570) in the margins of which are Dee's personal memeoranda covering the period January 1577 to December 1600.

Ashmole MS 488. The Ephemerides of Maginus for 1581-1620 (Venice 1582) in the margins of which are Dee's personal memoranda covering the period September 1586 to April 1601.

Ashmole MS 972. A copy of Ashmole's Theatrum Chemicum with his own notes and corrections. The copy contains a number of notes by Ashmole concerning Dee and Kelly.

Ashmole MS 1142, II. Ashmole's copy of Dee's library list.

Ashmole MS 1446. Townesend's annotated copy of Theatrum Chemicum with various notes about Dee.

Ashmole MS 1788, arts 1-16. Ashmole's copy of A Compendious Rehearsal; a copy of 'Praefatio Latina in actionem' (published by C.H. Josten as 'An Unknown Chapter'); letter from Dr. N. Bernard to Meric Casaubon and some ensuing correspondence; copy of a letter from Dee to William Camden, 7 August 1574; list of contents of 'Of Famous and Rich Discoveries'; copy of the Supplication to Queen Mary; miscellaneous notes on Dee; copy of a letter from William Aubrey to Dee; 'Medicina ad cancrum curandum'; two horoscopes for Dee; horoscope for Edward Kelly; Ashmole's comments on Dee's horoscope; information about Dee from Hollinsworth's book of antiquities; John Aubrey's account of Dee gathered from Goodwife Faldo; notes by Ashmole on his discourse with Goodwife Faldo.

Ashmole MS 1790, arts 1-4. 'Praefatio Latina in actionem'; various papers relating to the Actions with spirits; Ashmole's notes concerning the Actions with spirits; Ashmole's correspondence relating to Dee.

Douce MS 363, fol. 125. A record that Lasky arrived in England on 30 April 1583.

Rawlinson MS D 923, arts A12 and B10. Family tree taken from Dee's grandson Rowland; letter by Casaubon undated.

Selden Supra MS 79, fols 171-187. Notes copied by Brian Twyne from various manuscripts written by Dee.

Smith MS 95, fols 131-146. Thomas Smith's notes on Dee.

Printed Works

Acts of the Privy Council, 1554-1556.

Agricola, Georgius, De re metallica (1556), translated and edited by Herbert Clark Hoover and Lou Henry Hoover (New York 1950).

Agrippa, Henry Cornelius, Three Books of Occult Philosophy, translated by J[ames] F[rench] (London 1651).

Agrippa, Henry Cornelius, attrib., Henry Cornelius Agrippa his Fourth Book of Occult Philosophy, translated by Robert Turner (London 1655).

Agrippa, Henry Cornelius, Of the Vanitie and Uncertaintie of Artes and Sciences, translated by Ja[mes] San[ford] (London 1569).

Agrippa, Henry Cornelius, Opera, 2 vols facsimile edition of Lyons c.1600 (Hildesheim 1970).

Allen, Don Cameron, The Star-Crossed Renaissance (Durham, North Carolina 1941).

Ashmole, Elias, Elias Ashmole, his Autobiographical and Historical Notes, his Correspondence, and other Contemporary Sources Relating to his Life and Work, edited by C.H. Josten, 5 vols (Oxford 1966).

Aubrey, John, Letters Written by Eminent Persons in the Seventeenth and Eighteenth Centuries, 2 vols (London 1813)

Aubrey, John, Three Prose Works, edited by John Buchanan-Brown (Fontwell 1972).

St. Augustine, The Confessions of St. Augustine, translated by Sir Tobie Matthew, revised by Dom Roger Hudleston (London and Glasgow 1957)

Bacon, Francis, The Advancement of Learning and New Atlantis, edited by Arthur Johnston (Oxford 1972).

Bacon, Roger, Frier Bacon his Discovery of the Miracles of Art, Nature, and Magick, 'faithfully translated out of Dr. Dees own copy, by T.M.', facsimile edition (Lodon 1659).

Bailey, John E., 'Dee and Trithemius's "Steganography"', Notes and Queries, 5th series, vol. XI (1879), pp. 401-402 & 422-423.

Barrett, Francis, The Celestial Intelligencer (London 1801).

Besterman, Theodore, Crystalgazing: a Study in the History, Distribution, Theory and Practice of Skrying (London 1924).

Blau, Joseph Leon, The Christian Interpretation of the Cabala in the Renaissance (New York 1944).

Bibliotheca Ashmoliana, a Catalogue of the Library of the Learned and Famous Elias Ashmole Esq., BM collection of sale catalogues 1680-1696, shelf-mark S-C 92319.

Blount, Thomas, Glossographia: or a Dictionary (London 1656).

Bongus, Petrus, Mysticae numerorum significationis liber (Bergamo 1585).

The Book of Enoch, edited by R.H. Charles (Oxford 1893).

Boulenger, Jules César, Opusculorum systema, 2 tomes (Lyons 1621).

Bourne, William, A Regiment for the Sea and Other Writings, edited by E.G.R. Taylor, Hakluyt Society Series II, vol. CXXI (London 1963).

Boutell's Heraldry, edited by C.W. Scott-Giles and J.P. Brooke Little, revised edition (London and New York 1966).

Brahe, Tycho, Learned: Tico Brahae his Astronomicall Coniectur of the New and Much Admired [Star] which Appered in the Year 1572 (London 1632), facsimile edition, The English Experience No. 86 (Amsterdam and New York 1969).

Brooke, Iris, A History of English Costume (London 1957).

Browne, Sir Thomas, Works, edited by Geoffrey Keynes, 4 vols (Chicago 1964).

Bullinger, Henry, The Decades of Henry Bullinger (1587 edition), edited by Rev. Thomas Harding, Parker Society, 4 vols (Cambridge 1849-1852).

Butler, Christopher, Number Symbolism (London 1970).

'Calcuttensis', 'MS. Notes in Printed Books', Notes and Queries, 4th series IV (1869), pp. 69-70.

Calder, I.R.F., 'John Dee Studied as an English Neo-Platonist', unpublished University of London Ph.D. dissertation, 1952.

Calendar of Patent Rolls, Edward VI 1553.

Calendar of State Papers, Domestic 1547-1580, Domestic 1580-1625, Foreign 1583-1584.

Casaubon, Meric, Of Credulity and Incredulity in Things Divine and Spiritual (London 1670).

Casaubon, Meric, ed., A True and Faithful Relation of What Passed for Many Yeers Between Dr: John Dee...and Some Spirits (London 1659).

Cassirer, Ernst, ed., The Individual and the Cosmos in Renaissance Philosophy, translated by Mario Domandi (Oxford 1963).

Cassirer, Ernst, ed., The Renaissance Philosophy of Man (London and Chicago 1967).

Chaucer, Geoffrey, The Works of Geoffrey Chaucer, edited by F.N. Robinson, second edition (London 1970).

Cirlot, J.E., A Dictionary of Symbols (New York 1962).

Columna, Petrus Galatinus, Opus de arcanis Catholicae veritatis (Basle 1561).

Cooper, Charles Henry and Thomson, eds, Athenae Cantabrigiensis, 2 vols (Cambridge 1861, republished 1967).

Cuming, H. Syer, 'On Crystals of Augury', The Journal of the British Archaeological Association, V (1850), pp. 51-53.

Curtis, R., The Care of a Christian Conscience (London 1600).

Dalton, O.M., 'Notes on Wax Discs used by Dr. Dee', Proceedings of the Society of Antiquaries of London, XXI (1906-7), pp. 380-383.

Davidson, Gustav, A Dictionary of Angels (New York & London 1967).

Deacon, Richard, John Dee: Scientist, Geographer, Astrologer and Secret Agent to Elizabeth I (London 1968).

Debus, Allen G., The English Paracelsians (New York 1966).

Dee, John, Autobiographical Tracts of Dr. John Dee, Warden of the College of Manchester, edited by James Crossley, Chetham Society Publications, vol. XXIV (Manchester 1851).

Dee, John, 'Mathematicall Preface' to The Elements of Geometrie of the Most Auncient Philosopher Euclide of Megara, translated by Sir Henry Billingsley (London 1570).

Dee, John, General and Rare Memorials Pertayning to the Perfecte Arte of Navigation (London 1577), facsimile edition, The English Experience No. 62 (Amsterdam and New York 1968).

Dee, John, _A Letter, Containing a Most Briefe Discourse Apologeticall_ (London 1599).

Dee, John, _A Letter Nine Years Since_ (London 1603).

Dee, John, _Monas hieroglyphica_, translated by C.H. Josten, _Ambix_, XII (1964), pp. 84-221.

Dee, John, _The Private Diary of Dr. John Dee_, edited by James O. Halliwell, Camden Society Publications, vol. XIX (London 1842).

Dee, John, _Propaedeumata aphoristica_ (London 1558, reprinted London 1568).

Dee, John, _To the Honorable Assemblie of the Commons in the Present Parlament_ (London 1604).

Dee, John, _To the King's Most Excellent Majestie_ (London 1604).

Delrio, Martino, _Disquisitionum magicarum libri sex_ (Lyons 1608).

Digges, Leonard, _A Geometrical Practise named Pantometria_ (London 1571).

Digges, Thomas, _Alae seu scalae mathematicae_ (London 1573).

D'Israeli, Isaac, _Amenities of Literature_, 3 vols (London 1841).

'Dr. Dee's Magic Mirror—Reflecting Two Elizabethan Worlds', _The Listener_, 23 & 30 December 1976, pp. 824-826.

Encyclopaedia Biblica, edited by Rev. T.K. Cheyne and J. Sutherland Black, 4 vols (London 1899-1907).

Evans, R.J.W., _The Making of the Habsburg Monarchies, 1550-1780_ (Oxford 1979).

Evans, R.J.W., _Rudolf II and his World_ (Oxford 1973).

Evelyn, John, _Sculptura_, edited by C.F. Bell (Oxford 1906).

Forman, Simon, _The Autobiography and Personal Diary of Dr. Simon Forman_, edited by James Orchard Halliwell (London 1849).

Foxe, John, _Actes and Monuments_ (London 1563 and London 1576).

French, Peter J., _John Dee_ (London 1972).

Friedman, William F. and Elizabeth S., _The Shakespearean Ciphers Examined_ (Cambridge 1957).

Fulton, Thomas, The Sovereignty of the Sea (Edinburgh 1911).

Gaster, M., 'Jewish Divination', Encyclopaedia of Religion and Ethics, 12 vols (Edinburgh 1908-1921), pp. 806-814.

Ginsburg, Christian D., The Kabbalah, its Doctrines, Development, and Literature (London 1865).

Greg, W.W., Collected Papers, edited by J.C. Maxwell (Oxford 1966).

Halliwell, J.O., ed., Letters on Scientific Subjects (London 1841, reprinted London 1965).

Halliwell, J.O., ed. Rara Mathematica (London 1839).

Harsnett, Samuel, A Declaration of Egregious Popish Impostures (London 1603).

Hearne, Thomas, Johannis confratris et monachi Glastoniensis, chronica, sive historia rebus Glastoniensis, 2 vols (Oxford 1726).

The History of Reynard the Fox, edited by Donald B. Sands (Cambridge,Mass. 1960).

Hooke, Robert, The Posthumous Works of Robert Hooke, edited by R. Waller (London 1705).

James, M.R., Manuscripts Formerly Owned by Dr. John Dee, with Preface and Identifications, Supplement to the Bibliographical Society's Transactions (London 1921).

Jones, Richard Foster, Ancients and Moderns (University of California Press, Berkeley & Los Angeles 1965).

ben Joseph, Rabbi Akiba, The Book of Formation, translated by Knut Stenring (London 1923).

Josten, C.H., ed., 'An Unknown Chapter in the Life of John Dee', JWCI, 28 (1965), pp. 223-257.

Keller, H.A., ed., Le Roman des Sept Sages (Tübingen 1836).

Kahn, David, The Codebreakers (London 1966).

King, C.W., 'Talismans and Amulets: Mediaeval Talismans', Archaeological Journal, XXVI (1869), pp. 225-235.

Koestler, Arthur, The Sleepwalkers (London 1959, reprinted Harmondsworth 1972).

Laycock, Donald C., ed., The Complete Enochian Dictionary (London 1978).

Lilly, William, *William Lilly's History of his Life and Times*, published from the original MS, London 1715, (London 1822).

MacMichael, J. Holden, 'Bishopsgate Street Without', *Notes & Queries*, 11th series III (1911), pp. 2-3.

Meadows, Denis, *Elizabethan Quintet* (London 1956).

Nashe, Thomas, *The Works of Thomas Nashe*, edited by Ronald B. McKerrow, revised by F.P. Wilson, 5 vols (Oxford 1958).

Nichols, John Gough, ed., *Narratives of the Days of the Reformation*, Camden Society Publications (London 1859).

North, Martin, *Exodus, a Commentary* (London 1962).

Osborn, James M., *Young Philip Sidney 1572-1577* (New Haven & London 1972).

Original Letters Illustrative of English History, edited by Sir Henry Ellis, 3rd series, 4 vols (London 1846).

Philpot, John, *The Examinations and Writings of John Philpot*, edited by Robert Eden, Parker Society (Cambridge 1842).

della Porta, Gianbattista, *Natural Magick*, edited by Derek J. Price, facsimile edition, Collectors' Series in Science (New York 1957, reprinted 1959).

Postel, Guillaume, *Le Thresor des Prophéties de L'Univers*, edited by François Secret (The Hague 1969).

Prideaux, W.R.B., 'Books from John Dee's Library', *Notes & Queries*, 9th series VIII (1901), pp. 137-138.

Queen Elizabeth's Prayer Book (Edinburgh 1909).

Raine, J., 'Divination in the Fifteenth Century by Aid of a Magical Crystal', *Archaeological Journal* XIII (1856), pp. 372-374.

Read, Conyers, *Mr. Secretary Walsingham and the Policy of Queen Elizabeth* (Oxford 1925).

Recorde, Robert, *Grounde of Artes* (London 1543).

Reuchlin, Johannes, *De verbo mirifico* and *De arte cabalistica*, facsimile edition (Stuttgart, 1964).

Salisbury, John of, *Polycraticus*, edited by C.C.J. Webb (Oxford 1909).

Scholem, G.G., *Major Trends in Jewish Mysticism* (New York 1941, 3rd edition 1967).

Scholem, G.G., *On the Kabbalah and its Symbolism*, translated by R. Manheim (London 1965).

Scriptores historiae Augustae, translated by David Magie, Loeb Classical Library, 3 vols (Cambridge, Mass. 1960).

Scot, Reginald, The Discoverie of Witchcraft, facsimile edition (Arundel & London 1964).

The Second Volume Conteinyng those Statutes whiche haue ben made in the Tyme of the Most Victorious Reigne of Kynge Henrie the Eight (London 1543).

Shah, Sayed Idries, ed., The Secret Lore of Magic (London 1957, reprinted 1974).

Shakespeare, William, The First Folio of Shakespeare, prepared by Charlton Hinman (New York 1968).

Shumaker, Wayne, The Occult Sciences in the Renaissance (Berkeley, Los Angeles & London 1972).

Smith, Charlotte Fell, John Dee: 1527-1608 (London 1909).

Smith, D.E., A History of Mathematics, 2 vols (London 1925).

Smith, Thomas, Vitae quorundam eruditissimorum et illustrium virorum (London 1707).

Smith, Thomas, Catalogus librorum manuscriptorum bibliothecae Cottonianae (Oxford 1696).

Spenser, Edmund, The Works of Edmund Spenser, edited by E. Greenlaw, C.G. Osgood, F.M. Padelford and R. Heffner, variorum edition, 11 vols (Baltimore 1932-1957, reprinted 1958-1966).

Stanley, Sir Thomas, History of Philosophy (London 1656).

Strype, John, Annals of the Reformation and Establishment of Religion...in the Church of England, 7 vols (Oxford 1824).

Tahureau, Jacques, Les Dialogues (Anvers 1574).

Tait, Hugh, 'The Devil's Looking Glass: the Magical Speculum of Dr. John Dee', in Horace Walpole, Writer, Politician, and Connoisseur, edited by Warren Hunting Smith (New Haven & London 1967), pp. 195-212.

Tannenbaum, Samuel A., The Handwriting of the Renaissance (republished New York 1967).

Taylor, E.G.R., Tudor Geography: 1485-1583 (London 1930).

Taylor, E.G.R., Late Tudor and Early Stuart Geography: 1583-1650 (London 1934).

Taylor, F. Sherwood, The Alchemists (London 1951).

Thorndike, Lynn, *A History of Magic and Experimental Science*, 6 vols (New York 1923-1941).

Trismegistus, Hermes, attrib., *Corpus Hermeticum*, translated by A.J. Festugière with text established by A.D. Nock, 4 vols (Paris 1945-1954).

Trithemius, Johannes, *De septem secundeis* (Cologne 1567).

Trattner, Walter I., 'God and Expansion in Elizabethan England: John Dee, 1527-1583', *JHI*, XXV (1964), pp. 17-34.

Van Durme, M., ed., *Correspondence Mercatorienne* (Anvers 1959).

Waite, A.E., trans & ed., *The Alchemical Writings of Edward Kelly* (London 1893, second edition 1970).

Walker, D.P., *The Ancient Theology* (London 1972).

Walker, D.P., *Spiritual and Demonic Magic from Ficino to Campanella* (London 1958, reprinted 1969).

Webster, John, *The Displaying of Supposed Witchcraft* (London 1677).

Weever, John, *Ancient Funerall Monuments* (London 1631).

West, Robert Hunter, *The Invisible World* (Athens, Georgia 1939).

Westcott, William Wynn, *An Introduction to the Study of the Kabbalah* (London 1910, second edition 1926).

Whitney's Choice of Emblemes, edited by Henry Green, facsimile reprint (London 1846).

à Wood, Anthony, *Athenae Oxoniensis*, edited by Philip Bliss, 4 vols (London 1913-1820).

Worsop, Edward, *A Discoverie of Sundrie Errours and Faults Comitted by Landemeaters Ignorant of Arithmetike* (London 1582).

Yates, Frances A., *The Art of Memory* (London & Chicago 1966).

Yates, Frances A., 'The Art of Ramon Lull: An Approach to it through Lull's Theory of Elements', *JWCI* XVII (1954), pp. 115-173.

Yates, Frances A., *Astraea* (London 1975).

Yates, Frances A., *Giordano Bruno and the Hermetic Tradition* (London & Chicago 1964).

Yates, Frances A., *The Occult Philosophy in the Elizabethan Age* (London 1979).

Yates, Frances A., *Theatre of the World* (London & Chicago 1969).

Zika, Charles, 'Reuchlin's *De verbo mirifico* and the Magic Debate of the Late Fifteenth Century', *JWCI*, XXXIX (1976), pp. 104-138.

The Zohar, translated by Harry Sperling, Maurice Simon and Dr. Paul Levertoff, 5 vols (London & New York 1933-1934).